UNIVERSITY TREATISE SERIES

FEDERAL INCOME TAXATION OF S CORPORATIONS

Third Edition

John K. McNulty
Late Roger J. Traynor Professor of Law, Emeritus
University of California, Berkeley
School of Law

Karen C. Burke
Professor and Richard B. Stephens Eminent Scholar in Taxation
University of Florida Levin College of Law

FOUNDATION
PRESS

© 1992 By John K. McNulty
© 2015 LEG, Inc. d/b/a West Academic
© 2023 LEG, Inc. d/b/a West Academic
    444 Cedar Street, Suite 700
    St. Paul, MN 55101
    1-877-888-1330

Printed in the United States of America

ISBN: 978-1-63659-357-9

Preface

This book provides an introduction to federal income taxation of S corporations and their shareholders. It is intended to be used by law students and lawyers in the United States, as well as lawyers and scholars from other legal systems. It may be used as a supplement to traditional courses and teaching materials on taxation of business entities or as part of a specialized course on taxation of S corporations and other passthrough entities.

The emphasis is on explaining the law, its purposes and uses. Some alternatives, history, policy and criticism or evaluation are mentioned, but in small doses. Examples are offered to make more focused the meaning and implication of the general principles. Frequent references to the statute and regulations highlight the importance of having those sources available and reading them along with this book.

Since the publication of the first edition of this work, the number of businesses organized as S corporations has grown steadily, and the desirability of S corporations has been further enhanced by statutory amendments that have made them more accessible and flexible. The popularity of S corporations stems in part from the 1986 repeal of the *General Utilities* rule, which exposes distributions of appreciated property by a non-electing C corporation to tax at both the corporate and shareholder levels. In an S corporation, by contrast, such distributions normally incur only a single level of tax, at the shareholder level.

Choice of entity considerations comprise a fundamental theme of this book. An S corporation is often the preferred form of business organization, offering many of the income tax advantages of the partnership form (such as passthrough treatment of losses and deductions) as well as the limited liability of the corporate form. Sometimes, however, a partnership or non-electing C corporation may be more advantageous. Technical requirements, disadvantages and costs of using an S election must also be understood and weighed in evaluating use of Subchapter S. The most important rival to the S corporation as the business entity of choice is the limited liability company (LLC), which may offer the best of both worlds: classification as a partnership for federal tax purposes, combined with the non-tax advantages of a corporation. The continuing attractiveness of S corporations may hinge in large part on Congress's willingness to enact further revisions to Subchapter S.

This book begins with an extended introduction and overview of Subchapter S and S corporations (Chapter 1). The next two chapters focus on electing and maintaining S status (Chapter 2) and the effects of the S election during operation of the corporation (Chapter 3), including rules governing determination of corporate income, permissible accounting methods and tax years. Chapter 4 turns to the effects of distributions to shareholders. Chapter 5 discusses special taxes imposed on the S corporation itself. Chapter 6 considers the effects of an S election on shareholders, especially the passthrough of income and losses and accompanying basis effects. Chapter 7 covers the routine stages in the life of an S corporation—including formation, liquidation, redemptions, dispositions and acquisitions—which are governed to a large extent by Subchapter C rules, but often with a special twist. Chapter 8 addresses the more advanced and specialized topic of tax-free reorganizations involving S corporations.

Chapters 9 and 10 examine more fully the income tax choices and opportunities surrounding the choice of form, contrasting the tax treatment of S corporations with that of C corporations on the one hand and that of partnerships on the other hand. Chapter 11 concludes with a few observations about the future of Subchapter S, possible reforms to improve or expand S corporations, and the relationship of Subchapter S to other forms of passthrough integration. This look toward the future concludes a major theme of this book—how the more than half century of experience with Subchapter S may enhance understanding of the need for integration of corporate-shareholder taxation and may suggest a compulsory or elective model of such integration.

Citations to the Internal Revenue Code generally appear in the form "I.R.C. §" to distinguish them from cross references to other sections in this book. Treasury regulations are cited as "Reg. §" throughout; administrative pronouncements are cited to the Cumulative Bulletin (abbreviated as C.B.) or the IRS Revenue Bulletin (abbreviated as I.R.B.).

This book will hopefully prove helpful to students, practitioners, and foreign scholars seeking an introduction to the taxation of S corporations and their shareholders. It cannot substitute for, but can only supplement, a thoroughgoing examination and analysis of the Code, regulations, cases and rulings which are the sources of U.S. tax law. Those interested in pursuing specific topics in greater detail should consult the leading treatises on taxation of S corporations.

I note with sadness the passing of Jack McNulty, the original author of this book, who died in 2020. Jack was a good friend and a gracious collaborator, and I am grateful to him for inviting me to join as a co-author on the second edition of this book. This third edition continues to reflect his thorough knowledge and expertise in the area of federal income taxation that laid the groundwork for the first edition.

KAREN C. BURKE

Gainesville, FL
August 2022

Table of Contents

FEDERAL INCOME TAXATION OF S CORPORATIONS

Third Edition

Chapter 1

INTRODUCTION TO SUBCHAPTER S AND S CORPORATIONS; SUBCHAPTER S IN GENERAL

¶ 1.01   INTRODUCTION AND OVERVIEW

Subchapter S, which consists of §§ 1361 through 1379 of the Internal Revenue Code (I.R.C.), contains a special tax regime that applies to any qualified, electing corporation and its shareholders.[1] This alternative to Subchapter C's normal system of corporate and shareholder taxation enables a qualifying business to avoid the "double tax" on a C corporation and its shareholders.

An electing corporation, called an "S corporation," is treated as a passthrough entity very much like a partnership for federal income tax purposes, while remaining a corporation for all non-tax purposes (such as limited liability) under state law. It avoids a separate (federal) entity-level tax on its income. Generally, corporate gains and losses pass through to shareholders and are directly taxed to (or deducted by) them.

Subchapter S and S corporations have steadily increased in importance. Since 1997, S corporations have been the most popular form of business organization.[2] In 2016, there were 4.6 million S corporations, compared to 3.8 million partnerships (including LLCs), and 1.6 million C corporations. The single-level tax regime available to S corporations and partnerships has proven quite attractive. Currently, over half of all business income is earned by passthroughs, including sole proprietorships, partnerships, LLCs, and S corporations.

An S corporation is not separately taxable on its income. Instead, income passed through to S shareholders is taxed only once (by the *federal* income tax) at applicable individual shareholder rates. By contrast, income of a non-electing C corporation is taxed twice—once at the applicable C corporation rate and again, on the amount distributed, at individual shareholder rates.

The choice of business entity may be heavily influenced by the relationship between the individual and corporate tax rates. Under legislation enacted in 2017 (the "2017 Act"), the corporate rate dropped sharply from a maximum rate of 35% to a flat rate of 21%, and the maximum individual rate fell more modestly from 39.6% to 37%. Congress left intact the maximum 20% rate for qualified dividends under § 1(h).

Assume that a corporation earns income of $100. After paying $21 of corporate tax, the corporation has $79 available for distribution. The distribution triggers a shareholder-level tax of $15.80 ($79 × 20%) and leaves shareholders with $63.20 after tax. Thus, the maximum combined burden on distributed corporate earnings is currently 36.8%, or slightly less than the maximum individual rate (37%).

---

[1]   Unless otherwise indicated, all I.R.C. citations refer to the Internal Revenue Code as amended through 2023.

[2]   Between 1980 and 2006, the percentage of businesses organized as S corporations tripled.

Net investment income of high-income individuals is subject to a 3.8% tax, which is intended to mirror the Medicare tax on "earned income."[3] For high-income individuals, the overall tax rate for qualifying dividends and long-term capital gain is 23.8% (20% plus 3.8%). As a result, the combined tax burden on distributed corporate earnings is 39.8% for such individuals ($21 plus $18.80 ($79 × 23.8%)).

To level the playing field, Congress also enacted § 199A in 2017. This provision allows a deduction of up to 20% for "qualified business income" earned by passthrough entities (including estates and trusts) or sole proprietorships.[4] If a high-income passthrough owner (including an S corporation shareholder) is entitled to the maximum 20% deduction, qualified business income is taxed at a rate of only 29.6% (80% × 37%).

After the 2017 Act, the choice between an S corporation and a C corporation is much closer. Based solely on a comparison of tax rates, a C corporation will be preferable if the shareholder-level tax can be avoided entirely; in other situations, the relative benefit or detriment of a C corporation depends on various factors, including whether earnings are distributed or retained. Particularly given uncertainty concerning future corporate tax rates, the 2017 legislation is unlikely to drastically alter the choice of business entity. S corporations and partnerships remain attractive because they provide flexibility in accommodating a wide range of business arrangements.

In addition, electing S status can produce tax savings during loss years, since corporate losses are passed through to shareholders and can be deducted immediately by an individual shareholder who has income from other sources (subject to limits at the individual level). In contrast, a C corporation is allowed to use its losses only against its gains when realized (or in a permitted carryover year).

Eliminating the "double tax" on distributed corporate earnings and allowing shareholders to use corporate losses comprise two of the three main goals Congress sought to achieve when it first enacted Subchapter S in 1958. The third and overarching goal was to grant to those contemplating a business enterprise the freedom to choose the form of organization desired (as between a corporation and a partnership, for example) for business reasons, without major differences in federal income tax consequences.[5] As will become clear later, this third goal continues to prove elusive as taxes are likely to play an important, and even dominant, role in the choice-of-entity decision.

Subsequent legislation has significantly improved and liberalized Subchapter S. In recent years, Congress has increased the flexibility of S corporations as estate planning vehicles and expanded the number and kinds of eligible shareholders. In addition, S corporations are now permitted to own all of the stock of a qualified Subchapter S subsidiary. Such modifications have made S corporations a more attractive vehicle for small (and even some quite large) businesses. Congress has also imposed some additional constraints, particularly on the ability of corporations converting to S status to avoid corporate-level tax on built-in gains following repeal of the *General Utilities*

---

[3]   In the case of an individual, the 3.8% tax is levied on the lesser of net investment income or the excess of modified adjusted gross income over a threshold amount ($250,000 for married filers, $200,000 for single filers). I.R.C. § 1411(a)(1), (b).

[4]   *See* I.R.C. § 199A(b)(2), (c)(1).

[5]   *See* S. Rep. No. 1983, 85th Cong., 2d Sess. 87, *reprinted in* 1958–3 C.B. 922, 1008.

doctrine in 1986.[6] Congress continues to seek to balance the concern for administrative simplicity and the need to expand the scope and utility of S corporations.

This first chapter continues with its brief helicopter overview of Subchapter S, how it works, and what to be on the lookout for.

¶ 1.02   AN OVERVIEW OF SUBCHAPTER S—§§ 1361–1379

Subchapter S allows a qualified corporation, whether newly formed or preexisting, to elect a special tax regime. If a corporation is eligible and makes the election under § 1362(a), it becomes known as an "S corporation."[7] Any other corporation, that is, any corporation that is *not* an S corporation, is denominated a "C corporation."[8] Thus, Subchapter S does not create any new form of business organization, and no different state-law form is required to become subject to Subchapter S rather than Subchapter C. To have an S corporation, it is necessary merely to form or acquire a regular corporation under a state's corporation law and then to cause it to elect, in accordance with the provisions of § 1362, to be an S corporation.

¶ 1.03   ELIGIBILITY—§ 1361

In order to make a valid § 1362 election, a corporation must meet eligibility requirements which may be summarized by saying that it must be a "small business corporation," as that term is used in § 1361(a)(1) and defined in § 1361(b). Notwithstanding this terminology, the defined corporation need not be small in financial size, or in market or geographic scope.[9] Even a very large corporation (in terms of revenue and assets) can be eligible for Subchapter S treatment, if it otherwise meets the eligibility requirements of § 1361 and its corollary rules.[10] (The eligibility requirements will be described and analyzed in Chapter 2.)

¶ 1.04   ELECTION—§ 1362

Subchapter S applies to an eligible corporation only if it makes an effective election under § 1362. In other words, S corporation treatment does not apply automatically. The Code and regulations contain detailed technical rules that must be satisfied for an election to be valid. The election is made by the corporation, with certain formalities; in addition, all shareholders must consent to the election. The initial election is generally effective for the year for which it is made and for each succeeding year until terminated. Termination can occur by voluntary revocation or by involuntary or inadvertent failure to comply with the tax law's eligibility or other requirements. The election and

---

[6]   *See General Utilities & Operating Co. v. Helvering,* 296 U.S. 200 (1935). Under current law, a corporation (whether C or S) is taxed on appreciation in distributed assets. *See* I.R.C. §§ 311, 336; *see also* Chapter 5 (discussing the § 1374 built-in gain tax).

[7]   I.R.C. § 1361(a)(1).

[8]   I.R.C. § 1361(a)(2).

[9]   Originally, Subchapter S was enacted mainly to minimize the tax differences between the partnership and corporate form for small businesses. Even at the outset, however, it was not confined to *small* businesses (in terms of assets). The term "small business corporation" refers more accurately to the limit on the number of shareholders (100) and the requirement of a simple capital structure. It is a vestigial remnant of Subchapter S's original focus on small businesses that previously were almost forced into partnership form to avoid the burdensome double-tax system of Subchapter C.

[10]   Indeed, many S corporations are today quite large businesses. In 2009, S corporations with $100 million or more in assets constituted only .08% of all S corporations but held more than 36% of all S corporation assets; .3% of S corporations with total receipts in excess of $50 million accounted for 35% of total S corporation receipts. *See* Joint Comm. on Tax'n, Selected Issues Relating to Business Entities 11 (2012) (JCX–66–12).

termination rules, which contain many pitfalls for taxpayers and their advisors, will be covered in detail in Chapter 2.

¶ 1.05   TAXATION OF CORPORATION; EFFECTS OF ELECTION ON THE CORPORATION—§ 1363

If an eligible corporation has made an effective election, § 1363 states that—except as otherwise provided in Subchapter S—the S corporation shall not be subject to the taxes imposed by Chapter 1 of the Code. This means that (unless an exception applies) the S corporation does not have to pay the normal corporate income tax under § 11. An S corporation also avoids the accumulated earnings tax of § 531 and the personal holding company tax of § 541.

The S corporation, rather like a partnership, must *compute* its taxable income, under § 1363(b). Except in special circumstances explained in Chapters 3 and 5, however, it need not pay tax at the entity level. The main effect of an S election is to treat the entity somewhat like a conduit or an aggregate of investors, rather than as a separate payer of income tax.

¶ 1.06   EFFECT OF ELECTION ON SHAREHOLDERS—§ 1366

Subchapter S has largely achieved the second goal of the S form—to provide the business and its investors the benefits of a passthrough system.[11] Generally speaking, an S corporation's profit or loss passes through to the shareholders (regardless of any actual distributions) who report their pro rata shares of such profit or loss on their individual tax returns.[12] Consequently, corporate profits are taxed once, when earned, to the shareholders at their individual rates. Corporate items of deduction or loss also pass through and can be used by the shareholders against other income on their returns, subject to any limitations applicable at the shareholder level. (As discussed in Chapter 6, there are several such limitations on the use of losses at the shareholder level—found both within and outside Subchapter S—that turn out to be very important.) When passed through to shareholders, the character of items of income or loss (as determined at the corporate level) remains the same in the shareholders' hands.[13] Later distributions made by the S corporation are generally tax free to the shareholders to the extent they reflect previously taxed income.[14]

¶ 1.07   BASIS AND BASIS ADJUSTMENTS—§ 1367

The Subchapter S mechanism for relieving the corporation of tax while passing through undistributed income to shareholders (and preserving non-taxability of actual distributions of previously taxed income) uses shareholder basis and basis adjustments to obtain "correct" tax results. The basis system also ensures that passthrough of corporate losses produces one, and only one, tax benefit to the shareholders. Shareholders of an S corporation must never lose sight of their stock basis, as adjusted to reflect their share of undistributed corporate income, losses, and actual distributions of cash or property.

---

[11] I.R.C. § 1366.

[12] I.R.C. §§ 1366(c), 1377(a).

[13] I.R.C. § 1366(b).

[14] I.R.C. § 1368.

In general, under the rules of § 1367, a shareholder's basis in shares is *increased* for income passed through to the shareholder (including tax-exempt income) and any additional contributions. It is *decreased* for distributions not includable in the shareholder's income by virtue of § 1368 and for items of loss or deduction passed through under § 1366. With accompanying technical details, these basis rules keep track of the amount a shareholder should be able to take out of the S corporation, in addition to amounts previously withdrawn, without further tax. Basis in stock (and debt) also limits the amount of S corporation losses that each shareholder can deduct. Basis rules are discussed more fully in Chapter 6.

An example will help focus the basic rules, as summarized briefly here, for passthrough of income and losses and the impact of distributions.

Example 1.1: Under the law of state X, A and B form AB Corp. which issues 100 shares of common stock, 50 to each stockholder. At the outset, AB Corp. properly elects Subchapter S treatment. In Year 1, it earns $160,000 and has deductible expenses of $60,000.

If AB Corp. had not made an S election, it would have paid tax on $100,000 of taxable income, $160,000 of gross income less $60,000 in deductions. No tax would be imposed upon shareholders on the corporate earnings unless and until the entity distributed cash or property to them. If AB Corp. distributed $50,000 at the end of Year 1 ($25,000 to each shareholder) as a dividend, the distributed profits would be taxable again at the shareholder level, since AB Corp. would have at least $79,000 ($100,000 less $21,000 corporate tax) of current earnings and profits. The (fully taxable) distribution would have no effect on the shareholders' stock bases.

Because AB Corp. made an S election, the corporate gross income and deductions will not be taxed at the entity level. They will flow through ratably and be taxed immediately to the shareholders. The shareholders will be taxable, in the aggregate, on $100,000 of taxable income, even if they receive no actual distribution. As a consequence of this taxability, each shareholder will be entitled to increase stock basis by $50,000.

An actual distribution of $25,000 to each shareholder at the end of Year 1 would incur no additional tax at the shareholder level, because each shareholder's stock basis (as adjusted upward prior to the distribution) is sufficient to "absorb" the distribution without tax. As a consequence of the distribution, however each shareholder's stock basis would be reduced from $50,000 to $25,000.

Suppose, in Year 2, the AB S corporation loses $10,000. Although losses cannot be deducted or carried back or forward by the S corporation, the loss passes through to the shareholders pro rata. Each shareholder may deduct half of the corporate loss ($5,000 each) on the shareholder's own individual tax return. Because of the loss passthrough, each shareholder's stock basis would be reduced by $5,000. Indeed, full deductibility of the loss depends on each shareholder having at least $5,000 of stock basis (after upward adjustments for income and downward adjustments for any distributions during the year), so that the entire loss can be absorbed by basis without going below zero.

¶ 1.08   SUMMARY OF INTRODUCTORY MATERIAL

An S election by an eligible corporation relieves the corporation of the regular corporate income tax under § 11 and also of surtaxes and penalty taxes imposed by Subchapter C. It also affords passthrough treatment for the corporation and its shareholders. The result is a single tax (or deduction) premised on "transparency" principles that resemble those of partnership taxation. Because passthrough relief under Subchapter S is subject to numerous conditions, however, the end result is a special S regime that is not perfectly identical to Subchapter K, the partnership counterpart. While the results are often similar or parallel, comparisons between the tax treatment of S corporations and partnerships are essential. Indeed the choice-of-form issues facing a tax advisor demand just such close comparison.

Formation of a corporation and election of Subchapter S treatment may prove preferable to use of a partnership (or LLC) taxed under Subchapter K. But this is certainly not always true. Partnerships are inherently more flexible than S corporations and enjoy many advantages (for example, the generous partnership rules for including debt in "outside" basis), though partnerships and partners also pay a considerable price in terms of inordinate complexity. At various points, this book will attempt to elicit the respective advantages and disadvantages of each form.

Similarly, formation of a corporation and election of Subchapter S treatment often will prove advantageous compared to formation or use of a non-electing C corporation. Nevertheless, S corporations do not always have the edge over their C counterparts. Similarly, midstream conversion of an ongoing C corporation to the S form may be desirable but can entail serious costs or risks.

In deciding whether a business should be organized as a corporation (S or C) or instead as a partnership taxable under Subchapter K, the tax advisor faces important choice-of-entity issues. Chapters 9 and 10 provide an extended comparative overview of the use of S corporations versus C corporations, on the one hand, and partnerships, on the other hand.

¶ 1.09   WHEN IS AN S ELECTION INDICATED—GENERALIZATIONS

The main advantages of the S form indicate when an S election may be most useful. For a closely held profitable business that can use the non-tax benefits of incorporation, an S election will avoid the separate corporate income tax under Subchapter C; thus, its distributed earnings will be taxed once, not twice. The two levels of tax imposed on C corporations and their shareholders will generally produce a heavier combined tax burden than if an S election is made and the § 199A deduction is fully available. If a business expects start-up losses, or a period of later losses, the corporate form with an S election will afford passthrough of losses that can generate immediate tax savings by offsetting other income on the shareholders' individual tax returns.

¶ 1.10   IMPORTANCE OF THE S CORPORATION AS A PLANNING INSTRUMENT

By combining the non-tax benefits of the corporate form and the tax benefits of the partnership form of business, the S corporation has always been an important vehicle for the minimization of taxes. Changes in the taxation of C corporations following the

Tax Reform Act of 1986 (the "1986 Act") made S status even more desirable. The legislative repeal of the statutory *General Utilities* rule and its corollaries means that every corporation must recognize gain or loss on distribution of its appreciated assets to shareholders or upon a liquidating sale of the assets.

Following the 1986 Act, passthroughs (including partnerships, LLCs, and S corporations) were the entity of choice. Passthrough owners enjoyed the benefit of reduced individual rates while avoiding the double tax burden on distributed corporate earnings. Between 1986 and 2016, the number of C corporations generally declined, while the number and type of passthrough entities steadily increased. Beginning in 2012, the higher individual (but not corporate) tax rate and continued preferential treatment of qualified dividends tilted the balance somewhat back toward C corporations. Because C status entailed a potential second level of tax, however, operating in C form was still likely to be unappealing when S (or partnership) status was freely available. Although the 2017 reduction in the corporate tax rate has increased the relative attractiveness of C corporations, passthrough treatment is likely to remain attractive, especially for business income eligible for the § 199A deduction.

For an unprofitable business, an S election may offer substantial benefits. The shareholder in a regular C corporation is not permitted to report the corporation's loss on the shareholder's return; only upon disposition of the stock will the shareholder realize and be able to deduct any recognized loss. By contrast, under the S passthrough regime shareholders report the tax results of corporate activity on their own returns. Income is included but losses pass through as well, so that the shareholders essentially claim the corporate deductions or losses as their own. These losses are available to offset the shareholders' other income, subject to certain restrictions on the deductibility of such losses. Therefore, if a business anticipates losses in the early years, an S election affords the shareholders important tax advantages.[15] Under Subchapter S, an electing corporation obtains passthrough tax treatment, without sacrificing its entity character as a regular corporation for state law and all non-tax purposes.[16]

Comparison with Non-Electing C Corporations. One may ask why a C corporation is ever used if an S corporation could be elected. Sometimes the reason lies in the special conditions imposed on S corporations or the special needs of the investors. The eligibility requirements (such as the numerical shareholder limit) may preclude some S elections, particularly when capital must be raised from a large number of investors. Although the judicious use of debt may sometimes solve this problem, the S corporation is simply not the appropriate vehicle for widely held companies.

Sometimes the answer lies in the few residual tax advantages of C corporations versus passthroughs.[17] Today, S corporations (and partnerships) stand on just about the same footing as C corporations when it comes to qualified deferred compensation.[18] Although 2%-or-more shareholder-employees of an S corporation cannot enjoy the same

---

[15] The various loss limitations are discussed more fully in Chapter 6.

[16] In fact, it will bear separate corporate income tax under state income tax law, unless that tax system has adopted an S corporation regime for which the corporation qualifies, or unless state law determines state income tax liability for a corporation by reference to federal tax liability.

[17] Note that a C corporation can earn and retain income taxed at the 21% rate, which may fall below the shareholder's marginal rate. Section 1014 may eventually allow escape from a second tax on such earnings.

[18] *See* Eustice, Kuntz & Bogdanski, Federal Income Taxation of S Corporations ¶ 11.06[1] (5th ed. 2015).

fringe benefits as their C counterparts,[19] this relatively insignificant form of compensation is unlikely often to tip the balance against an S election.

For businesses that do not plan to distribute earnings currently, the ability to invest retained earnings at the low corporate tax rate provides a substantial advantage that increases the longer the earnings are retained. Deferral of the shareholder-level tax will be especially beneficial if a § 1014 death-time basis step-up is anticipated, eliminating tax on unrealized appreciation in a shareholder's shares.

Too often there is no satisfactory answer to the question raised, or at least any answer better than outmoded habits—such as that investments of this or that kind have "always" been done in corporate form.

Comparison with Partnerships (and LLCs). The decision whether to use a partnership or an S corporation involves questions of both tax and non-tax law. Of primary importance from a non-tax perspective, of course, is the availability of limited liability for S shareholders (unlike general partners), but that feature is also available to limited partners and members of a limited liability company (LLC). In the 1980s, the rise of LLCs called into question the appropriateness of distinguishing between double-tax and passthrough entities based on factors such as limited liability.[20] LLCs offer investors potentially the best of all possible worlds—the flexibility of the partnership tax rules combined with the limited liability of the corporate form. By operation of law, an LLC ensures protection for all of its owners (called members) from entity-level liabilities.

Newer forms of business organization include limited liability partnerships (LLPs) and limited liability limited partnerships (LLLPs). LLPs and LLLPs are simply variants of general partnerships and limited partnerships, respectively, with special limited liability shields. In contrast to the joint-and-several liability of general partners, each LLP member is typically shielded from liability for negligence or misconduct of other partners (and nonpartners not directly under such member's supervision). LLPs are especially popular among professional service partners who seek to insulate themselves from malpractice claims arising from other partners' misconduct. LLLP status is likely to be most attractive to existing limited partnerships that wish to provide limited liability for the general partner.

Under the check-the-box regulations, issued in 1996, a newly-formed domestic unincorporated entity (an "eligible entity") with at least two members is automatically classified as a partnership unless it elects to be treated as an association taxable as a corporation.[21] Given the rise of LLCs and the check-the-box regulations, some commentators predicted the demise of S corporations. Nevertheless, S corporations have continued to expand, in part because they may provide an advantage over other business forms in minimizing liability for employment taxes.[22]

---

[19] *See* ¶ 3.10.

[20] *See* Rev. Rul. 88–76, 1988–2, C.B. 360. LLC members can freely participate in management without losing limited liability.

[21] Reg. § 301.7701–3(b)(1). Proposed regulations also provide guidance concerning "series LLCs" engaged in multiple business or investment activities; under state law, obligations relating to one series may be enforceable only against the assets of that series and not against other series. *See* Prop. Reg. § 301.7701–1(a)(5) (generally treating each series as a separate entity for federal tax purposes, regardless of its status for state law purposes).

[22] *See* ¶ 3.11.

From a tax perspective, although both partnerships and S corporations enjoy a passthrough regime, the rules applicable to them differ in important ways. Generally speaking, Subchapter K offers a greater degree of flexibility to the participants than does Subchapter S, and partnerships are not subject to the eligibility restrictions that apply to S corporations. On the other hand, the Subchapter S rules provide greater certainty and simplicity than the comparable Subchapter K rules. The particular differences that matter in choosing between a partnership, LLC, or S corporation are discussed in Chapter 10.

¶ 1.11   APPLICATION OF SUBCHAPTER C TO S CORPORATIONS FOR SOME PURPOSES

Although Subchapter S invites corporations to elect an alternative tax regime, Subchapter S is not entirely autonomous and self-contained. As § 1371(a) specifies, except as otherwise provided or inconsistent with Subchapter S, Subchapter C continues to apply to an S corporation and its shareholders.

For example, Subchapter C rules play an important role in connection with formation of an S corporation, stock redemptions, liquidating and nonliquidating distributions, and reorganizations (acquisitive and divisive). Consequently, Chapters 7 and 8 examine how an S corporation is formed, operates, reorganizes or liquidates under the governing rules of Subchapter C. Particular attention is given to those Subchapter C rules that have special significance when the corporation has made an S election.

¶ 1.12   A REMINDER ABOUT STATE AND FOREIGN TAXES

A Subchapter S election affects only the *federal* income tax treatment of the corporation and its shareholders. The treatment under state, local and foreign tax laws is not affected. Consequently, the S corporation may be left to compute and pay state income tax as an entity to its state of incorporation or to other taxing authorities. Shareholders then may also find themselves taxable on dividends. Nearly all states that have income taxes permit a parallel S election and treat S corporations in ways corresponding closely with federal law. In those few states lacking special rules that parallel Subchapter S, the result may be a "double tax" on distributed income, an inability to pass through losses, and other "normal" corporate tax effects.[23]

State taxation of S corporations becomes quite complicated when interstate business or investment occurs, and a "host" (incorporation) state faces the problem of how to tax nonresident shareholders. There is no constitutional bar against a state taxing nonresident shareholders on income that is either sourced in the taxing state or is attributable to a corporation domiciled in a taxing state, although sourced elsewhere. Some states condition S corporation treatment (and thus exemption from state corporate income tax) on all (nonresident) shareholders consenting to such taxation. Some states prohibit S treatment if there are nonresident shareholders—paralleling the federal prohibition against foreign shareholders in an S corporation.

To ensure collection of taxes imposed on shareholders, other states require the S corporation to withhold and pay over an appropriate percentage of every nonresident's pro rata share of S corporation income. Still others require the S corporation to pay the

---

[23] Sometimes, a double *advantage* may be obtained if the state allows a parallel state-law S election and does *not* tax individual income.

tax if the shareholders fail to do so. Since innocent shareholders can therefore be hurt by the failure of another shareholder to pay or consent, the shareholders' agreement should contain provisions addressing these issues and related protections. Basis problems also beset nonresident S corporation shareholders. A shareholder's basis in S shares will be reduced by passthrough of losses, increasing realized gain on sale of the shareholder's stock. Such gain will be taxed by the S shareholder's resident or domiciliary state, not the host state. To help solve some of these and related problems, some states have adopted the proposed Model S Corporation Income Tax Act, as discussed briefly in Chapter 11.

Foreign income taxes may apply to an electing S corporation's foreign source income (with no relief for its S status), since another country may treat the electing S corporation as having "normal" corporate status. If so, the United States usually will grant a foreign tax credit under § 901 to relieve *international* double taxation.[24]

¶ 1.13 THE FUTURE OF SUBCHAPTER S

Past experience suggests that Subchapter S is likely to continue to grow and gain importance in the future, although reductions in the corporate tax rate could adversely affect the incentives to elect passthrough treatment. As a matter of future tax policy, Subchapter S could serve as a model for the taxation of all corporations, either on an elective or a mandatory basis. Eligibility for the S election could gradually be expanded until it embraced or pre-empted Subchapter C.

If the corporate income tax on C corporations were to become completely integrated with the individual income tax, Subchapter S could wither or be repealed. Or, depending on the integration model chosen, it could serve as an alternative, elective method of integrating corporate-shareholder taxation. If partial integration or dividend relief were enacted for C corporations,[25] Subchapter S could remain as a further option for eligible electing corporations. Or, Subchapter S could be made mandatory for some class of corporations, such as all those now eligible to elect.

While Subchapter S continues to serve as a potential integration model (in what one commentator has called "the search for the pass-through paradigm"),[26] it also provides a major choice for U.S. business and investment in an increasingly global economy.

---

[24] The rules of Subchapter S provide that any foreign tax will be passed through pro rata and credited (or deducted) by the shareholders. *See* I.R.C. §§ 1366(a)(1), 1373(a), 901(b)(5).

[25] In 2003, Congress enacted a form of partial integration by taxing dividends at a reduced rate. For more ambitious corporate-shareholder integration proposals, see Integration of Corporate and Individual Income Taxes: An Introduction to the Issues, in Integration of the U.S. Corporate and Individual Income Taxes: The Treasury Department and American Law Institute Reports 3 (Graetz & Warren eds., 1998).

[26] *See* Eustice, Subchapter S Corporations and Partnerships: A Search for the Pass-Through Paradigm, 39 Tax L. Rev. 345 (1984).

Chapter 2

ACQUIRING S STATUS AND MAINTAINING IT

¶ 2.01   SUBCHAPTER S REQUIREMENTS, PROCEDURES AND TAX RESULTS

To first avail itself of Subchapter S, a corporation and its shareholders must meet the eligibility requirements and a valid S election must be made.[1] To remain under Subchapter S, the qualifying attributes of the corporation and its shareholders must be maintained and the election must not be revoked or terminated.

Termination of S status, whether intended, inadvertent or involuntary, can take place under a plethora of rules. The tests for initial eligibility also serve as requirements for continued eligibility, though they may be applied differently for these two purposes.

All these subjects are the focus of the following sections on: qualification (¶¶ 2.02–2.10), election (¶¶ 2.11–2.12), revocation and termination (¶¶ 2.13–2.18), and the effects of termination and options for re-electing (¶¶ 2.19–2.24).

¶ 2.02   QUALIFYING FOR S CORPORATION TREATMENT—§ 1361

To qualify for S corporation treatment, the corporation must be an eligible corporation (not "ineligible," as the statute puts it); it must have only the permitted kinds of shareholders, not exceeding a specified maximum number; and it must have only the permitted kind of stock outstanding. In addition, it must have a permitted taxable year and must meet certain other requirements, often within particular time periods. Only if it is eligible, under all these tests, can the corporation make an S election.

¶ 2.03   ELIGIBLE CORPORATIONS—§ 1361(a)

To become a § 1361(a) "S corporation," a corporation must be a "small business corporation" for which an election under § 1362(a) is in effect for the year in question.[2] What constitutes a "small business corporation" is specified by the Code as a *domestic* corporation which is "not an ineligible corporation" *and* which does not violate certain conditions.[3]

To be a "domestic corporation," the corporation must be one created or organized in the United States or under the law of the United States or of any state.[4] Most ordinary domestic corporations will not be "ineligible." (Note again that there is no qualification or condition related to financial size.)

---

[1]   *See* I.R.C. §§ 1361, 1362.

[2]   I.R.C. § 1361(a)(1). A "corporation" includes any association taxable as a corporation, whether or not organized as a corporation under local laws. *See* I.R.C. § 7701(a)(3); Reg. §§ 301.7701–2(b), 1.1361–1(c). Under the check-the-box regulations, even an unincorporated association may be a "small business corporation" if it elects to be taxed as a corporation.

[3]   I.R.C. § 1361(b)(1).

[4]   I.R.C. § 7701(a)(4). Although a foreign corporation is ineligible to be an S corporation, a "domestic corporation" *may* be one that does business abroad or has foreign income.

To avoid being an "ineligible corporation," the domestic corporation must not be a financial institution that uses the reserve method of accounting described in § 585, an insurance company or a DISC or a former DISC.[5]

¶ 2.04   INELIGIBLE CORPORATIONS: AFFILIATED CORPORATIONS (PRIOR LAW)

Prior to 1996, an S corporation was ineligible to be a member of an "affiliated group" (determined under § 1504 with certain modifications). Thus, an S corporation could not be an 80% parent of another corporation.[6] (An S corporation could never be a "controlled" subsidiary because of the prohibition against having a corporate shareholder (even another S corporation), as discussed below.) Even under prior law, "transitory" ownership was sometimes ignored.[7] In 1996, Congress allowed S corporations to own stock in another corporation without any limit, so that an S corporation is now free to have a wholly-owned subsidiary. At the same time, Congress amended § 1504 to make an S corporation ineligible to be included within a consolidated group.[8]

Under current law, an S subsidiary may be a non-electing C corporation or an entity that meets the requirements of a "qualified subchapter S subsidiary" (QSub).[9] If the S parent so elects, a QSub is essentially ignored as a separate entity for federal tax purposes, and the assets and liabilities of the QSub are treated as assets and liabilities of the S parent. The check-the-box regulations further expand the possibilities. For example, an S corporation may have as a subsidiary a single-member LLC that is treated as a disregarded entity under § 7701.[10]

¶ 2.05   OTHER INELIGIBLE CORPORATIONS

There are three categories of corporations that the Code explicitly makes ineligible to be S corporations. First, a financial institution may not elect under Subchapter S if it uses the reserve method of accounting for bad debts described in § 585.[11] This rule is intended to prevent special corporate tax benefits from passing through to shareholders. Second, insurance companies subject to tax under Subchapter L are ineligible to be S corporations.[12] Third, a DISC or former DISC is ineligible to be an S corporation.[13]

---

[5]   I.R.C. § 1361(b)(2). "DISC" stands for Domestic International Sales Corporation. *See* I.R.C. § 992(a) (defining a DISC or former DISC).

[6]   *See* I.R.C. § 1504(a) (80% or more ownership of *both* voting power and total value).

[7]   *See, e.g.,* Rev. Rul. 73–496, 1973–2 C.B. 312 (transitory subsidiary); Rev. Rul. 72–320, 1972–1 C.B. 270 (spin-off of controlled corporation). The prohibition on affiliation was aimed mainly at avoiding complications involving passthrough of income and losses with multiple corporations and cross ownership. Momentary ownership did not implicate these concerns.

[8]   I.R.C. § 1504(b)(6). If a C corporation subsidiary of an S corporation has its own C corporation subsidiaries, these entities can file a consolidated return.

[9]   I.R.C. § 1361(b)(3); *see* ¶ 2.08.

[10]   *See* Reg. § 1.1361–2(d) (ex. 2).

[11]   I.R.C. § 1361(b)(2)(A). Note that a bank (defined in § 581) may generally elect Subchapter S if it does not use the reserve method of accounting for bad debts.

[12]   I.R.C. § 1361(b)(2)(B).

[13]   I.R.C. § 1361(b)(2)(C). The successor to the DISC, the FSC (Foreign Sales Corporation) could never be an S corporation because it was a foreign corporation. The FSC provisions were repealed in 2000.

¶ 2.06   AN ELIGIBLE CORPORATION'S OWNERSHIP RESTRICTIONS—§ 1361(b)

If a corporation is *not* an ineligible corporation, under the rules of § 1361(b)(2), it will be allowed to make an effective S election only if doing so does not violate any of the *prohibitions* of § 1361(b)(1). This cluster of rules, to be discussed in turn, specifies: (1) the maximum number of shareholders permitted to hold stock in an S corporation, (2) what kinds of persons and types of entities can be shareholders, and (3) the type of stock an S corporation may have outstanding. Also, another rule provides that a corporation cannot elect to be an S corporation if that corporation (or its predecessor) lost its S status within the four previous tax years.[14]

¶ 2.07   NUMBER OF SHAREHOLDERS

It is an absolute rule that an S corporation may not have more than 100 shareholders.[15] This limitation applies to the number of shareholders at any one time during the taxable year. (Thus, a corporation will not lose its S status if any of its 100 shareholders transfers her interest to a new shareholder during the year, as long as at any one time there are not more than 100 shareholders.[16]) For purposes of the 100-shareholder limit, a married couple (and their respective estates) is treated as a single shareholder, regardless of whether the spouses hold stock jointly or separately.[17] In addition, all members of a family (and their estates) are automatically treated as a single shareholder.[18] Family members are defined as a common ancestor (going back six generations) and all lineal descendants (and their spouses or former spouses) of such common ancestor.[19]

It is the *beneficial* owners of certain entities holding shares in an S corporation[20] who are treated as the shareholders for purposes of calculating the limitation on the number of shareholders under § 1361(b)(1). Technical title alone does not determine ownership for these purposes. Thus, in the case of certain trusts which are treated under Subpart E of Part I of Subchapter J (the "grantor trust" and § 678 trust rules) as wholly owned by an individual who is a U.S. citizen or resident (hereinafter referred to as "subpart E trusts"),[21] the deemed owner of the trust is treated as the shareholder.[22] After the death of the deemed owner, the deemed owner's estate is treated as the shareholder for up to two years.[23] In the case of a trust holding shares of an S corporation transferred

---

[14] I.R.C. § 1362(g) (unless the Secretary consents to an earlier election). *See* ¶ 2.21.

[15] I.R.C. § 1361(b)(1)(A).

[16] *See* Rev. Rul. 78–390, 1978–2 C.B. 220.

[17] I.R.C. § 1361(c)(1)(A)(i).

[18] I.R.C. § 1361(c)(1)(A)(ii).

[19] I.R.C. § 1361(c)(1)(B).

[20] *See, e.g., Kean v. Comm'r*, 469 F.2d 1183 (9th Cir. 1972) (unregistered person who would be required to include dividends in income is a shareholder whose consent is required); *see* Reg. § 1.1361–1(e)(1). The rules on what types of entities are permitted to hold shares in an S corporation are discussed immediately below.

[21] *See* Reg. § 1.1361–1(h)(1)(i) (using the term "Subpart E trust" to refer to a trust all of which is treated as owned by one U.S. citizen or resident individual).

[22] I.R.C. § 1361(c)(2)(B)(i).

[23] I.R.C. § 1361(c)(2)(B)(ii), (c)(2)(A)(ii). In a community property state, the decedent's estate is treated as the shareholder only of the portion of the trust included in the decedent's gross estate; the surviving spouse continues to be treated as the shareholder of the portion of the trust owned by the spouse under community property law. Reg. § 1.1361–1(h)(3)(i)(B).

to it pursuant to the terms of a will, the estate of the testator is treated as the shareholder for up to two years.[24]

Each beneficiary of a voting trust (a trust created primarily to exercise the voting power of the stock transferred to it) is treated as a shareholder.[25] If shares are held by a nominee, custodian or agent, the beneficial owners are the shareholders.[26] Since neither § 1361 nor §§ 671–678 (subpart E trusts) invokes the constructive ownership rules of § 318, stock attribution rules are not used in determining the number of shareholders.

The IRS has ruled that a partnership of S corporations does not violate the purpose of the 100-shareholder limit.[27] According to the IRS, the 100-shareholder limit is intended to preserve administrative simplicity. Under this "purpose" analysis, the S status of corporate partners should be respected, since a partnership arrangement does not introduce complexity at the S corporation level. It might be simpler to eliminate the 100-shareholder limit and merely deny S eligibility to publicly traded corporations.[28]

¶ 2.08   PERMITTED SHAREHOLDERS IN AN S CORPORATION

In General. In keeping with Congressional intent to offer the benefits of passthrough treatment only to relatively simple forms of corporate organization, § 1361 imposes significant limitations on the types of shareholders an S corporation may have. Careful attention must be paid to the eligibility of shareholders, as the penalty for noncompliance is termination of the S election. As described in more detail below, shareholders of S corporations must be either individuals, certain estates (including the estate of an individual in bankruptcy),[29] certain trusts,[30] or certain tax-exempt organizations.[31] Not permitted are: corporations (C or S type),[32] nonresident aliens,[33] partnerships, and foreign trusts.[34] (The rules for determining who is treated as the shareholder when an entity other than an individual holds shares in an S corporation were discussed in ¶ 2.07.)

In 1996, Congress allowed pension trusts and charitable organizations to be S shareholders. Special rules may, however, subject the tax-exempt entity's share of S

---

[24] I.R.C. § 1361(c)(2)(B)(iii), (c)(2)(A)(iii). If the trust continues to hold S stock beyond the two-year period, it may nevertheless remain a permitted shareholder if it otherwise qualifies as a QSST or ESBT, discussed below.

[25] I.R.C. § 1361(c)(2)(B)(iv), (c)(2)(A)(iv).

[26] *See* Reg. § 1.1361–1(e)(1).

[27] Rev. Rul. 94–43, 1994–2 C.B. 198. Whether partnerships may be used to circumvent other S limitations may depend on the purpose of the particular provision.

[28] *See* I.R.C. § 7704(b) (defining "publicly traded partnership").

[29] The term "estate" in § 1361(b)(1)(B) refers only to a decedent's estate or an individual's bankruptcy estate, not to the estate of an infant, incompetent or disabled person. Rev. Rul. 66–266, 1966–2 C.B. 356; I.R.C. § 1361(c)(3) (expressly allowing estate in bankruptcy to be an S corporation shareholder). If the estate is held open too long, it may be deemed to terminate. *Old Virginia Brick Co. v. Comm'r*, 44 T.C. 724 (1965), *aff'd*, 367 F.2d 276 (4th Cir. 1966).

[30] I.R.C. § 1361(b)(1)(B), (c)(2).

[31] I.R.C. § 1361(b)(1)(B), (c)(6).

[32] I.R.C. § 1361(b)(1)(B).

[33] I.R.C. § 1361(b)(1)(C). Hence an individual owner must either be a U.S. citizen or a resident alien. *Cf.* Reg. § 1.701–2(d) (ex. 2) (allowing use of partnership to avoid S restriction on nonresident aliens).

[34] I.R.C. § 1361(b)(1)(B), (c)(2).

income to the unrelated business income tax.[35] In general, traditional IRAs and Roth IRAs are not eligible S shareholders, since income is not taxed currently to the beneficiaries.[36] A limited exception exists for certain stock of banks that are S corporations.[37] An "employee stock ownership plan" (ESOP) may be an S shareholder, but certain special benefits are disallowed if the employer is an S corporation.[38]

Trusts. Not every kind of trust will be permitted to hold shares in an S corporation, probably out of fear that trusts generally could be used to allocate earnings of S corporations other than strictly according to stock ownership. The only types of trusts that are eligible to hold shares in an S corporation are (1) trusts all of which are treated (under Subpart E of Part I of Subchapter J, "grantor trusts" and "§ 678 trusts") as owned by an individual who is a U.S. citizen or resident ("Subpart E trusts"), (2) trusts receiving testamentary transfers of S corporation stock—but only for two years, (3) voting trusts, (4) qualified Subchapter S trusts (QSSTs), and (5) electing small business trusts (ESBTs).[39] Foreign trusts are not permitted to hold shares in an S corporation.[40]

Subpart E Trusts. A subpart E trust may hold shares in an S corporation.[41] A subpart E trust is a grantor trust or any other trust all of which is treated (under subpart E of Part I of Subchapter J) as owned by an individual who is a U.S. citizen or resident.[42]

> *Example 2.1:* X Corp. is an S corporation. X Corp.'s shares are held in trust by AB Trust with A as grantor and B as beneficiary. If either A or B (but only one of them), acting alone, has the power to vest the entire corpus and income in him or herself, then the AB Trust is a subpart E trust and may properly hold X Corp. stock. A or B (whoever holds the unilateral power to claim the trust) will be treated as the shareholder.[43]

Trusts Receiving Testamentary Transfers. A trust may hold shares of an S corporation transferred to it pursuant to the terms of a will, but only for two years from the date of such transfer.[44]

---

[35]   *See* I.R.C. § 512(e). The IRS has indicated that it will challenge abusive transactions designed to artificially shift the tax incidence (but not the economic benefit) of S corporation income to a tax-exempt entity. IRS Notice 2004–30, 2004–1 C.B. 828.

[36]   *See Taproot Admin. Serv., Inc. v. Comm'r,* 679 F.3d 1109 (9th Cir. 2012).

[37]   I.R.C. § 1361(c)(2)(A)(vi); Reg. § 1.1361–1(h)(1)(vii).

[38]   For example, the special deduction, under § 404(a), for contributions used to pay principal and interest is not available. *See* I.R.C. § 404(a)(9)(C). Unlike other tax-exempt entities, ESOP shareholders of an S corporation are not required to treat income of the S corporation as income from an "unrelated trade or business" for purposes of § 512. *See* I.R.C. § 512(e)(3). Thus, any tax on an ESOP shareholder's share of S income is deferred until the ESOP distributes such income.

[39]   I.R.C. § 1361(c)(2), (d), and (e).

[40]   I.R.C. § 1361(c)(2)(A); Reg. § 1.1361–1(h)(2). *See* I.R.C. § 7701(a)(31) (defining a "foreign trust").

[41]   I.R.C. § 1361(c)(2)(A)(i); Reg. § 1.1361–1(h)(1)(i).

[42]   *Id.*

[43]   A trust that was treated as a subpart E trust prior to the death of the deemed owner and which continues in existence after that individual's death, but ceases to be a Subpart E trust, may continue holding shares in the S corporation for two years. Thus, if the AB Trust is a subpart E trust and A is the deemed owner because A has the power to reclaim both income and corpus, but A dies before exercising such power, then A's estate is treated as the deemed owner of the X Corp. stock (for up to two years). *See* I.R.C. § 1361(c)(2)(A)(ii).

[44]   I.R.C. § 1361(c)(2)(A)(iii). Presumably, the trusts referred to in clauses (iii) and (iv) refer to trusts other than subpart E trusts.

Voting Trusts. In principle, a trust created primarily to exercise the voting power of stock transferred to it may hold shares of an S corporation.[45] Because the beneficial owners of a voting trust are treated as the shareholders, it is indispensable that each beneficial owner comply with the rules regarding persons eligible to be an S corporation shareholder.[46]

Qualified Subchapter S Trusts. A tightly-restricted trust exclusively for S corporations, known as a Qualified Subchapter S Trust ("QSST"), is permitted to hold shares in an S corporation.[47] To do so, a beneficiary of the trust (or the beneficiary's legal representative) must make an election for the trust to qualify as a QSST.[48] Once made, such an election is revocable only with the consent of the Secretary.[49] The beneficiary of the trust is treated as the owner of the S corporation stock.[50]

In order to qualify as a QSST, the trust terms must meet *all* of the following five requirements:[51]

(1)   During the life of the current income beneficiary, there can be only one income beneficiary. (However, a "substantially separate and independent" share of a trust, within the meaning of § 663(c), is treated as a separate QSST.[52])

(2)   Any corpus distributed during the life of the current income beneficiary may be distributed only to such beneficiary.

(3)   The income interest of the current income beneficiary must terminate on the earlier of that person's death or the termination of the trust.

(4)   Upon termination of the trust during the life of the current income beneficiary, the trust must distribute all of its assets to such beneficiary.

(5)   All of the trust's income (as defined by the trust instrument and local law)[53] must be distributed (or be required to be distributed) to one individual who is a U.S. citizen or resident.[54]

---

[45]   I.R.C. § 1361(c)(2)(A)(iv).

[46]   *See* I.R.C. § 1361(c)(2)(B)(iv). Thus, nonresident aliens and corporations cannot be the beneficial owners of S corporation shares held by a voting trust. For the requirements to qualify as a voting trust eligible to hold shares in an S corporation, see Reg. § 1.1361–1(h)(1)(v).

[47]   I.R.C. § 1361(d). Under § 1361(d)(1)(A), a QSST will be treated at a Subpart E trust for purposes of § 1361(c)(2)(A)(i).

[48]   I.R.C. § 1361(d)(2)(A). The requirements for making an election to be treated as a QSST are discussed below.

[49]   I.R.C. § 1361(d)(2)(C).

[50]   I.R.C. § 1361(d)(1)(B).

[51]   *See* I.R.C. § 1361(d)(3). If the trust fails to meet any of requirements (1) through (4), the trust will cease to be a QSST as of the date such requirement ceases to be met. I.R.C. § 1361(d)(4). If the trust fails to meet requirement (5), but continues to meet all of the other requirements, then the trust will fail to qualify as a QSST as of the first day of the following tax year. *See* I.R.C. § 1361(d)(4)(B).

[52]   I.R.C. § 1361(d)(3) (flush language). Thus, a trust may have more than one current income beneficiary and still qualify as a QSST, as long as each income beneficiary is treated as holding a substantially separate share of the trust. Reg. § 1.1361–1(j)(3); Rev. Rul. 93–31, 1993–1 C.B. 186. Although multiple income beneficiaries at any one time are prohibited, the trust may provide for multiple income beneficiaries after the death of the current income beneficiary. In that event, however, the trust will cease to be a QSST upon the death of the single income beneficiary.

[53]   *See* I.R.C. § 643(b).

[54]   *See* I.R.C. § 1361(d)(3)(B).

The regulations set forth the manner in which a beneficiary of a trust must make an election for the trust to qualify as a QSST.[55] They also provide narrow time limits for electing to be treated as a QSST.[56]

Why Use a QSST? Trusts can be made to qualify as QSSTs while accomplishing common and important estate planning objectives. These include obtaining the marital deduction and creating a power of appointment trust (§ 2056(b)(5)), a QTIP trust (§ 2056(b)(7)), or one qualifying for the annual gift tax exclusion (§ 2503(c)).[57]

Electing Small Business Trusts. Stock of an S corporation may also be held by an "electing small business trust" (ESBT), as defined in § 1361(e)(1)(A). The beneficiaries of an ESBT are limited to individuals, estates, and certain charitable organizations. Furthermore, no interest in the trust may be acquired by "purchase," *i.e.*, acquired with a cost basis under § 1012.[58]

An ESBT may be particularly useful for estate planning purposes, since it is permitted to have multiple beneficiaries and accumulate income. Each potential current beneficiary of the trust is treated as a single shareholder.[59] If there is no current beneficiary for a particular period, the ESBT is treated as a single shareholder.[60] Beginning in 2018, a nonresident alien can be a potential current beneficiary of an ESBT; such a beneficiary is not treated as a prohibited shareholder for purposes of § 1361(b)(1)(C).[61] A corporation's S election terminates if a potential current beneficiary is an ineligible shareholder.[62] Although potential current beneficiaries count toward the numerical shareholder limit, the special rule treating family members as a single shareholder applies.[63]

Except for net capital gains and qualified dividends taxed under § 1(h), an ESBT is taxed at the highest rate applicable to trusts (37%) on its ratable share of S income.[64] No amount is included, however, in the beneficiaries' income when distributed. Taxing income at the highest rate ensures that an ESBT will be used for estate planning purposes other than tax avoidance.

Qualified Subchapter S Subsidiaries. A qualified subchapter S subsidiary ("QSub") is a domestic corporation (other than an ineligible corporation) whose stock is wholly

---

[55] *See* Reg. § 1.1361–1(j)(6). For the rules relating to revoking a QSST election, see Reg. § 1.1361–1(j)(11).

[56] Generally, the election must be made within a period of two months and sixteen days beginning with the later of either (1) the transfer to the trust of shares of the S corporation or (2) the first day of the first year in which the corporation's election to be treated as an S corporation becomes effective. Reg. § 1.1361–1(j)(6)(iii). A successive income beneficiary is treated as having consented to the election unless that beneficiary affirmatively refuses to consent to the election. *See* Reg. § 1.1361–1(j)(9). Under certain circumstances, an invalid QSST election may be waived. *See* ¶ 2.24.

[57] *See* Reg. § 1.1361–1(j)(4) (QTIP trust).

[58] I.R.C. § 1361(e)(1)(C).

[59] A potential current beneficiary is an individual who is eligible to receive income or principal of the trust (determined without regard to any power of appointment that remains unexercised). I.R.C. § 1361(e)(2).

[60] I.R.C. § 1361(c)(2)(B)(v).

[61] *Id.* (second sentence). *See* Reg. § 1.1361–1(m)(4)(i).

[62] Reg. § 1.1361–1(m)(5)(iii).

[63] I.R.C. § 1361(c)(1)(A)(ii).

[64] *See* I.R.C. § 641(c). This treatment applies only to the "S portion" of the ESBT that consists of S stock; the "grantor portion" of an ESBT is subject to the normal rules applicable to subpart E trusts. *See* Reg. § 1.641(c)–1. If a nonresident alien is the deemed owner of the grantor portion, however, items are reallocated to the S portion and remain subject to U.S. federal income tax. *See* Reg. § 1.641(c)–1(b)(1)(ii), (2)(ii).

owned by an S corporation (the "S parent") which makes a QSub election for the subsidiary.[65] If QSub status is elected, the subsidiary is treated as a "disregarded entity," and its assets and liabilities are treated as assets and liabilities of the S parent.[66] The election is generally treated as giving rise to a deemed liquidation of the QSub into the S parent, which will be tax free under the normal Subchapter C rules governing subsidiary liquidations.[67]

The consequences of the deemed liquidation (and any accompanying larger transaction) are determined under general tax principles, including the step-transaction doctrine. For example, if an S corporation forms a subsidiary and simultaneously makes a valid QSub election for the subsidiary, the subsidiary is simply treated as a QSub from the outset; under the step-transaction doctrine, the incorporation (and deemed liquidation) are disregarded.[68] Thus, a QSub election that occurs as part of a larger transaction will not always result in a deemed liquidation. If a deemed liquidation does occur, the liquidation is generally treated as occurring the day *before* the QSub election becomes effective.[69]

As long as QSub status is maintained, the S parent will include any income and deductions of the QSub in determining its own taxable income, just as if the QSub were a division.[70] A QSub resembles a single-member LLC treated as a disregarded entity. Indeed, an S corporation may consider forming a disregarded single-member LLC as an alternative to a QSub, given the relative flexibility and ease of operation of LLCs. Nevertheless, owning a QSub will often be preferable to owning a separate C subsidiary. The QSub arrangement offers the practical benefits of consolidation, since any dealings between the QSub and its S parent will be ignored.

Foreign Trusts. A foreign trust may not own shares in an S corporation.[71] A trust is classified as a foreign trust unless it qualifies as a domestic trust, as defined in § 7701(a)(30)(E).[72] Under the two-pronged definition of a domestic trust, two requirements must both be satisfied concurrently: a U.S. court must be able to exercise primary supervision over administration of the trust (the "court test") and one or more U.S. persons must have authority to control all substantial decisions of the trust (the "control test").[73] While the statutory test provides relative certainty, reclassification of a domestic trust as a foreign trust may have adverse consequences under § 1361, potentially terminating the corporation's S election.[74]

---

[65]   I.R.C. § 1361(b)(3)(B); Reg. § 1.1361–3(a) (election mechanics). The 100% ownership test can be satisfied directly or indirectly, and the S parent may own a chain of two or more QSubs. *See* I.R.C. § 1361(b)(3)(A); Reg. § 1.1361–2(d) (ex. 1–3).

[66]   I.R.C. § 1361(b)(3)(A). The QSub's stock is generally ignored, and debt of the QSub is treated as debt of the parent. The QSub may nevertheless be treated as a separate entity for certain purposes, such as employment taxes. *See* Reg. § 1.1361–4(a)(7).

[67]   *See* I.R.C. §§ 332, 334(b), 337; Reg. § 1.1361–4(a)(2). The election is treated as the adoption of a plan of complete liquidation for purposes of § 332. *See* Reg. § 1.1361–4(a)(2)(iii).

[68]   *See* Reg. § 1.1361–4(a)(2).

[69]   *See* Reg. § 1.1361–4(b)(1); *see also* Reg. § 1.1361–4(b)(3)(i) (deemed liquidation occurs immediately after S parent first owns 100% of the subsidiary's stock).

[70]   I.R.C. § 1363(b)(3)(A)(ii).

[71]   I.R.C. § 1361(c)(2)(A) (flush language).

[72]   I.R.C. § 7701(a)(31)(B).

[73]   *See* Reg. § 1.7701–7(a)(1).

[74]   *See* I.R.C. § 1361(b)(1)(B). Under § 679, the grantor of the trust may also be subject to tax as the grantor of a foreign trust having U.S. beneficiaries; this provision generally treats a U.S. person who transfers

Commentators have argued that the restrictions on foreign owners of S corporations (*i.e.*, foreign trusts and nonresident alien individuals) should be abolished. According to this argument, it would be possible to adapt for Subchapter S purposes the rules under § 875, which tax a foreign partner on such partner's share of a partnership's "effectively connected income" when the partnership engages in a U.S. trade or business. Under current law, the prohibition on foreign owners may be a trap for the unwary. For example, an inadvertent termination of a corporation's S status could occur by reason of a marriage by a shareholder to a nonresident alien subject to community property laws.[75]

Guardians and Custodians. Stock held by a custodian under the Uniform Transfers to Minors Act will be deemed to be owned by the minor shareholder, who is a permitted S corporation shareholder. Similarly, stock held by a guardian or a conservator for a minor or incompetent person will be deemed held by the individual beneficial owner.[76] Presumably a foreign custodian, guardian or conservator for a U.S. person would be permissible. Similarly, a bankrupt individual's Title 11 case will not be disqualifying; the individual's bankruptcy estate is a permitted shareholder.[77]

¶ 2.09   PERMITTED STOCK: ONE-CLASS-OF-STOCK RULE—§ 1361(b)

To be eligible to elect Subchapter S treatment, a corporation must confine itself to a simple and rather inflexible capital structure. It may have both debt and stock, but only one class of stock may be outstanding.[78] The rule is designed to prevent the use of the S corporation to "steer" income and losses to particular shareholders. Thus, the one-class-of-stock rule is somewhat analogous to the "special allocation" rules applicable to partnerships. As described below, the rule has rather technical contours. Moreover, the regulations elaborating the one-class-of-stock rule must be studied carefully when evaluating the capital structure of an S corporation. As with any of the eligibility requirements, a particular danger is that an electing S corporation will either be deemed ineligible or will inadvertently lose its S status as a result of failure to meet these requirements.

An eligible corporation simply may not have more than one class of stock outstanding. This rule requires very strict compliance, as a number of unhappily litigated cases have demonstrated. The general rule is subject to two helpful qualifications: one, for kinds of stock that differ *only* with respect to voting rights, and two, for "straight debt" which will not be treated as a second class of stock. By virtue of § 1361(b)(1)(D), no second class of stock that is preferred, as to dividends or liquidation distributions, is compatible with a Subchapter S election.

The one-class-of-stock requirement is designed to ensure that each share of stock represents an equal share in the profits and assets of the corporation, and obviates the need to allocate income among different classes of stock. Generally, a corporation has

---

property to a foreign trust as the owner of the portion of the trust attributable to such property if, for that year, there is a U.S. beneficiary of the foreign trust. See I.R.C. § 679.

[75]   *See* Eustice, Kuntz & Bogdanski, Federal Income Taxation of S Corporations ¶ 1.03[2][b][iv] (5th ed. 2015).

[76]   *See* Rev. Rul. 66–266, 1966–2 C.B. 356.

[77]   *See* I.R.C. §§ 1361(c)(3), 1398.

[78]   I.R.C. § 1361(b)(1)(D). A corporation with more than one class of stock outstanding may still become eligible for treatment as an S corporation by recapitalizing, by redeeming all outstanding shares of all but one class or by merging into a wholly-owned subsidiary that has only one class of stock.

only one class of stock if "all outstanding shares . . . confer identical rights to distribution and liquidation proceeds."[79] Only issued and outstanding stock is considered when determining whether a corporation has more than one class of stock.[80] Thus, an S corporation may have authorized but *unissued* preferred stock.

Stock issued in connection with services that is not transferable and is subject to a substantial risk of forfeiture is not considered outstanding stock unless the holder makes a § 83(b) election with respect to such stock (thus treating receipt of the stock as a taxable event).[81] If a § 83(b) election is made, the holder of restricted stock is treated as a shareholder. Conversely, a call option[82] is treated as a second class of stock if it is "substantially certain" to be exercised by the holder and has a strike price substantially below the fair market value of the underlying stock when issued (or at certain other times).[83]

Identical Rights to Distributions and Liquidating Proceeds. The determination of whether all outstanding shares of stock confer identical rights to distribution and liquidation proceeds is based on the "governing provisions" (*i.e.*, the corporate charter, articles and bylaws, binding agreements relating to distribution and liquidation proceeds, and applicable state law).[84] Normal commercial arrangements (*e.g.*, leases, employment contracts, and loans) are generally not treated as governing provisions unless a principal purpose of the arrangement is to circumvent the one-class-of-stock requirement. Provided that the governing provisions confer identical rights, distributions that differ in timing or amount do not give rise to a second class of stock, but they may be recharacterized for other tax purposes (*e.g.*, as a below-market loan under § 7872).[85]

When a change in stock ownership occurs, distributions that reflect the shareholders' varying interests during the year do not violate the one-class-of-stock requirement.[86] A state-law requirement that the corporation withhold state income taxes on behalf of some shareholders does not give rise to a second class of stock if it affects only the timing (not the amount) of distributions.[87] In effect, the corporation's payment of state income tax on behalf of some shareholders is treated as a constructive distribution, which must be taken into account in determining whether all shareholders are entitled to equal distributions.[88] The one-class-of-stock requirement is violated, however, if a corporation attempts to equalize the shareholders' after-tax burdens by distributing greater amounts to those shareholders with heavier state tax burdens.[89]

---

[79]   Reg. § 1.1361–1(*l*)(1).

[80]   Reg. § 1.1361–1(*l*)(3).

[81]   Reg. § 1.1361–1(b)(3), (*l*)(3). *See Austin v. Comm'r*, T.C. Memo 2017–69 (2017) (S stock issued for services was initially nonvested because subject to a substantial risk of forfeiture; the stock subsequently became vested when the restrictions lapsed).

[82]   A call option is an option to acquire stock of a corporation at a specified price, known as the "strike price." *See* Rev. Rul. 58–234, 1958–1 C.B. 279.

[83]   Reg. § 1.1361–1(*l*)(4)(iii)(A). Under a safe harbor, an option is not treated as a second class of stock if the strike price is at least 90% of the fair market value of the underlying stock on the relevant testing dates. Reg. § 1.1361–1(*l*)(4)(iii)(C).

[84]   Reg. § 1.1361–1(*l*)(2)(i).

[85]   Reg. § 1.1361–1(*l*)(2)(vi) (ex. 5); *see id.* (ex. 3) (excessive compensation).

[86]   Reg. § 1.1361–1(*l*)(2)(iv).

[87]   Reg. § 1.1361–1(*l*)(2)(ii).

[88]   Reg. § 1.1361–1(*l*)(2)(vi) (ex. 7).

[89]   *Id.* (ex. 6).

Even though the shareholders receive identical after-tax distributions, the arrangement alters their right to equal pre-tax distributions.

Voting Differences. Perhaps unexpectedly, a corporation will *not* be treated as having more than one class of stock solely because there are differences in voting rights among its shares of common stock.[90] Thus, a corporation can have outstanding both voting and nonvoting common stock and still qualify to be treated as an S corporation.

The use of nonvoting stock can be useful to facilitate estate planning and permit taxpayers to shift income among family members without transferring control.

Example 2.2: D wishes to share some of her wealth in wholly-owned X Corp. (an S corporation) with F, but is not willing to give up exclusive control. D could cause X Corp. to issue nonvoting common stock with respect to her common stock and give the nonvoting stock to F, without causing X Corp. to violate the one-class-of-stock rule.

Buy-Sell and Redemption Agreements. The regulations generally disregard buy-sell agreements and redemption plans unless (1) a principal purpose of the agreement is to circumvent the one-class-of-stock requirement and (2) the agreement establishes a purchase price that, when the agreement is entered into, is significantly above or below fair market value.[91] Because a test based on fair market value may be difficult to apply, the regulations provide two safe harbors.[92] First, bona-fide agreements fixing a redemption or purchase price equal to book value or an amount between book value and fair market value are treated as establishing an acceptable price (and hence ignored). Second, the IRS will accept a "good faith" determination of fair market value unless the value is substantially erroneous or the taxpayer failed to exercise reasonable diligence. To ensure that a buy-sell or redemption agreement does not run afoul of the one-class-of-stock rule, S shareholders would be well advised to obtain an appraisal.

Debt Reclassified. If an S corporation has any type of debt outstanding, the issue can arise whether the debt will be recharacterized as equity and treated as a second class of stock, thus terminating the corporation's S election.[93] Section 1361(c)(5) provides a reliable safe harbor for "straight debt" that will not be deemed to be a second class of stock. In other words, even if such debt is reclassified as stock, it will not constitute a *second class* of stock.

In order to fall within the safe harbor, the debt must meet the following criteria: (1) there must be a written unconditional promise to pay on demand, or on a specified date, a sum certain in money, (2) the interest rate and payment dates must not be contingent on profits, the borrower's discretion or similar factors, and (3) the debt must not be convertible into stock.[94] Unless the creditor is regularly and actively engaged in the business of lending money, the creditor must be an individual or entity eligible to hold

---

[90]   *See* I.R.C. § 1361(c)(4).

[91]   *See* Reg. § 1.1361–1(*l*)(2)(iii)(A). In addition, agreements to redeem or purchase stock upon the occurrence of certain events (death, disability or termination of employment) are disregarded in determining whether stock conveys identical rights. *See* Reg. § 1.1361–1(*l*)(2)(iii)(B).

[92]   *See* Reg. § 1.1361–1(*l*)(2)(iii)(A).

[93]   As discussed below, the regulations explicitly state that debt reclassified as equity does not always constitute a second class of stock under Subchapter S. For prior case law, *see, e.g., Portage Plastics Co. v. U.S.,* 486 F.2d 632 (7th Cir. 1973), *aff'g,* 301 F. Supp. 684 (W.D. Wis. 1969).

[94]   Reg. § 1.1361–1(*l*)(5)(i). An obligation may qualify as straight debt even if it is subordinated to other debt of the corporation. Reg. § 1.1361–1(*l*)(5)(ii).

shares of an S corporation.[95] Such safe harbor debt will not constitute a second class of stock even if, under § 385 and case-law principles, it would be reclassified as equity or stock.[96]

In addition to the safe harbor for straight debt, the regulations provide a safe harbor for debt that is held in proportion to stock.[97] Such debt will not be treated as a second class of stock.

Example 2.3: S Corp. has three individual shareholders. A holds 50 shares and B and C each hold 25 shares of the only class of stock outstanding. Proportionately-held corporate debt of $100,000 ($50,000 by shareholder A, and $25,000 each by B and C) would not give rise to a second class of stock. If all the debt were owed to A, or if it were owed $10,000 to shareholder A and $45,000 each to B and C, the debt would not be held in proportion to stockholdings. If it were reclassified as equity, it could thus potentially give rise to a disqualifying second class of stock.

The regulations provide that a debt instrument generally will not be treated as a second class of stock unless (1) the debt instrument constitutes equity under general principles of federal tax law, and (2) a principal purpose of issuing the debt instrument (or entering into the arrangement) is to circumvent the requirement for identical rights to distribution and liquidation proceeds or to circumvent the limitation on eligible shareholders.[98] Thus, most hybrid debt-equity instruments will not create a second class of stock which would disqualify an S corporation. This liberal approach seems justified because the one-class-of-stock requirement is intended primarily to ensure that an S corporation's capital structure remains relatively simple.

Deferred Compensation Plans. The question inevitably arises whether deferred compensation plans or phantom stock for employees, when used by S corporations, result in a fatal second class of stock. The regulations provide a safe harbor for certain types of deferred compensation arrangements. An instrument, obligation or arrangement is not treated as creating outstanding stock (and thus will not create a second class of stock) if it: (1) does not convey the right to vote, (2) is an unfunded, unsecured promise to pay money in the future, (3) is issued to an employee (or independent contractor) in connection with services (and is not excessive), and (4) is issued pursuant to a plan under which the employee (or independent contractor) is not currently taxable on income.[99] Perhaps because of the 100-shareholder rule, actual stock bonus plans seem relatively rare in the S corporation context; instead, compensation plans are typically tied to the value of the stock, giving employees the right to additional deferred compensation, not actual stock.

¶ 2.10   IMPORTANCE OF SHAREHOLDER AGREEMENTS

The many Subchapter S restrictions on eligibility may represent booby traps for an eligible corporation. Such a corporation may find that it has become *ineligible* because

---

[95]   I.R.C. § 1361(c)(5)(B)(iii); Reg. § 1.1361–1(*l*)(5)(i)(C).

[96]   Reg. § 1.1361–1(*l*)(5)(iv).

[97]   Reg. § 1.1361–1(*l*)(4)(ii)(B)(2). The regulations also contain a safe harbor for short-term unwritten advances (not in excess of $10,000). *See* Reg. § 1.1361–1(*l*)(4)(ii)(B)(1).

[98]   Reg. § 1.1361–1(*l*)(4)(i), (ii).

[99]   Reg. §§ 1.1361–1(b)(4), 1.83–3(e) (unfunded, unsecured promise to pay does not constitute "property").

of a change in the number, identity or characteristics of the shareholders, or the kind of stock or securities outstanding. Some event as "innocent" as a sale by one shareholder of all her shares to two buyers could terminate S status if it causes there to be more than 100 shareholders at any one time. If a resident alien becomes a nonresident, or if a shareholder transfers a share to a corporation or to an ineligible trust, the S status would terminate.

One key protection against unexpected or inadvertent (or hostile and deliberate) disqualification lies in the making of shareholder agreements. Such agreements may be contained in separate contracts and (if permissible) in corporate by-laws, regulations or articles or certificates of incorporation. Often desirable for non-tax reasons in any closely held corporation, restrictions on the transfer of shares, first-refusal rights and buy-sell agreements will help prevent undesired and disqualifying sales or gifts or transfers in trust of S corporation stock. (Such limits or notice of them probably should also be placed on the share certificates.) Repurchase rights or forfeitures could be triggered by disqualifying events such as nonresidency. All parties should agree not to do anything that would disqualify the corporation or terminate its election. The corporation, in addition, can be prohibited from issuing more than one class of stock, at least if state law does not invalidate such restrictions. (Other concerns upon which shareholder agreements should touch are discussed at ¶ 7.06.) Forms for such agreements are reproduced in leading reference books.

Care must be taken when shareholder agreements or corporate-shareholder agreements contain buy-sell provisions or other terms that could be treated as creating a second class of stock. Traditional buy-sell agreements should not violate the statutory requirement.

¶ 2.11   ELECTING AND REVOKING S CORPORATION TAXATION—§ 1362

An eligible corporation will receive S treatment only if it makes an effective election.[100] The rules governing the election and its revocation or termination are found in the Code[101] and regulations.[102] These rules must be followed with the greatest of care. Since an effective S election requires both corporate and shareholder action, attention must be given to the rules bearing on both levels. The next section summarizes those provisions, focusing on the mechanics of making a corporate election and the requirements regarding shareholder consents.

¶ 2.12   WHO MUST ELECT; FILING REQUIREMENTS

In order to elect to be an S corporation, the corporation must timely file IRS Form 2553, and the form must contain all the required information.[103] (The form must be signed by a person authorized to sign the S corporation's tax return that is required to be filed under § 6037.[104] Such authorized persons include the president, treasurer, assistant treasurer and chief accounting officer of the corporation.[105]) As discussed more

---

[100] I.R.C. § 1361(a)(1).

[101] I.R.C. § 1362.

[102] Reg. §§ 1.1362–1 to –6.

[103] *See* Reg. § 1.1362–6(a).

[104] *See id.*

[105] See instructions to Form 2553.

fully below, all persons who are shareholders at the time the election is made must properly consent to such election.[106] A valid election is effective for the year for which it is made and for all succeeding years until terminated.[107] The IRS will notify the corporation whether the election is accepted and when it will take effect.[108]

The election may be made at any time during the taxable year *preceding* the year for which the election is being made (assuming that all other applicable requirements are met), or at any time before the 16th day of the third month of the year for which the election is being made.[109] If an election is made during the year for which such election is to apply (*i.e.*, before the 16th day of the third month of the taxable year), the election will apply to the entire year, provided that the corporation was a "small business corporation" for that entire year and all persons who were shareholders at any time during that year consent to the election.[110]

Each person who is a shareholder at the time the election is made must consent to the election, probably so that no unwilling shareholder can be placed in the position of being taxed on income not distributed when the shareholder lacks the means to pay the tax.[111] *In addition*, all persons who were shareholders *at any time* during the taxable year must consent, *whether or not* they are shareholders when the election is made, if the corporation is electing during the year for which the election is to apply.[112] In contrast, if an election is made to be effective for the *following* taxable year, no consent need be filed by anyone who was not a shareholder on the date the election was made.[113]

Once a valid election is made, new shareholders need not consent to the election.[114] Thus, a new shareholder must accept the S corporation's status as is; the shareholder cannot refuse to consent (and possibly extort consideration from other shareholders to leave the S status undisturbed), unless the new shareholder becomes a more-than-50% shareholder. Such an owner can force a formal revocation of S status.[115]

Consents by shareholders to elect S status must be made either on Form 2553 or on a separate signed statement in which the shareholder consents to the election.[116] The shareholder's consent is binding and may not be withdrawn after a valid election has

---

[106] *See* Reg. § 1.1362–1(a). Use of a single statement of shareholder consent or use of the consent statement on Form 2553 will tend to guard against failure to obtain consents from all shareholders.

[107] Reg. § 1.1362–1(b). Termination of an election is discussed more fully at ¶¶ 2.15–2.24.

[108] A Form 2553 will be considered timely filed if the U.S. postmark on the envelope is on or before the due date. *See* I.R.C. § 7502.

[109] In other words, the election must be made either within the first two months and 15 days of the taxable year for which the election is intended, or during the preceding taxable year. *See* Reg. § 1.1362–6(a)(2)(ii).

[110] *Id.* If the election is made after the first 2½ months of the year, it will be treated as made for the following taxable year. I.R.C. § 1362(b)(3). The election may not be made before the corporation is deemed to be in existence for these purposes. The first month of a corporation's taxable year begins whenever the corporation first has shareholders, acquires assets or begins doing business. Reg. § 1.1362–6(a)(2)(ii)(C).

[111] *See* Reg. § 1.1362–6(b)(3)(i); *see also* ¶ 2.08.

[112] *Id.*

[113] *Id.* A person who is treated as a shareholder under state law solely by reason of her status as an incorporator is not treated as a shareholder for purposes of § 1362. *Id.*

[114] Reg. § 1.1362–6(a)(2)(i).

[115] To revoke S status, holders of more than one half of all outstanding shares must consent. *See* I.R.C. § 1362(d)(1)(B); Reg. § 1.1362–2(a)(1).

[116] *See* Reg. § 1.1362–6(b)(1).

been made by the corporation.[117] If any of the corporation's stock or the income from such stock is owned in joint form (such as community property or joint tenancy), each person having an interest in the stock must consent.[118]

In general, the corporation's election will not be valid unless all shareholder consents are filed correctly in accordance with the regulations.[119] However, the regulations grant an extension of time for filing consents, if certain conditions are met.[120]

¶ 2.13   REVOCATION OF AN S ELECTION—§ 1362(d)

An S election may be terminated either (1) by revocation, (2) by the corporation ceasing to be a "small business corporation" and thus losing its eligibility for S status, or (3) if the corporation has excess passive investment income for three consecutive years.[121] The third termination cause is relevant only if the corporation has accumulated Subchapter C earnings and profits.[122] An S corporation that has always been an S corporation generally cannot have any Subchapter C earnings and profits and therefore its S election cannot be terminated for excess passive investment income. The Code provides that in the event of certain inadvertent terminations, a corporation will continue to be treated as an S corporation.[123] The causes and results of terminating an S election are discussed more fully in ¶¶ 2.14 and 2.19.

After termination, a corporation (or its successor)[124] will not be eligible to make a new election until its fifth taxable year following after the taxable year for which the termination is effective, without the consent of the Secretary.[125] Such consent is more likely to be granted if either (1) more than 50% of the corporation's stock has changed hands since the date of the termination or (2) it can be shown that the event causing termination was not reasonably within the control of the corporation or of shareholders having a substantial interest in the corporation.[126]

¶ 2.14   REVOKING THE S ELECTION; TERMINATION OF S STATUS

When an eligible corporation has made an effective S election and all shareholders have consented in timely fashion, Subchapter S treatment continues to apply unless and until revocation of the election or termination of S corporation status. No annual re-election is needed.

---

[117] Reg. § 1.1362–6(b)(3)(i).

[118] *See* Reg. § 1.1362–6(b)(2)(i). *See also Kean v. Comm'r*, 469 F.2d 1183 (9th Cir. 1972) (though not a shareholder of record, beneficial owner of portion of stock was required to file consent).

[119] Reg. § 1.1362–6(b)(1).

[120] Reg. § 1.1362–6(b)(3)(iii). The IRS may also require new consents to be filed by any other shareholders during the extended period. *Id.*

[121] I.R.C. § 1362(d).

[122] I.R.C. § 1362(d)(3)(A)(i).

[123] I.R.C. § 1362(f).

[124] For example, Y Corporation will be deemed a successor corporation to X Corporation if (1) 50% or more of the stock of Y Corporation is owned by persons who owned 50% or more of the stock of X Corporation on the date its S status terminated, and (2) Y Corporation acquired a substantial portion of X Corporation's assets. *See* Reg. § 1.1362–5(b).

[125] I.R.C. § 1362(g); Reg. § 1.1362–5(a).

[126] *See* Reg. § 1.1362–5(a).

The Code sets forth rules for termination or voluntary revocation in § 1362(d).[127] *Revocation* is a voluntary election by the corporation. *Termination* occurs by operation of law. Nevertheless, termination sometimes is desired and intended. In other instances, termination occurs involuntarily, when a condition of continued S treatment is violated. These eligibility conditions therefore constitute triggers for termination and a potentially disappointing loss of S status. They must be examined in order to guard against unintended disqualification.

The material below (¶¶ 2.15 through 2.24) sets forth the provisions for voluntary revocation or termination, special rules for mistaken or inadvertent termination, the consequences of termination, the terms for re-election after termination, and some practical planning ideas.

¶ 2.15   KINDS OF REVOCATION AND TERMINATION

The circumstances surrounding termination of S status fall into three main categories. The first category consists of voluntary revocation—when shareholders holding more than 50% of the stock explicitly revoke the election.[128] The second category consists of the rules that make the *corporation* ineligible, because it no longer meets the definitional terms for a "small business corporation" in § 1361(b).[129] The third category is a special rule for an S corporation that has at some time in its life been a C corporation, has (leftover) Subchapter C earnings and profits, and has passive investment income in excess of 25% of gross receipts for three consecutive S years.[130]

¶ 2.16   VOLUNTARY SHAREHOLDER REVOCATION

Section 1362(d)(1) states that an S election may be terminated by revocation. Shareholders holding *more than* one half of the shares outstanding on the date of revocation must consent. Both voting and nonvoting shares are counted for the 50% test. Shareholders may revoke even for the first year of election, if they act within the first 2½ months of that year. Alternatively, they may revoke for the next tax year or may specify a prospective date.[131] (If a revocation specifies a prospective date other than the first day of a tax year, it will produce an S short year and a C short year.)[132] A revocation may be rescinded at any time before it becomes effective.[133] The regulations require that the rescission be requested in writing and be accompanied by shareholder consents.[134]

If such explicit, voluntary shareholder action cannot be secured, deliberate violation of eligibility rules or of the excess passive investment income rule could be considered as a planning technique to force termination of S status.

---

[127] *See* Reg. § 1.1362–2, –3.

[128] I.R.C. § 1362(d)(1); *see* ¶ 2.16.

[129] I.R.C. § 1362(d)(2); *see* ¶ 2.17.

[130] I.R.C. § 1362(d)(3). "Leftover" Subchapter C earnings and profits also can come from another corporation that merged into the S corporation. *See* ¶ 2.18.

[131] I.R.C. § 1362(d)(1)(D).

[132] I.R.C. § 1362(e).

[133] Reg. §§ 1.1362–2(a)(4), –6(a)(4)(ii).

[134] *See* Reg. § 1.1362–6(a)(4).

¶ 2.17   DISQUALIFICATION; FAILURE TO MEET ELIGIBILITY RULES

The second statutory way in which S status may terminate is if the corporation no longer qualifies as a "small business corporation," as strictly defined by the terms of § 1361(b) and discussed in ¶ 2.03 above.[135] Section 1362(d)(2) states that an S election shall be terminated at any time if and when the corporation ceases to be a small business corporation, effective upon cessation. Each of these ineligibilities will be mentioned in turn.

First, eligibility will cease and S status will be lost if the corporation ever, at any one time, has more than 100 shareholders.[136] The regulations must be consulted again, in special cases, to determine whether the numerical limit is exceeded. In general, beneficial ownership is what matters. (Recall ¶ 2.07.)

Second, the corporation cannot be a small business corporation if it has a prohibited kind of shareholder in violation of § 1361(b)(1)(B) and (C), such as a corporation, non-resident alien, partnership, or non-qualified trust. (Recall ¶ 2.08.) Consequently, a shareholder can terminate S status by giving, selling or bequeathing her shares to an unacceptable person (which makes a shareholder agreement not to do so imperative).[137]

Third, since an S corporation is allowed to have only one class of stock outstanding, issuance of a second class of shares or a change in the terms of some shares so as to create two classes of stock will terminate the election. Recall that some differences— such as voting rights—do *not* constitute different classes of stock for these purposes.[138] Differences or preferences in dividend or liquidation rights do violate the one-class-of-stock rule. Debt recharacterized as equity can also do so (except for safe harbor "straight debt" or debt proportionately held). Only stock that is outstanding is taken into account.

Fourth, if an S corporation becomes an "ineligible corporation" as defined in § 1361(b)(2), it will cease to be a "small business corporation" as defined in § 1361(b)(1), and its S status will terminate.[139] So, the S corporation may not become one of the entities described in § 1361(b)(2)(A) to (C).[140]

If termination under any of these rules has occurred, the corporation is obliged to notify the IRS.[141] Often, however, the corporation or its shareholders do not learn of, or recognize, the disqualification until it is brought to their attention.

Termination for violation of the qualification requirements generally takes effect on the date the corporation ceases to qualify.[142] Termination results in two short tax years: the first an S short year which ends on the day before the termination event, and the

---

[135] *See* I.R.C. § 1362(d)(2); Reg. § 1.1362–2(b)(1).

[136] I.R.C. § 1361(b)(1)(A).

[137] Momentary ownership of an S corporation's stock in the course of an asset acquisition may not terminate the election. *See* Rev. Rul. 73–496, 1973–2 C.B. 312.

[138] *See* I.R.C. § 1361(c)(4); ¶ 2.09.

[139] I.R.C. § 1362(d)(2). Presumably this means that if the corporation, by any means, ceased to be a domestic corporation, it would cease to be eligible and would lose its S status.

[140] *See* ¶ 2.05.

[141] *See* Reg. § 1.1362–2(b)(1).

[142] I.R.C. § 1362(d)(2)(B).

second a C short year which ends on the date the corporation's taxable year would have ended had there been no termination.[143]

¶ 2.18   TERMINATION BECAUSE OF EXCESS PASSIVE INVESTMENT INCOME

The third statutory way in which S status may end is if an S corporation with Subchapter C earnings and profits realizes too much passive investment income for three consecutive S years.[144] An S corporation that has always been an S corporation (sometimes referred to as a "virgin S corporation") has nothing to fear from this rule, since it *cannot* have any Subchapter C earnings and profits of its own.[145] Technically, an S corporation that was formerly a C corporation but "zeroed out" its earnings and profits from its C years before electing S treatment also could proceed without concern.

Even one dollar of leftover Subchapter C earnings and profits will trigger this termination rule: passive investment income in excess of 25% of gross receipts for three consecutive taxable years causes termination of S status, if the corporation has *any* earnings and profits. Consequently, one minor miscalculation, or one redetermination on audit, could cause an unwanted termination. (Section 1362(f) may afford relief, as mentioned in ¶ 2.24.) Thus, as a planning matter, a new corporation electing S status will prove safer than a former C corporation that converts by making an S election.

Of course, if a vulnerable former C corporation sees trouble coming in the form of one or two years of excess passive investment income, it may be able to escape involuntary termination. It can wiggle out of the "three consecutive years" part of the rule (either by ridding itself of Subchapter C earnings and profits or by reducing its passive investment income) or otherwise ensure that it is not technically caught by the termination rule. Even if it succeeds, however, and does not suffer termination of its S election, it may still suffer the § 1375 sting tax. (For more on this penalty tax, see Chapter 5.) If termination occurs because of the passive investment income limit, the election is terminated immediately after the end of the third consecutive year.[146]

¶ 2.19   EFFECTS OF TERMINATION

If an S election is terminated, a number of effects will follow; the effects may differ according to the reason for termination.[147] The following sections discuss the implications of termination for determining applicable tax years (¶ 2.20), for options for re-electing S status (¶¶ 2.21 and 2.24), for the post-termination transition period (¶ 2.22), for QSubs (¶ 2.23), and for carryover of net operating losses (NOLs) and other tax attributes (¶ 2.25).

¶ 2.20   TERMINATION EFFECTS; TAX YEARS; ALLOCATION OF EARNINGS

Termination of an S election results in the end of passthrough treatment for the shareholders and the beginning of taxation of the corporation as a Subchapter C entity.

---

[143] I.R.C. § 1362(e); Reg. § 1.1362–2(b)(2). *See* ¶ 2.20.

[144] I.R.C. § 1362(d)(3); Reg. § 1.1362–2(c).

[145] The sources of Subchapter C earnings and profits are discussed at ¶ 4.02.

[146] I.R.C. § 1362(d)(3)(A)(ii).

[147] *See* Reg. §§ 1.1362–3, –4.

When a termination is timed to be effective as of the first day of a taxable year of a corporation, the new year is a "C" year and the prior year is an "S" year, which raises no difficult tax accounting problems. However, when the termination occurs during a taxable year, the situation is more complex, since the passthrough system will apply only during the period when the S election was in effect. Some allocation of income and loss items between the C and S years, therefore, will be necessary. Whether such an allocation will be required is often a function of the type of termination that occurs. The effect on the corporation's tax year of various types of terminations is described in this section.

Section 1362(c) provides that an S election is effective for the taxable year of the corporation for which it is made and for all succeeding taxable years until the election is terminated under § 1362(d), whether by revocation,[148] by ceasing to be a "small business corporation," or for excess passive investment income.[149]

If the termination is by *revocation* and unless a particular prospective date is specified, the revocation is effective as of the first day of the *current* taxable year only if made on or before the 15th day of the third month of that year.[150] In that event, a C year will begin as of that first day. If not made within that first 2½ months of the year, a revocation will be effective on the first day of the *following* taxable year,[151] which will also be the first day of a new C year.

> *Example 2.4:* X Corp., a calendar-year S corporation, decides to revoke its election in 2023. If it files the revocation on or before March 15, 2023, then X Corp. will be treated as a C corporation for all of 2023. If X Corp. files a revocation on March 16, 2023 (or anytime thereafter until March 15, 2024), it will be taxed as a C corporation beginning January 1, 2024. X Corp. may also file a revocation specifying a day, month and year for revocation (be it the day of filing, or any *future* day).

If the revocation specifies a particular prospective date, the revocation will be effective on and after that date.[152] Thus, if X Corp., on June 15, 2024, files a revocation "to take effect June 15, 2024" then June 14 will be the last day of an S short year and June 15 will be the first day of a C short year. Again, a revocation may be rescinded at any time before becoming effective.[153]

If the termination occurs because the corporation ceases to be a small business corporation, the termination is effective as of the date of cessation and a C short year begins on that date.[154] If the termination occurs because the S corporation has Subchapter C earnings and profits and excess passive investment income for three consecutive years, the S election will terminate under § 1362(d). The termination will

---

[148] I.R.C. § 1362(d)(1). *See* ¶ 2.16.

[149] I.R.C. § 1362(d)(2), (3). *See* ¶¶ 2.17–2.18.

[150] I.R.C. § 1362(d)(1)(C)(i). So, a slightly retroactive revocation can be made.

[151] I.R.C. § 1362(d)(1)(C)(ii).

[152] I.R.C. § 1362(d)(1)(D). *See* Reg. § 1.1362–2(a)(2)(ii) (revocation date must be expressed in terms of specific day, month and year, not a particular event).

[153] Reg. § 1.1362–2(a)(4)

[154] I.R.C. § 1362(d)(2); Reg. § 1.1362–2(b)(2). *See* ¶ 2.17.

take effect at the close of the third year in which the corporation has such disqualifying income,[155] and a new C year will commence on the first day of the next taxable year.

Allocations of Earnings to Different Tax Years. When revocation or termination takes place other than at the *very* beginning or end of the corporation's tax year, two short tax years will result, the first an S short year and the second a C short year.[156] When that happens, obviously the passthrough effect of the S election will end. But, the *general* rule—subject to an election and certain restrictions—provides that the corporation does not "close its books" on the termination date.[157] Instead it must compute for the *entire* year all its separately and non-separately stated items that it would have passed through if S status had not terminated. Then, it must *prorate*, on a daily basis, these items (for the entire year) between its S short year and its C short year. The shareholders must include their share of S items for the S short year in their taxable year with which (or within which) the S short year ends.[158] The corporation must take the amount allocated to the C short year into income to compute its tax as a Subchapter C corporation for the C short year.[159]

> *Example 2.5:* In 2023, X Corp., a calendar-year S corporation, files a revocation in June to take effect on July 15, 2023. In this event, 2023 will be an S termination year composed of an S short year (January 1 to July 14) and a C short year (July 15 to December 31). For ease of calculation, assume X Corp.'s only tax item for all of 2023 is income of $3,650. Under the general rule, X Corp. will make a pro rata allocation of $1,950 (195/365ths of its separately and non-separately stated items) to the S year and $1,700 (170/365ths of the same) to the C year. Then, under § 1362(e)(5), the C year figure must be "annualized" for purposes of computing corporate tax.[160] Under prior law, the purpose of annualizing the corporation's income was to restrict the benefits of the lower corporate tax brackets for the partial year.[161]

In the case of an S *termination* year, § 1362(e) provides three exceptions to the general rule of per-share, per-day allocation of the entire year's tax items. If these exceptions apply, some or all tax items will be assigned under the interim closing method to each short year, using a corporation's normal tax accounting methods. First, the corporation may elect, with unanimous shareholder consent, to have the interim closing method apply.[162] Second, if 50% or more of the S corporation's stock is sold or exchanged

---

[155] I.R.C. § 1362(d)(3)(A)(ii); Reg. § 1.1362–3(a).

[156] Reg. § 1.1362–3. The corporation's taxable year in which the termination occurs is referred to as an "S termination year." Reg. § 1.1362–3(a).

[157] I.R.C. § 1362(e)(2).

[158] *See* Reg. § 1.1362–3(c)(6).

[159] *Id.* To compute its tax, the C corporation must annualize its income for the short year. The corporate tax returns for both short years are not due until the due date for the C short year. The two short years are treated as a single year for purposes of exhausting loss carryovers. I.R.C. § 1362(e)(5), (6).

[160] For purposes of annualizing X Corp.'s income, the C earnings ($1,700) must be multiplied by the number of days in the S termination year over the number of C days (365/170). The result ($3,650), is then treated as a taxable income figure to compute what X Corp.'s tax liability would have been if it had a full C year rather than a C short year. The result ($766.50, or 21% of $3,650) is then multiplied by the number of C days over the number of days in the S termination year (170/365) to reach an actual tax liability ($357).

[161] Since the proration method was used, the annualized income figure here is simply the total income for the S termination year. If instead the corporation used the interim closing method, the annualized income for the C portion of the year would depend on the income actually allocated to the C short year (and then annualized).

[162] I.R.C. § 1362(e)(3); Reg. § 1.1362–3(b)(1).

during the S termination year, the interim closing method is mandatory.[163] Third, as discussed later (¶ 7.13), specific allocation (rather than proration) is required for items arising from a § 338 election.[164]

If the interim closing method applies, the corporation allocates its separately and non-separately stated items between each of the two short years under normal tax accounting principles. In this event, such items are attributed to the short year (S or C) in which they were realized or incurred.[165] In the case of an election to use the interim closing method, shareholder consent must be obtained from each person who was a shareholder at *any time* during the S year *and* all those who were shareholders at the outset of the C year.[166] Whether the election will prove advantageous will depend on the relative tax brackets of the shareholders and the corporation, as well as the timing of events during the two short taxable years.

¶ 2.21   RE-ELECTING AFTER TERMINATION

One of the most serious consequences of revoking or terminating an S election is that, under § 1362(g), a new S election cannot be made by the same or a successor corporation for any taxable year until the fifth taxable year (short or otherwise) after the taxable year in which the termination is effective, unless the Secretary consents to an earlier election.[167] Thus, an S corporation whose election terminates in Year 1 must wait until Year 6 to re-elect S status. Accidental and innocent loss of S status makes the most appealing case for permitting an early re-election. Indeed, even *retroactive* reinstatement may be available under § 1362(f), as described in ¶ 2.24.

¶ 2.22   POST-TERMINATION TRANSITION PERIOD

Another effect of a termination is to start the post-termination transition period (PTTP), defined in § 1377(b)(1)(A). During the PTTP, special rules provide for tax-free cash distributions, under § 1371(e), not in excess of the accumulated adjustment account (AAA) balance.[168] These rules and planning ideas will be taken up with the general rules on distributions, discussed in Chapter 4.

¶ 2.23   QSUB TERMINATIONS

A QSub election may terminate as a result of revocation, termination of the S parent's election, or the occurrence of an event that causes the subsidiary to be ineligible for QSub status.[169] Special rules apply if termination results from a sale of QSub stock.[170]

---

[163] I.R.C. § 1362(e)(6)(D); Reg. § 1.1362–3(b)(3).

[164] I.R.C. § 1362(e)(6)(C); Reg. § 1.1362–3(b)(2).

[165] Reg. § 1.1362–3.

[166] I.R.C. § 1362(e)(3)(B); *see* Reg. § 1.1362–6(a)(5).

[167] For purposes of the five-year waiting period, a short taxable year apparently counts as a year. A successor corporation is one that has acquired a substantial portion of the terminating corporation's assets and is owned substantially (at least 50%) by the same persons. *See* Reg. § 1.1362–5(b).

[168] *See* I.R.C. § 1371(e); Reg. § 1.1377–2. Cash distributions may be received tax free and applied against basis only up to the AAA. *See* ¶¶ 4.04–4.05.

[169] Reg. § 1.1361–5(a)(1); *see* Reg. § 1.1361–3(b) (revocation). The effective date depends on the cause of the termination. For inadvertent termination of QSub status, see ¶ 2.23.

[170] *See* I.R.C. § 1361(b)(3)(C)(ii) (treating sale of QSub stock as an asset sale); *see also* ¶ 7.15.

If QSub status ceases, the subsidiary is treated as a new corporation that is deemed to acquire its assets and liabilities from the S parent in exchange for its stock.[171] The former QSub (and any successor) is generally not eligible to make another QSub election or an S election for five years, unless the Secretary consents to an earlier election.[172] Nevertheless, the regulations permit an automatic waiver of the five-year rule if (1) immediately after the termination, the former QSub (or its successor) is otherwise eligible to make an S election (or have a QSub election made for it) and (2) the election takes effect immediately after the termination. In this case, the former QSub (or its successor) will not be treated even momentarily as a C corporation.[173]

¶ 2.24   SALVAGING THE ELECTION: INADVERTENT TERMINATIONS AND INVALID ELECTIONS

In some limited circumstances, § 1362(f) allows a termination to be waived or cured, if the termination is inadvertent and innocent. Congress has authorized the IRS to waive the effects of an *inadvertent* termination if (1) the corporation corrects the terminating foot fault within a reasonable time and (2) the corporation and all of its shareholders agree to be treated as if the election had remained in effect for the period in question and to make such adjustments (consistent with S status) as the Secretary may require. Appealing examples include innocent violation of the one-class-of-stock rule (with no tax avoidance) or the unwitting transfer of stock to a corporation or a partnership. Relief is also available for inadvertent termination of QSub status.

Section 1362(f) also authorizes the IRS to waive an invalid S election (or QSub election).[174] The conditions for waiver of an invalid election parallel those for waiver of an inadvertent termination. The reason for "ineffectiveness" of the election must be inadvertent, immediate steps must be taken to remedy the problem (*e.g.*, obtaining shareholder consents), and the corporation and all of its shareholders must consent to any required adjustments. Under some circumstances, automatic relief may be granted for certain late elections under Subchapter S.[175] In the case of a late S election, relief is generally available only if (1) the corporation intended to be classified as an S corporation as of a particular effective date, (2) relief is requested within three years and 75 days after the intended effective date, (3) the reason for failure to qualify was solely because a timely S election was not filed, and (4) there was reasonable cause for the late filing and diligent action was taken to correct the mistake upon discovery.

An S election may also be invalid because of the lack of a timely election with respect to a trust. The trustee of an ESBT or current beneficiary of a QSST may be granted relief for the late election, causing the S corporation's election to be valid. If automatic relief for a late election is not available, the taxpayer may request a letter ruling.

---

[171] I.R.C. § 1361(b)(3)(C)(i); Reg. § 1.1361–5(b).

[172] I.R.C. § 1361(b)(3)(D).

[173] *See* Reg. § 1.1361–5(c)(2). For example, if S1 (an S corporation) sells 100% of the stock of Y (a QSub) to S2 (an unrelated S corporation), S2 may immediately elect to have Y treated as a QSub, without requesting consent to the re-election. Reg. § 1.1361–5(c)(3) (ex. 2); *see id.* (ex. 1) (same result if QSub stock distributed to S parent's shareholders).

[174] If the conditions for waiver are satisfied, the corporation will be treated as an S corporation (or QSub) during the period specified by the Secretary. I.R.C. § 1362(f) (flush language).

[175] *See* Rev. Proc. 2013–30, 2013–36 I.R.B. 173 (late S elections, ESBT elections, QSST elections, QSub elections, and late entity classification elections).

¶ 2.25   CARRYOVERS

Revocation or termination of the S election raises the subject of carryovers from C to S years and from S to C years. In general, an S corporation cannot use an NOL (or other loss or credit carryover) generated during earlier C years.[176] So, for example, a C corporation with a large NOL may be well advised to exhaust it before electing S status, perhaps by accelerating income or deferring expense. Otherwise, it may wish to defer the S election. The opposite problem (carrying over an NOL from an S year to a C year) cannot arise. The reason is that an S corporation does not generate NOLs during its S years. Instead, any entity-level loss is passed through to its shareholders.[177]

---

[176] I.R.C. § 1371(b)(1).

[177] *See* I.R.C. § 1371(b)(2). The loss limitation rules applicable to S shareholders are discussed at ¶¶ 6.08–6.15.

Chapter 3

EFFECTS OF THE S ELECTION DURING OPERATION OF THE S CORPORATION—TAX CONSEQUENCES OF THE ELECTION

¶ 3.01   GENERALLY

Chapter Three examines the effects of an S election on the corporation during its operation. Chapters Four and Six explore the effects on its shareholders, particularly with respect to distributions and the passthrough of income, loss, and deduction items. Chapter Five discusses special taxes imposed on the S corporation itself. Chapter Six also discusses the impact of sales, exchanges or other dispositions of equity interests by the shareholders. Chapters Seven and Eight will relate this material to the tax issues and law on various topics of general corporate concern: forming and capitalizing the S corporation; corporate events such as liquidations, redemptions and reorganizations; and planning considerations.

¶ 3.02   EFFECTS OF THE S ELECTION ON THE CORPORATION—§ 1363

The general rule exempting an S corporation from entity-level income taxation[1] applies to a new corporation that elects Subchapter S treatment from the outset and, with a few exceptions, to a converting C corporation after it elects S treatment. Business net income (income and gains less losses and deductions) is not taxed to the S corporation under § 11. Nevertheless, the S corporation must compute its taxable income; in fact it must compute its taxable income "in the same manner as in the case of an individual," with specified exceptions.[2] It does so because its income is passed through and taxed to individuals, much as if the individuals themselves owned the assets or engaged in the business activities without use of a separate business organization. Thus, to some extent, the individuals will be treated as if the income were attributable to them directly, rather than through the artificial passthrough mechanism of Subchapter S.

There are several exceptions to the general rule that the S corporation computes its income as if it were an individual. Section 1363(b) provides that:

(1)   items of income, loss, deduction or credit must be separately stated if they could affect differently the tax liability of any shareholder;[3]

(2)   deductions listed in § 703(a)(2) (including the deductions for charitable contributions and foreign taxes) are disallowed to the S corporation;[4]

(3)   the § 248 election to amortize organizational expenditures applies;[5] and

---

[1]   *See* I.R.C. § 1363(a); Reg. § 1.1363–1(a).

[2]   I.R.C. § 1363(b).

[3]   I.R.C. § 1363(b)(1).

[4]   I.R.C. § 1363(b)(2).

[5]   I.R.C. § 1363(b)(3).

(4) the § 291 cutback on certain corporate preference items applies, but only if the S corporation or its predecessor was a C corporation during any of the three preceding taxable years.[6]

Thus, the S corporation essentially computes its taxable income as if it were an aggregate consisting of all the individual shareholders to whom its income is passed through pro rata and taxed. Although it is not usually regarded as a separate taxpaying entity,[7] the S corporation *does* act as an entity taxpayer in *some* respects. Generally, an S corporations makes all elections that affect the computation of items for purposes of determining taxability.[8]

An S corporation is not allowed a deduction for charitable contributions. Instead, the charitable deduction passes through to the S shareholders.[9] A special rule ensures that the shareholder's stock basis is reduced, under § 1367, by the *basis*, not *value*, of the contributed property.[10] Together, these rules allow shareholders to take advantage of the § 170 deduction for their share of the contributed property's appreciation, without regard to their stock (and debt) basis.[11] The shareholder avoids recognition of gain on the contributed property, and applies the § 170 limitations at the individual level, consistent with passthrough treatment.

Under the principle of § 1371(a), the S corporation is subject to all the normal entity-regarding rules of Subchapter C—except as otherwise provided or unless inconsistent with Subchapter S. Such rules include those governing formation, liquidation, and reorganization. Therefore, any Subchapter C rule that treats as a separate entity a business association that is taxable as a corporation presumptively applies, unless otherwise provided or inconsistent with Subchapter S.

An S corporation in its capacity as a shareholder of another corporation is not entitled to the §§ 243–246A deduction for dividends received.[12] This exception makes sense since there will not be any additional entity-level tax imposed on the dividends when received by the S corporation.

Because of its transparent or passthrough nature, an S corporation will also not be subject to the Subchapter C penalty taxes on corporations that improperly accumulate

---

[6] I.R.C. § 1363(b)(4). Section 291 imposes special limitations on the tax benefits available to a corporation from specified "preference items," such as the unrecaptured portion of accelerated depreciation deductions on certain real property under § 1250. *See Vainisi v. Comm'r*, 599 F.3d 567 (7th Cir. 2010).

[7] In certain respects, the S corporation is treated like a corporate taxpayer. Importantly, an S corporation that was formerly a C corporation is exposed to the special sting taxes on built-in gain from C years or on excess passive investment income. *See* I.R.C. §§ 1374, 1375. *See also* ¶¶ 5.01–5.04.

[8] *See* I.R.C. § 1363(c)(1). Examples of such elections include method of accounting and depreciation computations. Reg. § 1.1363–1(c); *see* ¶ 3.05.

[9] I.R.C. §§ 1363(b)(2), 1366(a)(1).

[10] I.R.C. §§ 1367(a)(2) (flush language), 1366(d)(4). Thus, the loss limit under § 1366(d)(1) applies only if the shareholder's ratable share of the basis of the contributed property exceeds the shareholder's total basis in stock (and debt). *See* ¶¶ 6.05, 6.09.

[11] For example, assume that an S corporation contributes long-term capital gain property with a basis of $50 and a fair market value of $200 to a charity. The passthrough of the charitable deduction to a 50% shareholder would be $100, but the shareholder's stock basis would only be reduced by $25. *See* Rev. Rul. 2008–16, 2008–1 C.B. 585.

[12] I.R.C. § 1363(b)(2); Reg. § 1.1363–1(b)(1).

earnings or surplus,[13] or that act as personal holding companies.[14] Given their tax policy purposes, it would not make sense to apply either of these penalty taxes to a passthrough entity.[15]

¶ 3.03   COMPUTATIONS OF CORPORATE INCOME

Like a partnership under § 703(a), an S corporation must compute and report its income (in the same manner as in the case of an individual) for passthrough purposes under § 1363(b).[16] Then, by virtue of § 1366, each shareholder of the corporation is obliged to take into account her pro rata share of the S corporation's separately and non-separately stated items of income, loss, deduction or credit.[17] The shareholders must report the S corporation's income or loss in the shareholder's taxable year in which the taxable year of the S corporation ends, or in the final taxable year of a shareholder who dies before the end of the corporation's taxable year.[18]

The character of passthrough items is generally determined at the entity level and is retained in the shareholder's hands. Thus, the character will be the same as if it were realized by the shareholder directly from the source from which realized by the corporation, or incurred in the same manner as incurred by the corporation.[19] Some special limitations apply, however, particularly with respect to deductions or losses passed through. These limitations are in addition to those generally applicable at the individual level, such as limits on passive activity losses and capital losses. In particular, losses will be allowed only to the extent of the shareholder's basis in her shares (with any disallowed losses carried over indefinitely).[20] Also, the Code specifically allows the IRS to reallocate items within a family group to prevent abusive shifting of income or losses (for example, by working for a family corporation without reasonable compensation).[21]

The amount of income passed through and taxed to shareholders must be reduced by the amount of any tax imposed on the S corporation itself, such as the sting taxes on built-in gains and excess passive investment income (discussed below in ¶ 3.04).[22]

¶ 3.04   SPECIAL ENTITY-LEVEL TAXES AND TAX COMPUTATION EFFECTS

Some S corporations must pay an entity-level tax on special items or in special circumstances. For example, a converted S corporation is subject to tax on "built-in gains" under § 1374. (This tax does *not* apply to a corporation that has always been an S corporation and has never acquired C assets with built-in gain in a tax-free transaction.)

---

[13]   *See* I.R.C. §§ 531, 532. The accumulated earnings surtax applies to corporations that improperly accumulate earnings and profits. Since an S corporation does not generate earnings and profits, it cannot fall within the scope of § 531.

[14]   *See* I.R.C. § 541.

[15]   Similarly, since the S corporation must be a domestic corporation, it can never be a § 951 controlled foreign corporation or a § 1291 passive foreign investment company.

[16]   *See* Reg. § 1.1363–1(b).

[17]   For discussion of items that must be separately stated, see ¶ 6.03.

[18]   I.R.C. § 1366(a), (c).

[19]   I.R.C. § 1366(b); Reg. § 1.1366–1(b).

[20]   I.R.C. § 1366(d)(1), (2).

[21]   I.R.C. § 1366(e).

[22]   I.R.C. § 1366(f)(2), (3).

If the § 1374 tax does apply, the corporation must pay the highest § 11(b) corporate tax rate on the lesser of its recognized built-in gains for the year or on the amount that would be taxable income if it were not an S corporation. The § 1374 built-in gain tax is discussed more fully at ¶ 5.01.

Also, if an S corporation has C corporation earnings and profits carried over from C years, it may be subject to the § 1375 tax on net passive investment income in excess of 25% of gross receipts for the year. The tax on excess passive investment income is discussed in greater detail at ¶ 5.02.

For purposes of the § 318 attribution rules, an S corporation is treated as a partnership, and any shareholder is treated as a partner of the "partnership."[23] This special rule does not apply, however, for purposes of determining whether stock *in* the S corporation is constructively owned by any person.[24]

¶ 3.05   ELECTIONS TO BE MADE BY THE S CORPORATION

An S corporation must generally make all elections affecting the computation of tax items, and such elections are binding on shareholders.[25] For example, the corporation elects its method of accounting[26] and choice of depreciation method.[27] The corporation must also make the election to deduct organizational expenses under § 248.[28] The statute reserves two tax elections to be made by the shareholders of an S corporation.[29] For example, each shareholder adds her distributive share of foreign taxes paid by the corporation to those foreign taxes she has paid, and individually elects either to deduct or credit them.[30]

¶ 3.06   THE S ELECTION AS A TAXABLE EVENT

The election of S status by a former C corporation does not involve any actual transfer of property from one corporation to another. Nevertheless, questions sometimes arise as to whether the change from C to S status triggers taxation as a result of recapture or similar rules. The tax consequences of making an S election may cause some C corporations to reconsider migrating to S status, or to defer conversion until the tax costs can be reduced.

Since the conversion from C to S status is treated as a mere change in form, the S election itself generally does not trigger recapture of investment tax credits allowed for prior C corporation years.[31] These investment tax credits may be recaptured later when

---

[23]   I.R.C. § 318(a)(5)(E).

[24]   *Id.*

[25]   I.R.C. § 1363(c)(1); Reg. § 1.1363–1(c)(1).

[26]   In computing its income for purposes of § 1363, the S corporation may use whatever accounting method is available under conventional principles, including the cash method, unless the S corporation is also a tax shelter. *See* I.R.C. § 448. In that case, the Code may limit the choices available by prescribing a method of accounting (usually the accrual method) for the corporation. *See* I.R.C. §§ 444, 461(i)(3).

[27]   *See* Reg. § 1.1363–1(c)(1).

[28]   I.R.C. § 1363(b)(3). Under § 108, the insolvency determination and reduction in tax attributes is also made at the entity-level. *See* I.R.C. § 108(d)(7); *see also* ¶ 7.05.

[29]   I.R.C. § 1362(c)(2) (elections related to the foreign tax credit under § 901 and the treatment of certain mining expenditures under § 617).

[30]   *See* Reg. § 1.1363–1(c)(2)(iii).

[31]   I.R.C. § 1371(d)(1).

property is disposed of (or ceases to be investment tax credit property). In that event, the S corporation must pay the *corporate-level* recapture tax.[32]

Similarly, § 1363(d) imposes a special tax on an S corporation that was formerly a C corporation and used the LIFO inventory method during its last C year. Upon conversion to S status, the corporation must include in gross income the "LIFO recapture amount" for the last taxable year of C status.[33]

¶ 3.07   METHODS OF ACCOUNTING

In computing its income for purposes of § 1363, an S corporation may use whatever accounting method is available under conventional principles unless the S corporation is a tax shelter.[34] Unlike most C corporations, an electing S corporation is permitted, under § 448(a), to use the cash method of accounting. The choice of accounting method may have important implications for the operation of other tax rules, such as the passive investment income rules of § 1362(d)(3), as well as for the timing, bunching or deferral of income or deductions.

Section 267(e) puts an S corporation on the cash method with respect to payments to related persons. As a result, an S corporation and its shareholders cannot arrange to defer taxation of income by having the corporation accrue a deduction in one year for an amount not paid to a cash-method shareholder until the next year.[35] The S corporation's deduction is deferred until the shareholder-payee includes the payment in income (under the payee's method of accounting).

¶ 3.08   TAX YEAR

As an entity, an S corporation chooses the taxable year for reporting its income (and calculating tax, if any). Shareholders must include corporate income in their individual returns for the year in which the tax year of the corporation ends, under § 1366(a)(1). The S taxable year must be a "permitted" year; the corporation is not free to choose any fiscal year solely as it wishes.[36] A permitted year includes a taxable year that ends on December 31st (*i.e.*, a calendar year), or any other accounting period (*i.e.*, a fiscal year) *only if* the corporation establishes a *bona fide* business purpose for using such a year, or if it makes a § 444 election (discussed below).[37] Not surprisingly, deferral of income to shareholders, often a reason that S corporations formerly elected a non-calendar year, is *not* treated as a business purpose.[38]

---

[32]   I.R.C. § 1371(d)(2). If corporate-level tax is triggered, the corporation's accumulated earnings and profits account will be adjusted to reflect the recapture tax. I.R.C. § 1371(d)(3).

[33]   I.R.C. § 1363(d). This requires recapture of the difference between FIFO and LIFO inventory amounts. The additional tax is payable in four installments.

[34]   *See* I.R.C. §§ 448 (limiting method of C, but not S, corporations), 461(i)(3) (defining tax shelter).

[35]   *See* I.R.C. § 267(a)(2), (e). Note that, by virtue of § 267(e)(1)(B)(ii), any shareholder (not just a more-than-50% shareholder) is treated as a related party for purposes of § 267(a)(2). Moreover, losses on a sale or exchange between related parties will not be deductible. *See* I.R.C. § 267(a)(1).

[36]   I.R.C. § 1378(a); Reg. § 1.1378–1. If the S corporation could elect a taxable year that would end shortly after the end of the shareholders' taxable years, shareholders could defer reporting S corporation income for almost a full year. This choice, formerly allowed, provided unacceptable latitude.

[37]   *See* I.R.C. § 1378(b).

[38]   I.R.C. § 1378(b)(2) (flush language).

Thus, calendar-year reporting is generally required for a new S corporation, placing it generally on a par with a partnership. If the corporation wishes to apply for permission to use a different taxable year, it must follow the procedures dictated by the IRS.[39]

Example 3.1: For example, a business such as a retail store with large Christmas sales may be granted permission to use a "natural business year" if at least 25% of its gross receipts fall within the last two months of the year. In this situation, a non-calendar year may be justified even if it results in some deferral of income.

Of course, if the S corporation will pass through losses, deferral is likely *not* desirable, and a *calendar* year will serve best the tax-saving purposes of individual shareholders.

In addition, § 444 offers an S corporation, a partnership, or a personal service corporation another option to avoid calendar-year taxation. To elect to use a year other than "the required taxable year," under § 444 an S corporation must make the payments required by § 7519. This section imposes an excise tax whose purpose is to defeat any tax benefit resulting from deferral.[40] In essence, the § 7519 payments amount to an interest-free deposit that compensates the government for the benefit of deferral.

¶ 3.09   QUALIFIED EMPLOYEE RETIREMENT PLANS

Qualified employee retirement plans of S corporations are generally subject to the same rules as those governing C corporations (and all other employers, including partners and proprietors).[41] A qualified plan loan to an S shareholder-employee is not treated as a "prohibited transaction" under § 4975.[42] Thus, S corporation shareholder-employees can borrow on the same terms as C corporation shareholder-employees. Permitting such loans eliminates a potential trap upon conversion of a C corporation to S status.

¶ 3.10   FRINGE BENEFITS—§ 1372

For purposes of employee fringe benefits, § 1372(a) provides that an S corporation and any shareholder-employees who own more than 2% of the outstanding stock (or stock having more than 2% of the total combined voting power of all of the stock) are subject to the same rules as those applying to partnerships and partners.[43] Consequently, "2% shareholders" of an S corporation are *not* eligible to receive tax-favored employee fringe benefits available to C corporation employees (including shareholder-employees). The

---

[39] *See* Rev. Proc. 2006–46, 2006–2 C.B. 859 (guidelines for requests to adopt, retain or change taxable years).

[40] *See* I.R.C. § 444(a). The "required taxable year" is defined by § 444(e) as the year determined under § 1378 without taking into account any year allowable by reason of business purposes. So, there are two avenues of escape from a calendar year. The first is the business-purpose rule of § 1378 and the second, separate method, is the § 444 election, with payment of the excise tax, regardless of whether the S corporation can establish a business purpose for the fiscal year.

[41] Such plans are those governed by I.R.C. §§ 401–417 (defined-contribution or defined-benefit plans). Nonqualified, unfunded, deferred compensation arrangements in an S corporation will be treated like those in a C corporation. *See* I.R.C. §§ 162, 404(a)(5).

[42] *See* I.R.C. § 4975(f)(6)(B)(iii). Congress considered that permitting loans to S shareholder-employees on a par with C shareholder-employees would help to foster qualified plans.

[43] *See* I.R.C. § 1372. Section 1372 invokes § 318 attribution rules.

disallowed fringe benefits include excludable health and accident plans or policies, group-term life insurance, and employer-provided meals and lodging.[44]

Employees who are *not* "2% shareholders" can receive these corporate fringe benefits with the normal tax preferences. For both categories of employees, the costs of these fringe benefits should be deductible to the S corporation as compensation paid, under general income tax principles. This treatment is consistent with the partnership analogy, where payments to partners under § 707(c) (guaranteed payments) or § 707(a) (payments to a partner not acting in her capacity as a partner) are deductible by the partnership under § 162. Accordingly, these fringe benefits should likewise be deductible by the S corporation.[45] The same treatment should apply for fringe benefits that do not receive any statutory preference, since the goal of § 1372 is to harmonize the treatment of S corporations and partnerships.

Stock option plans can also be used by an S corporation. If an option granted to an employee (or independent contractor) qualifies for safe harbor treatment, it will not create a second class of stock.[46]

¶ 3.11   REASONABLE COMPENSATION OF SHAREHOLDER-EMPLOYEES

For a C corporation, the payment of deductible compensation to shareholder-employees reduces the corporate-level tax; the result is the payment of a single tax by the shareholder-employee upon receipt of the compensation. In the C corporation context, recharacterization of compensation paid to a shareholder-employee as a dividend may result in denial of a corporate-level deduction and corporate tax on the disallowed amounts. For S corporations, in which corporate taxable income will be taxed—only once—to the shareholders, avoidance of the double tax is not a concern. However, reasonable compensation issues nevertheless arise in the S corporation context, as S corporation shareholders may be tempted to characterize payments as distributions with respect to stock rather than as compensation. Such characterization is highly desirable in order to avoid payment of employment taxes.

In Revenue Ruling 74–44, the IRS recognized the potential problems of such an arrangement.[47] In that ruling, an S corporation's two shareholder-employees arranged to take no salary from the corporation but, instead, to have the corporation pay out all net taxable income as a dividend. The IRS recharacterized the purported dividend payment as salary, on the theory that the payment to the shareholder-employees was in fact compensation for services rendered, since the amount of the dividend payment was actually the amount of reasonable compensation.

---

[44]   I.R.C. § 132. Some fringe benefits clearly fall within the purview of § 1372, including those mentioned in the legislative history such as the death benefit exclusion (§ 101(b)), the accident and health plan exclusions (§§ 105(b), (c), (d), 106), the group-term life insurance exclusion (§ 79), the meals and lodging exclusion (§ 119), and the § 132 exclusion for certain other fringe benefits.

[45]   *See* Rev. Rul. 91–26, 1991–1 C.B. 184 (treating accident and health insurance premiums for shareholder-employees (including 2% shareholders) as deductible under § 162); IRS Ann. 92–16, 1992–5 I.R.B. 53. *See also Hurst v. Comm'r*, 124 T.C. 16 (2005) (following Rev. Rul. 91–26; 2% shareholder taxable on premiums). However, some costs, such as for medical expenses, will *not* be deductible by the S corporation (or the partnership). *See* I.R.C. §§ 1363(b)(2), 703(a)(2)(E). Nevertheless, an S shareholder may be able to salvage a personal deduction for health insurance premiums under § 162(*l*)(5).

[46]   *See* ¶ 2.09

[47]   1974–1 C.B. 287.

Courts have agreed with the IRS's approach. In *Radtke*,[48] for example, an S corporation paid no salary to the shareholder-employee; instead, it distributed *all* taxable income as a dividend. The IRS recharacterized the distribution as salary and sought deficiencies in employment taxes. Both the District Court and the Seventh Circuit agreed with the IRS, on the theory that the function of the payments was to compensate the shareholder-employee for services rendered to the corporation.

As the IRS's victory in *Radtke* suggests, an S corporation tax return showing no compensation payments to shareholder-employees will, understandably, generate inquiry. If, however, the S corporation pays reasonable compensation (determined, presumably, in the same manner as in the C corporation context), any additional amounts should be classified as a distribution with respect to stock and taxed in the same manner as any other distribution. As in the C corporation context, it may be difficult to determine what constitutes reasonable compensation.[49]

More recently, courts have looked askance at S corporations that pay *some* compensation to shareholder-employees (in the hope of avoiding audit) but less than reasonable compensation. In *Watson*,[50] the taxpayer's professional service corporation (taxed as an S corporation) provided services to an accounting firm. The taxpayer reported a relatively small amount of wages and much larger distributions from the S corporation. Because the compensation was unreasonably low, the court treated a portion of the distributions (25%) as wages. Arguably, nearly all of the distributions represented disguised compensation, given the nature of the accounting firm's business.

If reasonable compensation is paid and the S shareholder has sufficient stock basis, distributions are normally tax free. If instead the payment were treated as salary, the S corporation would receive a deduction but the shareholder-employee would have a corresponding income inclusion. Thus, for income tax purposes, an S shareholder-employee may be indifferent to the characterization of the payment. Despite the "wash" for income tax purposes, however, distribution of amounts in lieu of salary may yield significant employment tax savings for shareholder-employees.[51] By arranging to receive lower compensation and higher distributions, such shareholders may avoid Social Security taxes, unemployment taxes and withholding taxes.

Example 3.2: A is the sole shareholder of S Corp., a calendar-year S corporation. In 2023, A received a salary of $100,000, on which she paid FICA taxes of $7,650 (7.65%). S Corp. paid the employer's share of the FICA taxes ($7,650)

---

[48] *Radtke v. U.S.*, 712 F. Supp. 143 (E.D. Wis. 1989), *aff'd*, 895 F.2d 1196 (7th Cir. 1990). The District Court emphasized that no salary was paid and that the taxpayer was the sole director, shareholder, and employee of the corporation. These factors suggested the opportunity and context for abuse. *See Spicer Accounting, Inc. v. U.S.*, 918 F.2d 90 (9th Cir. 1990); *Veterinary Surgical Consultants, P.C. v. Comm'r*, 117 T.C. 141 (2001).

[49] Considerable flexibility exists in determining what constitutes reasonable compensation. *See Menard, Inc. v. Comm'r*, 560 F.3d 620 (7th Cir. 2009) (applying "independent investor" test). *Cf. Mulcahy v. Comm'r*, 680 F.3d 867 (7th Cir. 2012) (independent investor test not satisfied when an accounting firm, organized as a C corporation, eliminated most of its taxable income by deducting consulting fees paid to entities controlled by the firm's founding shareholders).

[50] *Watson v. U.S.*, 668 F.3d 1008 (8th Cir. 2012), *cert. denied*, 568 U.S. 888 (2012). *See Glass Blocks Unlimited v. Comm'r*, T.C. Memo 2013–180 (distributions were deemed wages, not repayment of debt).

[51] As used here, the term employment taxes includes social security taxes and Medicare taxes. *See* I.R.C. §§ 3102, 3111, 3301. *See Dagres v. Comm'r*, 136 T.C. 263 (2011) (S corporation received fees for management services provided to partnership that advised and managed a venture capital fund). Presumably, the S corporation structure was intended to avoid self-employment taxes on the management fees allocable to its sole shareholder (who also held an interest in the partnership).

for total FICA taxes of $15,300. If A reduced her salary to $25,000 and received a distribution of $75,000, the corporate-shareholder FICA burden would be only $3,825 (15.3% × $25,000), resulting in combined tax savings of $11,475. Since distributions from an S corporation are not treated as self-employment income, the $75,000 distribution escapes FICA taxes unless some portion is recharacterized as salary.

The introduction of the § 1411 tax on net investment income (NII) increases the stakes.[52] If payments to a shareholder-employee are treated as compensation, the § 1411 tax will not apply (but the corresponding Medicare portion of the employment taxes will apply).[53] If instead the payment is characterized as a distribution, the § 1411 tax will apply but only if the S shareholder does not actively participate in the business (within the meaning of the § 469 passive loss rules).[54] Because the § 1411 tax does not apply to active business income derived from an S corporation, S shareholders who participate in the business and receive distributions in lieu of reasonable compensation potentially enjoy the best of all possible worlds: understating compensation avoids both employment taxes and the § 1411 tax.

Example 3.3: In Example 3.2 above, suppose that A materially participates in the business of S Corp. A again reduces her salary to $25,000 and receives a distribution of $75,000. Assuming $25,000 is a reasonable salary for A's services, the distribution avoids both FICA taxes and the § 1411 tax. If A did not materially participate in S Corp.'s business, then the $75,000 distribution would trigger tax under § 1411 (assuming A's modified adjusted gross income exceeds the threshold).

This S loophole also provides a significant advantage in comparison to other business forms. For example, sole proprietors must pay employment taxes on their net business income. Similarly, general partners are subject to self-employment tax on their entire share of partnership income, with certain limited exceptions. By contrast, limited partners enjoy an exclusion from self-employment taxes (except for certain guaranteed payments) but are generally subject to the § 1411 tax on their distributive share.[55] Distinguishing between passive and active members of an LLC for purposes of self-employment taxes presents difficult issues, since the traditional distinction between "general" and "limited" partners does not apply. Nevertheless, courts have sought to deny the limited partner exclusion from self-employment tax to active LLP members.[56]

Suppose an S corporation pays excessively *high* compensation to a shareholder who is also an employee? In that event, the unreasonable excess might be reclassified as a disproportionate distribution with respect to shares held by the shareholder-employee,

---

[52] NII includes capital gains, interest, dividends, annuities, royalties and rents, as well as income from a trade or business that is a § 469 passive activity with respect to the taxpayer. I.R.C. § 1411(c)(1), (2). *See* Reg. § 1.1411–4(a)(1), (b), –5. Under § 1366, such items (and allocable deductions) that pass through to an S shareholder must be separately stated.

[53] *See* I.R.C. § 3101(b)(2)(A) (imposing .9% Medicare surtax on high earners).

[54] The passive activity loss rules are discussed at ¶ 6.10.

[55] *See* I.R.C. § 1402(a)(13). Proposed regulations attempt to provide greater certainty in defining a "limited partnership interest" for purpose of the passive loss rules. *See* Prop. Reg. § 1.469–5(e)(3), (f).

[56] *See Renkemeyer v. Comm'r*, 136 T.C. 137 (2011). In the case of a professional service partnership, the IRS is likely to argue that the partner's entire distributive share is subject to self-employment tax rather than only a portion.

potentially resulting in a second class of stock and loss of S status.[57] Unless a principal purpose of the excess payment is to avoid the one-class-of-stock requirement, however, no second class of stock will arise.[58]

¶ 3.12   MAXIMIZING PASSTHROUGH DEDUCTION—§ 199A

In general, § 199A allows a deduction of up to 20% of a taxpayer's "qualified business income" (QBI).[59] The deduction is commonly referred to as the "passthrough deduction" because it is available only to noncorporate taxpayers. QBI excludes reasonable compensation paid to the taxpayer by a qualified trade or business for services rendered to the trade or business.[60] In addition, a qualified business does not include a "specified service trade or business" (SSTB) or the trade or business of performing services as an employee.[61]

The § 199A deduction reduces taxable income (but not adjusted gross income) regardless of whether the taxpayer itemizes.[62] Taxpayers with taxable income not exceeding a threshold amount ($315,000 for joint filers, $157,500 for other filers, adjusted for inflation) are eligible for a full 20% deduction without regard to the principal limitations that apply to higher-income taxpayers.[63] Above the income threshold, the "wage" and "wage-and-property" limitations may produce less than a full 20% deduction.[64]

Section 199A complicates compensation strategies for S shareholder-employees. Because reasonable compensation reduces QBI, minimizing compensation generally increases the amount of qualifying income eligible for the § 199A deduction. In some instances, however, increasing compensation to an S shareholder can increase the § 199A deduction if other limitations would otherwise be binding.

Example 3.4: A is the sole shareholder of a non-capital-intensive S corporation that has qualified business income of $400,000 after paying reasonable compensation of $100,000 to A for her services. Under the wage limitation, A's § 199A deduction is limited to the lesser of (i) $80,000 (20% of $400,000 QBI) or (ii) $50,000 (50% of $100,000 wages). A's deduction is limited to $50,000

---

[57]   *See* ¶ 2.09. Because of the one-class-of-stock rule, S shareholders can vary ratable sharing of net profits only through compensation arrangements.

[58]   *See* Reg. § 1.1361–1(*l*)(2)(vi)(ex. 3). *See also* § 1366(e) (reallocation to curb family-income shifting).

[59]   QBI generally means net income (other than investment-type income) from a U.S. trade or business. *See* I.R.C. § 199A(c)(1). The § 199A deduction may never exceed 20% of the taxpayer's total taxable income (determined without regard to the § 199A deduction), reduced by net capital gain. *See* I.R.C. § 199A(a)(2).

[60]   *See* I.R.C. § 199A(c)(4)(A).

[61]   *See* I.R.C. § 199A(d)(1)(A) and (B). An SSTB generally includes any professional service business described in § 1202(e)(3)(A) (except for architecture and engineering), as well as certain investment-management businesses. *See* I.R.C. § 199A(d)(2). Under § 1202(e)(3)(A), the disfavored categories include professional services in the areas of health, law, and accounting, as well as any trade or business having the reputation or skill of one or more employees or owners as its principal asset. The SSTB disqualification reflects Congress's concern about the ability of high-income passthrough owners to convert ordinary labor income into capital income.

[62]   *See* I.R.C. § 63(b)(3).

[63]   *See* I.R.C. § 199A(e)(2). Within a phase-in range (up to $415,000 for joint filers, $207,500 for other filers, adjusted for inflation), the limitations are partially applicable (and reduce the § 199A deduction correspondingly). Also, the SSTB limitation does not apply to taxpayers below the income threshold.

[64]   *See* I.R.C. § 199A(b)(2).

because the wage limitation is binding.[65] A could potentially increase her § 199A deduction by paying herself a higher wage. This strategy is advantageous if the income tax savings from the increased § 199A deduction outweigh any increase in employment taxes.

Example 3.5: In Example 3.4 above, suppose that A pays herself 2/7 of net QBI (determined before taking into account any compensation deduction). Assuming A pays herself wages of $142,857 (2/7 × $500,000 pre-wage QBI), the S corporation would have post-wage QBI of $357,143, ignoring any employer deduction for employment taxes. At this point, the wage limitation (50% × 142,857 = $71,429) equals 20% of post-wage QBI (20% × $357,143 = 71,429); with rounding, A's § 199A deduction equals $71,429. Because the § 199A deduction is equal to the lesser of the wage limitation or 20% of QBI, paying more (or less) wages than $142,857 will reduce the allowable deduction.

When the wage limitation is binding, the "cost" of increasing compensation to a sole S shareholder-employee (up to the 2/7 breakpoint) is essentially the amount of any increase in employment taxes. Often, this additional cost will be less than 3.8% of the additional wage amount (2.9% Medicare tax plus the .9% additional Medicare tax), taking into account the employer deduction for half of the Medicare tax. By contrast, for a high-income taxpayer, the tax savings from the § 199A deduction will be worth 18.5% (50% × 37%) of the additional compensation.

To the extent the tax savings outweigh any additional cost, § 199A potentially provides an incentive to overstate the wages of S shareholder-employees. If the § 199A deduction disappears after 2025, as scheduled, excessively high compensation in the interim might make it more difficult later to claim unreasonably low compensation.[66]

---

[65] By contrast, if A's business owns tangible depreciable property that is not yet fully depreciated, the wage-and-property limitation may allow a § 199A deduction even though the business has no employees. In that case, A's § 199A deduction cannot exceed the lesser of (i) 20% of QBI or (ii) the sum of 25% of A's share of the wages of the business (zero) and 2.5% of the unadjusted basis of the business's depreciable property. The wage-and-property limitation is intended to benefit businesses (such as real estate) that have large capital investments and few employees.

[66] Excess compensation may also run afoul of the one-class-of-stock rule. *See* ¶¶ 2.09, 3.11.

Chapter 4

EFFECTS OF THE S ELECTION DURING OPERATIONS—DISTRIBUTIONS TO SHAREHOLDERS

¶ 4.01   TAXATION OF DISTRIBUTIONS BY THE S CORPORATION—§ 1368

Actual distributions of cash or property by an S corporation to shareholders with respect to their shares are treated differently from those by a C corporation. The differences reflect the flowthrough taxation of shareholders and the absence of any corporate-level tax. This subject can usefully be subdivided into sections contemplating actual distributions by S corporations of cash (¶ 4.02) and *other property* (appreciated or diminished in value) (¶ 4.07). It is also necessary to distinguish between distributions by S corporations *without* accumulated earnings and profits (an "always" S corporation) and those *with* accumulated earnings and profits left over from prior C years. As might be expected, S corporations with a prior C history are subject to more complex distribution rules.

To explore these topics fully, it will be necessary to make detours along the way to discuss the accumulated adjustments account (AAA) (¶ 4.05) and the post-termination transition period (PTTP) (¶ 4.06), both of which play an important part in characterizing distributions from S corporations.

¶ 4.02   CASH DISTRIBUTIONS; GENERALLY

The taxability of actual distributions of cash by an S corporation to its shareholders with respect to their shares is governed by two statutory systems, one for an S corporation *without* earnings and profits (from C corporation years) and one for S corporations *with* such earnings and profits.[1]

When does an S corporation have accumulated earnings and profits, upon which a number of tax determinations can depend, including the taxability of distributions? One answer is simple: An S corporation that was formed after 1982, was an S corporation from the outset, and has continuously been an S corporation and never acquired another entity or business that had C earnings and profits, cannot and will not have accumulated earnings and profits. This is so because, after 1982, an S corporation by law does not generate or accumulate earnings and profits.[2] Prior to 1983, it was possible for an S corporation to have earnings and profits from S corporation years, but Congress has eliminated pre-1983 earnings and profits for most S corporations.[3] Thus, distributions attributable to pre-1983 earnings and profits will no longer generate amounts treated as a dividend.

---

[1]   *Compare* I.R.C. § 1368(b) (S corporations without earnings and profits) *with* I.R.C. § 1368(c) (S corporations with earnings and profits).

[2]   I.R.C. § 1371(c)(1).

[3]   For S corporations that qualify under this rule, distributions in excess of AAA deemed to come out of pre-1983 S earnings and profits will now be applied first to reduce stock basis and then taxed as capital gain.

An S corporation may have accumulated earnings and profits if it has been operated as a C corporation sometime in its life. An S corporation may also inherit earnings and profits from a C corporation (or a converted S corporation) in a tax-free reorganization, by virtue of § 381(c)(2). As discussed in Chapter 8 on reorganizations, § 381(c)(2) provides for a carryover or "inheritance" of tax attributes when an S corporation is the acquiring, surviving or resulting corporation. Even such an S corporation can "zero out" its accumulated earnings and profits by making taxable distributions that reduce the accumulated earnings and profits account. But it runs the risk of miscalculating, or of suffering a redetermination on later audit. Consequently, an "untainted" S corporation (without any C attributes) is the best if freedom from accumulated earnings and profits will be a consideration—as it always can be, either as to taxability of future distributions or other issues. A "midstream" S election by a C corporation thus can raise the danger that an unknown or unanticipated determination of accumulated earnings can change the consequences of future events to a shareholder's disadvantage.

The simplest and most basic type of distribution (a cash distribution) is considered first.

¶ 4.03   CASH DISTRIBUTIONS BY S CORPORATION WITH NO ACCUMULATED EARNINGS AND PROFITS—§ 1368(b)

If an S corporation *without* Subchapter C earnings and profits makes a *cash* distribution, shareholders can receive the cash tax free up to the aggregate basis of their stock. Each shareholder's stock basis must be reduced by the amount of the cash received.[4]

Example 4.1: X Corp., an always S corporation, distributes $1,000 to each of its shareholders, A and B. Shareholder A has a basis of $5,000 in his shares, and Shareholder B has a basis of $2,500 in her shares. Neither shareholder pays tax on this distribution because each has sufficient basis to "cover" a $1,000 distribution. A must reduce his basis by $1,000 to $4,000, and B must reduce her basis by $1,000 to $1,500.

If and when a shareholder receives cash in excess of stock basis, the excess is treated as gain from the sale or exchange of property.[5] Such gain usually will be capital gain, short-term or long-term depending on how long each shareholder has held the stock. Under § 1(h), net long-term capital gain is taxed at a maximum rate of 20%. In addition, the shareholder may have some unused capital loss which can be used (dollar for dollar and with no ceiling) to offset any gain resulting from the distribution.

Example 4.2: In Example 4.1 above, assume X Corp. distributes another $2,000 to each of the two shareholders. A would not have to pay any tax because his basis of $4,000 would be sufficient to absorb the $2,000 distribution; B would have to pay tax on $500, the excess of her $2,000 distribution over her basis of $1,500. Provided the stock constitutes a capital asset in B's hands, the $500 gain would be long-term or short-term capital gain depending on B's holding

---

[4]   *See* I.R.C. §§ 1368(b)(1), 1367(a)(2)(A). A cash distribution may be disguised salary or wages, with implications also for employment taxes, social security taxes, and interest and penalties. *See, e.g., Radtke v. U.S.,* 712 F. Supp. 143 (E.D. Wis. 1989), *aff'd,* 895 F.2d 1196 (7th Cir. 1990). *See also* ¶ 3.11.

[5]   I.R.C. § 1368(b)(2).

period. After the distribution, A's stock basis would be $2,000 and B's stock basis would be zero.

The corporation's earnings are passed through and taxed to shareholders under § 1366, without regard to actual distributions. That taxability results in a *pro rata* increase in the shareholders' bases under § 1367(a)(1). In turn, the upward basis adjustment for the amount taxed but *not* distributed allows an actual distribution of the same amount, in the same or a later tax year, to be received by the shareholder(s) without further tax, under § 1368(b)(1). But the price of a tax-free distribution is a downward adjustment in basis by the amount received, placing the shareholder back where she started. (Hence, it is more likely that a further cash distribution will exceed basis and be taxable under § 1368(b)(2)). The basis rules, working in tandem with the taxability rules, thus accomplish the single-tax flowthrough regime that lies at the heart of Subchapter S.[6]

For purposes of determining the taxability of distributions, any adjustments to stock basis under § 1367(a)(1) for income passed through during the taxable year must be made *before* any distributions are taken into account.[7] Thus, it may be somewhat misleading to refer to stock basis on the actual date of distribution, since stock basis adjustments (and hence taxability of distributions) can only be determined at the end of the corporation's taxable year.

Example 4.3: X Corp. is a calendar-year S corporation with no accumulated earnings and profits. A owns 10% of X Corp.'s outstanding shares with a basis of $1,000. On November 1, A receives a $2,000 cash distribution. On this date, the tax consequences of the distribution cannot yet be fully determined. A must wait until year end. Suppose that X Corp. has no gains or losses to report for the year. Then, the first $1,000 of the distribution (not in excess of A's stock basis) will be tax free; A's stock basis will be reduced to zero and A will be taxed on the remaining $1,000 as gain from sale or exchange of A's shares.

However, if X Corp. had net ordinary income of $10,000 for the taxable year (10% of which passed through to A), A would be taxed on $1,000 of regular income (10% of $10,000) and receive a concomitant $1,000 increase in basis. Under these circumstances, the $2,000 distribution would be entirely tax free to A whose stock basis would again be reduced to zero ($1,000 initial basis increased by $1,000 income and decreased by $2,000 distribution).

Distributions reduce stock basis *before* losses are taken into account.[8] This ordering rule maximizes the amount of distributions that may be received by a shareholder tax free under § 1368, while potentially reducing the amount of losses that the shareholder may deduct currently.[9]

---

[6]   Income and loss must be allocated pro rata to shareholders. I.R.C. § 1366(a); *see* I.R.C. § 1377(a) (per-share, per-day allocation). Usually actual distributions will be made in the same ratios. Disproportionate distributions raise not only corporate law questions but may also violate the single-class-of-stock rule.

[7]   I.R.C. § 1368(d) (flush language); Reg. § 1.1368–1(c). By contrast, the taxability of partnership distributions is determined as of the date of the distribution, although the special rule for partnership draws achieves a similar result by deferring taxation until year end. *See* ¶ 4.05 n.29 *infra*.

[8]   I.R.C. §§ 1368(d), 1367(a)(2); *see* I.R.C. § 1366(d)(1) (loss limitation). This ordering rule is intended to conform the treatment of S corporations and partnerships when distributions and losses occur in the same year. *See* Reg. § 1.704–1(d)(2); Rev. Rul. 66–94, 1996–1 C.B. 166.

[9]   For the order of basis adjustments, see Reg. §§ 1.1367–1(f) and 1.1368–1(e)(2). *See also* ¶ 6.05.

Thus, in Example 4.3 above, if X Corp. reported $10,000 in net ordinary *losses* for the taxable year, the cash distribution of $2,000 would reduce A's stock basis to zero and trigger $1,000 of gain ($2,000 distribution less $1,000 pre-distribution basis) from the deemed sale of A's shares. A's share of the net ordinary loss ($1,000) would be "suspended."[10] A would not be allowed to use the suspended loss until a subsequent year when A's stock basis increased above zero.[11]

¶ 4.04   CASH DISTRIBUTION BY S CORPORATION WITH ACCUMULATED EARNINGS AND PROFITS—§ 1368(c)

If an S corporation *does* have accumulated earnings and profits derived from C years or from a predecessor corporation, a distribution of cash will be subject to a more complicated regime under § 1368(c), which partially displaces § 1368(b). Section 1368(c) is designed to produce proper taxation of distributions by a "tainted" S corporation, one that has not fully distributed accumulated earnings and profits attributable to a prior C history. The question raised by such a prior C history is what character and taxability to assign to a distribution of cash—taxable dividend up to earnings and profits, as in a pure C corporation, or tax-free distribution of previously taxed earnings, as in a pure S corporation, or some mix of the two. The goal is, after an S election, to preserve the taxability of Subchapter C earnings when such earnings (or their equivalent) are distributed.

Congress enacted special statutory rules, in § 1368(c), to segregate the Subchapter C earnings from the Subchapter S previously taxed income. This segregation is intended to ensure that the C earnings are taxed as dividends when distributed but that previously taxed S earnings remain tax free when distributed. Since the regime cannot trace or identify cash (which is fungible) to one source or another, it uses ordering rules or presumptions. This elegant system consists of the AAA set forth in § 1368(c) to (e), and described more fully in ¶ 4.05. Simply stated, the AAA measures previously taxed but undistributed S corporation income. It generally tracks the (undistributed) earnings and profits of a corporation while it has an S election in effect; special adjustments are needed if, for example, the corporation has tax-exempt income.

The key ordering rule set forth in § 1368(c) treats a cash distribution by an electing S corporation as coming first or presumptively out of previously taxed (and therefore now tax free) S corporation earnings (measured by the AAA). Once this source has been exhausted, cash is deemed to come out of the corporation's accumulated earnings and profits, and hence constitutes a taxable dividend to the recipient shareholders.[12]

Example 4.4: X Corp. is an S corporation having C accumulated earnings and profits of $1,600 and an AAA of $2,000. X Corp. distributes $2,000 to its two equal shareholders, A and B ($1,000 each). If each shareholder has a basis in her shares of at least $1,000, neither will have to pay any tax on this distribution, because it is deemed to come first out of previously taxed Subchapter S earnings as measured by the AAA ($2,000), not out of

---

[10]   I.R.C. § 1366(d)(1).

[11]   I.R.C. § 1366(d)(2).

[12]   I.R.C. § 1368(c). For purposes of determining the taxability of distributions, the year-end AAA is determined without regard to any "net negative adjustments." A net negative adjustment is generally the excess of all reductions to AAA (other than for distributions) in excess of upward adjustments to AAA for the taxable year. *See* I.R.C. § 1368(e)(1)(C); Reg. § 1.1368–2(a)(5).

accumulated earnings and profits. Moreover, each shareholder has sufficient stock basis to absorb the cash distribution.

To the extent of the AAA, a § 1368(c)(1) cash distribution to shareholders thus will be tax free and will reduce stock basis, just as if the corporation had no accumulated earnings and profits. Of course, if the amount distributed is covered by the AAA but *exceeds* a distributee shareholder's stock *basis*, the shareholder must recognize gain on the excess amount under the normal rule of § 1368(b). AAA is reduced by distributions to shareholders even if the distribution triggers gain because the shareholder has insufficient basis.

Example 4.5: In Example 4.4 above, each shareholder would reduce initial stock basis ($1,000) to zero to reflect the tax-free distribution of $1,000. In effect, stock basis is "used up" by absorbing the tax-free distribution of $1,000.

If each shareholder instead had a stock basis of only $500 before the distribution, then each would receive $500 tax free, reducing stock basis to zero. On the remaining distribution, each shareholder would report $500 taxable gain.

If any portion of a distribution exceeds the AAA, § 1368(c)(2) will apply; the excess portion will be taxable to shareholders as a dividend to the extent of any accumulated earnings and profits. The net result is much like the ordinary Subchapter C dividend regime. The dividend will be taxed at the 20% maximum rate applicable to qualified dividends.

Example 4.6: In Example 4.4 above, assume X Corp. distributed $1,800 to each shareholder. In this event, each shareholder would treat the first $1,000 as tax free up to basis. Each shareholder would treat the additional $800, however, as coming from accumulated earnings and profits (to the extent thereof). Accordingly, each shareholder would be taxable on an $800 dividend as if from a C corporation.

If a distribution exceeds both the AAA and accumulated earnings and profits, the excess portion is applied first against any remaining stock basis under § 1368(c)(3); then, any remaining amount in excess of basis is treated as gain from sale or exchange.[13]

Example 4.7: In Example 4.4 above, assume X Corp. distributed cash of $3,000 to each shareholder, when it had an AAA of $2,000 and accumulated earnings and profits of $1,600. If each shareholder had a stock basis of $2,000, each would be taxable as follows:

$1,000   tax free up to a ratable share of the AAA *and* covered by stock basis; each shareholder's stock basis reduced by $1,000;

$800   taxable as a dividend because "out of" accumulated earnings and profits; stock basis not reduced further;

---

[13]   I.R.C. § 1368(b), (c)(3).

$1,000   tax free as a return of capital and covered by
         remaining basis of $1,000; each shareholder's
         stock basis reduced to zero;

$200   taxable as gain from sale or exchange of
         shares.

(For more on the AAA, see ¶ 4.05.)

To sum up, § 1368(c) in effect creates three tiers or ordered categories of priority for distributions by an S corporation with accumulated earnings and profits. The distribution is treated first as coming from (or chargeable against) the AAA to the extent thereof (tax free up to basis); second, as coming from accumulated earnings and profits (taxable as a § 301 dividend); and third, as purchase price for shares (tax free up to basis and then taxable gain from sale or exchange). This amounts to a favorable ordering rule for taxpayers. The Code could have presumed a distribution to come first from accumulated earnings and profits and, only when *that* source was exhausted, thereafter from previously taxed Subchapter S earnings.

In fact, the statute gives the corporation a *choice* to opt out of the normal ordering rules if it chooses. Under § 1368(e)(3), the corporation may elect—with the consent of all affected shareholders—to have any year's distributions treated as coming first from of accumulated earnings and profits and only thereafter from Subchapter S earnings.[14] This election allows the corporation to "zero out" its accumulated earnings and profits, which will simplify life as to future distributions, as discussed in ¶ 4.05.

It remains to be seen just what comprises the accumulated earnings and profits and AAA and how the different accounts interact. As indicated earlier, an S corporation can have accumulated earnings and profits from its own prior Subchapter C years. It can also acquire accumulated earnings and profits from another C corporation (or a converted S corporation) in a reorganization.[15] Subchapter C year earnings and profits ride with a corporation into and through S years; they do not just disappear when a C corporation makes an S election.

During a corporation's S years, there usually will be no adjustments in earnings and profits carried over from C years. Thus, run-of-the-mill events in the life of an S corporation (such as earning profits and paying expenses) do not affect accumulated earnings and profits, unlike for a C corporation under § 316.[16] Nevertheless, some events during S years can affect accumulated earnings and profits, at least downward. For example, downward adjustments are needed for (1) distributions deemed (or electively) made out of earnings and profits,[17] (2) distributions by way of redemption, liquidation or reorganization,[18] or (3) tax paid by the S corporation on such things as LIFO recapture.[19] Generally speaking, *upward* adjustments will not occur during S years unless the S

---

[14]   Electing to draw down the AAA first is an all-or-nothing decision. *See* Reg. § 1.1368–1(e)(2).

[15]   *See* I.R.C. § 381.

[16]   *See* I.R.C. § 1371(c).

[17]   I.R.C. § 1371(c)(3). After taking into account all other adjustments, AAA is reduced (but not below zero) for distributions during the taxable year. *See* Reg. § 1.1368–2(a)(3)(i), (iii).

[18]   I.R.C. § 1371(c)(2); Reg. § 1.1368–2(d).

[19]   I.R.C. § 1363(d); Reg. § 1.1368–2(a)(3)(i)(C)(1) (reduction for federal taxes). *See* I.R.C. § 1371(d)(3) (recapture of investment credit).

corporation inherits earnings and profits through a tax-free acquisition of another corporation.

¶ 4.05   THE ACCUMULATED ADJUSTMENTS ACCOUNT (AAA)

The AAA, which is the touchstone for tax-free cash distributions by any S corporation, amounts to a cumulative total of all earnings during post-1982 S years that have been taxed to shareholders, less any amount of such earnings that have been distributed.[20] The AAA is a measure of the S corporation's capacity to make distributions whose taxability is tied to prior shareholder taxation (and to the shareholders' remaining basis in their shares). It measures the accumulation of previously taxed but undistributed earnings of the S corporation.

The AAA is defined by § 1368(e), technically, as an income account of the S corporation that is adjusted during the "S period" in a manner similar to the § 1367 basis adjustments, with certain exceptions.[21] One of the main differences is that the AAA, unlike § 1367 basis adjustments, does not include adjustments for tax-exempt income and related expenses.[22] If a redemption qualifies as an exchange under § 302 or § 303, AAA is reduced by the redeemed stock's percentage of the total outstanding stock immediately prior to the redemption.[23]

Keying the AAA to § 1367 basis adjustments makes sense, since passthrough of an S corporation's earnings should generally create a basis increase and an AAA increase of the same amount. The linkage is not absolute, however. For example, losses can cause the AAA to become negative, unlike basis which cannot be reduced below zero.[24] In this situation, future earnings are needed to restore the AAA to a positive amount before a tax-free distribution can be made. Consequently, the AAA will not necessarily always equal aggregate shareholder basis, particularly since they probably will have different starting points.[25] Nevertheless, both the AAA and aggregate shareholder basis will tend to move together in the same directions, and often in the same amounts. (Keeping the AAA can involve numerous technicalities and raise many questions, some of which are answered by the Code and regulations,[26] some by implication or accounting conventions, and some only by informed legal judgment.[27])

---

[20]   In a way, AAA parallels undistributed earnings and profits in a C corporation.

[21]   I.R.C. § 1368(e)(1)(A), (e)(2). Section 1368(e)(2) defines the "S period" as the most recent continuous period during which the corporation has been an S corporation after 1982.

[22]   By contrast, a shareholder's outside basis is adjusted to reflect tax-exempt income (and related expenses). Thus, distributions of tax-exempt income will be tax free to the shareholder once accumulated earnings and profits are exhausted.

[23]   I.R.C. § 1368(e)(1)(B). The AAA is adjusted first for distributions governed by § 1368(a) and then for redemptions treated as exchanges if both occur during the same taxable year. Reg. § 1.1368–2(d)(1).

[24]   See I.R.C. § 1368(e)(1)(A) (language disregarding the phrase "(but not below zero)" in § 1367(a)(2)). Although losses can reduce AAA below zero, distributions cannot create or increase a negative AAA.

[25]   Since the AAA is a corporate-level account, it is not affected by gifts or sales of S stock.

[26]   In particular, Reg. § 1.1368–2 provides important guidance concerning the technical adjustments to the AAA.

[27]   Under the IRS reporting requirements, every S corporation must complete annually a Form 1120S Schedule M, which calls for a beginning and year-end AAA computation and other adjustments. This applies even to an S corporation without accumulated earnings and profits which is not required to keep an AAA under § 1368(b). The "other adjustment account" is not mentioned in the Code but appears on the Form 1120S, Schedules L and M. In the case of S corporations with accumulated earnings and profits, it keeps track of adjustments for tax-exempt income and nondeductible expenses.

The AAA of an S corporation is determined at year end. Hence, the taxability of distributions during the year must await final determination until year end.[28] In this respect, such calculations resemble C corporation dividends (governed by current or accumulated earnings and profits). Distributions from an S corporation also resemble partnership "draws" which are treated as advances until year end; thus, a partnership draw (like an S distribution) will not be taxable if the upward basis adjustments for the year (as determined at year end) are sufficient to absorb the amount of the draw.[29] If distributions by an S corporation during the year exceed the amount of the AAA at year end, § 1368(c) (flush language) requires that *each* of the year's distributions be allocated to the AAA proportionately. The remainder of each distribution is then applied to reduce basis or taxed as gain from a sale or exchange, as the case may be.

¶ 4.06 DISTRIBUTIONS AFTER S TERMINATION; POST-TERMINATION TRANSITION PERIOD (PTTP)

A special rule involving the AAA provides relief when an S election terminates while the corporation has an AAA that would have been sufficient to permit a tax-free distribution prior to termination. Section 1371(e)(1) helpfully provides that a distribution of money with respect to stock during the "post-termination transition period" (PTTP) is not taxed but instead is applied against and reduces a shareholder's stock basis up to the amount of the AAA.[30] Thus, distributions by the once S corporation will be tax free up to the lesser of the shareholder's stock basis or the AAA. With the consent of all affected shareholders, the corporation may elect *not* to have this special rule apply and instead choose to distribute earnings and profits first (as taxable dividends).[31] The corporation may wish to make this election in order to purge itself of accumulated earnings and profits.

Under § 1371(e)(1), an S corporation whose S election has terminated can make tax-free distributions from the AAA (assuming sufficient shareholder basis), but only during the PTTP. This window of opportunity is defined as one of three periods. For S corporations currently terminated, the period starts the day after the last day of the corporation's last year as an S corporation and lasts one year or until the due date (including extensions) of the return for the last S corporation year, whichever is later.[32] In the case of an S corporation whose election is determined (retroactively, as by court decision or an agreement with the IRS) to have terminated in a previous taxable year, the period begins on the date of such determination and lasts 120 days.[33] A third 120-day "window" begins on the date of an audit determination that adjusts Subchapter S items of income or deduction following termination of a corporation's S status.[34]

---

[28] *See* Reg. § 1.1368–2(a)(5). When a fiscal-year S corporation makes a cash distribution to a calendar-year shareholder, it may not be possible to determine the distribution's taxability until after the year in which the shareholder must report income. An interim closing of the books may help to alleviate this problem.

[29] *See* Reg. § 1.731–1(a)(1)(ii) (partnership draw).

[30] Otherwise, such previously taxed earnings might be "locked in" and could not be distributed without tax until all current and accumulated earnings and profits had been distributed as taxable dividends.

[31] I.R.C. § 1371(e)(2).

[32] I.R.C. § 1377(b)(1)(A).

[33] I.R.C. § 1377(b)(1)(C).

[34] I.R.C. § 1377(b)(1)(B). With respect to the third period, AAA consists only of the net positive adjustment to AAA resulting from the audit determination.

In most instances, it will prove advantageous for an S corporation to make an actual distribution up to the AAA either before termination or within the PTTP window. The § 1371(e) rule for PTTP distributions avoids the problem of locking in previously taxed but undistributed earnings. Note that, while pre-termination distributions may consist of money or property, by contrast, a post-termination distribution sheltered under § 1371(e) must consist solely of money, not other property. Of course, the corporation can borrow money, if need be, in order to make a cash distribution qualifying under § 1371(e).[35]

To facilitate conversion of S corporations to C corporations, the 2017 Act provided relief for certain S corporations that voluntarily revoked their S status within two years after the date of enactment.[36] Following the post-termination transition period, cash distributions from the former S corporation will be treated indefinitely as distributions from accumulated earnings and profits or AAA on a pro rata basis. (Cash distributions during the PTTP will continue, under § 1371(e)(1), to be treated as coming first from AAA.)

¶ 4.07   DISTRIBUTIONS OF PROPERTY BY AN S CORPORATION

If an S corporation distributes property other than cash, some special issues arise. Nevertheless, the regime for determining shareholder-level taxability is basically the same as that applicable to cash distributions discussed at ¶¶ 4.02–4.06. The amount of any distribution to shareholders is the sum of any cash plus the fair market value of property other than cash.[37] Tentatively, the taxability of a property distribution to shareholders depends on their bases in their shares. If the S corporation has accumulated earnings and profits, the rules using the AAA for cash distributions continue to apply to distributions made in kind.

If the corporation's basis in the distributed property differs from its fair market value, the treatment is more complex both for the distributing S corporation and derivatively for its shareholders. Under § 311(b), which applies to S corporations as well as C corporations, a distribution of appreciated property triggers recognition of gain (at the corporate level) as if the property had been sold to the distributee at its fair market value.[38] Corporate-level loss on property that has declined in value is *not* recognized on a nonliquidating distribution.[39]

Gain recognized by the S corporation at the entity level passes through and is taxed immediately to the shareholders, under § 1366(a) and (b), with its character preserved intact. The passthrough gain increases the S corporation's AAA under § 1368, because the AAA measures previously taxed income. Each shareholder will increase her stock basis correspondingly under § 1367(a). This increase in basis will be treated as an adjustment taking effect *before* the distribution of the property; in other words, its effect

---

[35] The S corporation may elect to treat distributions during the post-termination transition period as coming first from accumulated earnings and profits. *See* I.R.C. § 1371(e)(2).

[36] An eligible S corporation must have the same shareholders with proportionately identical stock ownership on the dates of enactment and revocation. *See* I.R.C. §§ 1371(f), 481(d) (six-year adjustment period).

[37] *See* I.R.C. § 301(b). Thus, the general rule for C corporations applies. Proper adjustment must also be made for liabilities assumed. *See* I.R.C. §§ 301(b)(2), 357(d).

[38] I.R.C. § 311(b)(1).

[39] I.R.C. § 311(a). By contrast, § 336(a) generally allows recognition of corporate-level losses on liquidating distributions. *See* ¶ 7.09.

must be taken into account for purposes of determining the taxability to shareholders of the receipt of the distributed property itself.[40] Upon distribution of the gain property, the basis increase will reduce or eliminate any additional taxable gain at the shareholder level—a very important effect.

Example 4.8: X Corp., an always S corporation, has two assets, each with a fair market value of $5,000 and a basis of $2,000 in the corporation's hands. X Corp. makes a nonliquidating distribution in kind to each of its two equal shareholders; each shareholder has a pre-distribution stock basis of $1,000 and receives one of the two assets. Under § 311(b)(1), X Corp. must recognize $3,000 gain on the distribution of each asset or a total corporate-level gain of $6,000. The gain is not taxable to the S corporation but instead passes through and is taxed to the two equal shareholders ($3,000 each). That taxability entitles each shareholder to increase stock basis from $1,000 to $4,000. This $3,000 basis increase is taken into account before determining the taxability of the actual distribution.

Each shareholder (whose basis is now $4,000) receives an actual distribution of property worth $5,000. Hence, each shareholder receives a tax-free distribution of $4,000, reducing stock basis to zero, and is taxed on the remaining $1,000 of the property distribution. (If stock basis had not been increased first, each shareholder would have received only $1,000 tax free and would have been taxable on the balance of $4,000.)

When appreciated property is distributed, the character of gain recognized at the corporate level is preserved in the shareholders' hands. While such recognized gain will often be capital or § 1231 in nature, it may be ordinary income instead. For example, if the corporation distributes inventory or other non-capital assets, § 1221 will not afford capital gain treatment. Alternatively, if the corporation distributes depreciable property to a more-than-50% shareholder, § 1239 may convert what otherwise would be capital gain into ordinary income.[41]

The distributed property takes a fair-market-value basis in the shareholders' hands under § 301(d), so that they can sell it without further tax. The result is a single tax, at the *shareholder* level, on the gain inherent in the appreciated asset distributed by the S corporation.

Example 4.9: In Example 4.8 above, each shareholder has a post-distribution basis of $5,000 in the property distributed and a zero basis in her S corporation stock. A sale of the distributed property for $5,000 would not trigger any additional gain. The net result is a single tax on gain inherent in the distributed property, with the gain passed through and taxed at the shareholders' individual rates. Since each shareholder now has a zero basis, any further distribution of cash or property will be taxable unless and until the shareholders are entitled to increase the basis of their shares. Such a basis increase might result, for example, from the S corporation earning taxable income (which would pass through pro rata and be taxed to the shareholders),

---

[40]   I.R.C. § 1368(d); Reg. § 1.1368–1(e)(2).

[41]   *See* I.R.C. § 1239(a), (c). The requisite ownership may be direct or indirect within the meaning of § 267(c) (other than paragraph (3)). *See Fish v. Comm'r*, T.C. Memo 2013–270 (§ 351(b) distribution triggered ordinary income under § 1239; deemed sale of § 197 intangibles transferred to the corporation).

or it might result from another distribution of appreciated property, triggering corporate-level recognition of gain and a corresponding basis increase upon passthrough of the gain.

Distributions by an S corporation may thus affect the taxability of both shareholders and potentially the S corporation itself (for example, a distribution of appreciated property that triggers corporate-level tax under § 1374). Such distributions may also affect eligibility for continued S status. For example, a disproportionate distribution could cause the S corporation to be deemed to have a second class of stock outstanding, jeopardizing its S status. To ensure compliance with the one-class-of-stock rules, distributions by an S corporation should be monitored closely to avoid unequal treatment of shareholders. In general, the S corporation should attempt to distribute the same amount, at the same time, to shareholders with respect to their shares.

A distribution of appreciated property may trigger the "sting" taxes under §§ 1374 and 1375, which are covered in Chapter Five. These special taxes apply most obviously to straightforward realization of gain when an S corporation sells property to an outsider for cash, or exchanges such property for other property in a taxable transaction. But, what is crucial to observe here is that, following repeal of the *General Utilities* doctrine, these sting taxes can also apply when corporate-level gain is realized upon *distribution* of appreciated property.

Chapter 5

SPECIAL TAXES IMPOSED ON
THE S CORPORATION

¶ 5.01   S CORPORATION TAXATION OF BUILT-IN GAINS—
§ 1374 (THE "BIG" TAX)

Subchapter S contains two special corporate-level taxes that entail actual taxation of the S corporation itself (rather than a passthrough system) and *payment* (as well as reporting) by the S corporation. The first of these "sting taxes" is the § 1374 tax on "built-in gain" (the "BIG tax").

The § 1374 tax stems from Congress' anticipation that an S corporation election could be used by a C corporation to avoid corporate-level tax on unrealized appreciation in corporate assets during C years (or gain from sale of assets whose basis had been reduced to reflect depreciation deductions). Even before 1986, the problem existed of a "one-shot" S election made when a large capital or other gain was about to be realized by a C corporation on sale of an asset. This concern became more acute in 1986, however, when Congress repealed the *General Utilities* rule that had allowed a C corporation to distribute appreciated assets to shareholders (in a liquidating or nonliquidating distribution) without recognition of gain to the corporation.[1] This legislation tightened Subchapter C and extended the double-tax principle to distributions of appreciated property as well as to gain from sales or exchanges.[2]

The tightened double-tax system might have been easily avoided by a closely held C corporation if it could elect S treatment and distribute the appreciated assets to shareholders with only a shareholder-level tax.[3] The § 1374 tax blocks use of an S election by a C corporation to avoid corporate-level tax on gain that accrued *during Subchapter C years*. Section 1374 imposes a corporate-level tax for 5 years after an S election is made.[4] If the corporation is willing to wait out that recognition period, pre-election appreciation escapes the double-tax burden.

In accordance with its purpose, the § 1374 tax does not apply to an S corporation that has never been a C corporation, nor to gain on assets acquired during S status (unless such assets have a carryover basis from a C corporation or from a tax-free

---

[1]   In 1986, Congress modified §§ 311, 336, and 337 to require all corporations to recognize gain upon distribution of appreciated property.

[2]   Under the pre-1986 regime, a corporation did not recognize gain if it (1) distributed appreciated property in kind under former §§ 311 and 336 or (2) sold the asset and distributed the proceeds in liquidation under former § 337. Shareholders paid tax on their gain (dividend or exchange treatment), took a fair-market-value basis, and could resell the asset without further tax.

[3]   Even prior to repeal of the *General Utilities* rule, a distribution of appreciated property by an S corporation, unlike that by a C corporation, caused the corporation to recognize gain as if such property were sold at fair market value. *See* former I.R.C. § 1363(d).

[4]   I.R.C. § 1374(d)(7).

acquisition).[5] The § 1374 tax is reduced by certain net operating loss carryforwards and capital loss carryforwards.[6]

The § 1374 tax applies to an S corporation's "net recognized built-in gain" (NRBIG) during the five-year recognition period.[7] The tax rate applicable is the highest § 11(b) corporate tax rate.[8] An overall limitation restricts the amount of the NRBIG to the "net unrealized built-in gain" (NUBIG), *i.e.*, the excess of the aggregate fair market value of all of the corporation's assets over their aggregate adjusted basis at the time of conversion from C to S status.[9] Thus, the appreciation (or depreciation) in assets purchased after the conversion date and subsequent appreciation (or depreciation) in existing assets is generally not subject to the § 1374 tax. "Recognized built-in losses" (RBILs) can offset "recognized built-in gains" (RBIGs) to arrive at the net figure (NRBIG).[10] Moreover, the net taxable amount may not exceed the corporation's taxable income (as determined under § 1375(b)(1)(B)).[11]

The regulations provide a useful summary of the manner in which an S corporation's NRBIG is determined. NRBIG for any taxable year is the *least* of three amounts: (1) the amount of the S corporation's taxable income (applying C corporation rules), determined as if only recognized built-in gains, losses and carryovers were taken into account (the "pre-limitation amount"), (2) the taxable income limitation, or (3) the corporation's NUBIG reduced by NRBIG for all prior taxable years during the recognition period (the "NUBIG limitation").[12]

The § 1374 tax is not confined to capital gains. Ordinary income items, including accounts receivable, will be subject to § 1374 if such gain arose before an S election.

> *Example 5.1:* X Corp., a former C corporation, elects S status in 2023. At that time, its only asset has a fair market value of $10,000 and a basis of $7,500. The difference of $2,500 would all constitute built-in gain and there is no offsetting built-in loss.
>
> If X Corp. sells the asset for $12,500 in 2024 (when the asset's basis is still $7,500), it will recognize total gain of $5,000. Of that amount, only $2,500 is gain that was "built in" at the time of the S election. Assuming a 21% tax rate, X Corp. will owe tax of $525 (21% × $2,500) on the built-in gain under § 1374. The amount of gain passing through to the shareholders will be reduced, under § 1366(f)(2), by the tax paid at the corporate level. The shareholders will be taxable on a total of $4,475, consisting of $1,975 built-in gain ($2,500 less $525 corporate-level tax) and the remaining post-conversion gain of $2,500. Thus, the built-in portion of the gain (less the § 1374 tax) will be taxed twice.

Another example will show how the § 1374 tax works when there are both built-in gains and losses.

---

[5]   I.R.C. § 1374(c)(1), (8).

[6]   I.R.C. § 1374(b)(2), (d)(2)

[7]   I.R.C. § 1374(a). *See* I.R.C. § 1374(d) (defining key terms).

[8]   I.R.C. § 1374(b)(1).

[9]   I.R.C. § 1374(c)(2), (d)(1).

[10]   *See* I.R.C. § 1374(d)(3), (4) (defining recognized built-in gains and losses).

[11]   *See* I.R.C. § 1374(d)(2)(A)(ii) ("taxable income limit").

[12]   Reg. §§ 1.1374–2(a), –3(a).

Example 5.2: X Corp. is a former C corporation that elected S status beginning on the first day of 2023. When the S election took effect, X Corp. had two assets, Blackacre (with a fair market value of $100,000 and a basis of $60,000) and Whiteacre (with a fair market value of $50,000 and a basis of $70,000). In the aggregate, the fair market value of X Corp.'s assets ($150,000) exceeded their aggregate basis ($130,000) by $20,000. That difference ($20,000) is the amount of the NUBIG, as defined in § 1374(d)(1). If X Corp. sold both assets within the recognition period (assuming fair market value and basis remain unchanged), it would have a RBIG of $40,000 (on Blackacre) and a RBIL of $20,000 (on Whiteacre). As a result, the NRBIG of $20,000 would be taxed to the S corporation under § 1374, as long as the taxable income of the corporation was at least $20,000. In addition, both the $40,000 gain and the $20,000 loss would pass through to the shareholders, with a reduction for the § 1374 tax paid by X Corp.

Suppose X Corp. sold only the built-in gain asset (Blackacre) and continued to hold the built-in loss asset. On the sale, it would realize gain of $40,000 ($100,000 amount realized less $60,000 basis). Nevertheless, only $20,000 of the gain on Blackacre would be taxable to the S corporation under § 1374, because that was the total amount of the NUBIG at the time of the S election. Notwithstanding this NUBIG limit, the entire $40,000 gain (reduced by the § 1374 tax) would pass through to the shareholders.

If the taxable income of the S corporation were only $15,000 in the year both assets were sold, the taxable income limit would apply. As a result, X Corp. would be taxed on only $15,000 of RBIG (attributable to Blackacre) in the year of sale, and the remaining $5,000 would be carried over to a subsequent year during the recognition period. Under § 1374(d)(2)(B), the carried over amount would be treated as RBIG arising in the later year.

Any gain taxable to the S corporation under § 1374 will not also be taxed under § 1375, even if such gain consists of "passive investment income" otherwise taxable by § 1375.[13] Thus, NRBIG is subject only to the § 1374 tax.

Built-in gain will be recognized not only if the S corporation sells or exchanges a built-in gain asset during the recognition period, but also if it distributes the asset to shareholders.[14] In either event, the corporate-level gain taxed under § 1374 will also pass through to shareholders, just as it would if § 1374 did not apply.[15] However, under § 1366(f)(2), the corporate-level tax is treated as a *loss* for passthrough purposes. The character of the loss is determined by reference to the character of the built-in gain that gave rise to the § 1374 tax.[16] While this ameliorates the burden of the double tax— shareholders are relieved from paying tax on corporate gain used to pay the § 1374 tax— the gain recognition and second tax (at the shareholder level) occurs immediately. Thus,

---

[13] *See* I.R.C. § 1375(b)(4).

[14] *See* I.R.C. §§ 311, 336, 1374(d)(3).

[15] I.R.C. § 1367(a).

[16] Since the § 1374 tax is treated as a loss (rather than a tax), it reduces AAA under § 1368(e)(1), but not accumulated earnings and profits. *See* I.R.C. § 1371(c).

shareholder-level recognition is *not* deferred until distribution, as it would be if no S election had been made.[17]

Example 5.3: In Example 5.2 above, suppose X Corp. (holding both appreciated Blackacre and depreciated Whiteacre) distributed Blackacre to its shareholders within the recognition period. Under § 311(b), the distribution would trigger recognition of the $40,000 gain in Blackacre. Only $20,000 of this recognized gain consists of NUBIG, the amount taxable to X Corp. under § 1374 (assuming ample taxable income). All $40,000 of the gain, however, would be recognized and passed through to the shareholders (reduced by the amount of the § 1374 tax paid by X Corp.).

Some opportunities exist to escape or soften the § 1374 tax. One possibility is simply to wait out the recognition period before disposing of a built-in gain asset.[18] Another possibility is to use a nonrecognition transaction (such as a like-kind exchange)[19] to avoid triggering taxable gain within the recognition period. Under the installment sale method, realized built-in gain may be deferred until after the recognition period. To forestall this potential abuse, the regulations impose the built-in gain tax on installment sale proceeds reported during or after the recognition period, subject to the taxable income and other limitations.[20]

Because of its considerable "sting," the § 1374 tax must be considered carefully before a C corporation makes an S election. If such an election is to be made, contemporaneous appraisals are imperative in order to fix the amount of built-in gain at the time of conversion to S status. Post-election appreciation escapes the § 1374 tax, but the shareholder has the burden to show the amount of built-in gain upon conversion, and hence the amount of gain beyond the reach of the § 1374 tax.

In enacting § 1374, Congress may have had in mind the stereotypical case of a C corporation that, wanting to liquidate, would otherwise elect S status and then liquidate. The § 1374 tax, however, is not limited to such liquidation scenarios. It applies to gain recognized on nonliquidating sales or distributions, and even to such ordinary transactions as post-election sales of inventory or collection of accounts receivable. Thus § 1374 creates an added reason to elect S status at the *beginning* of a corporation's existence—to prevent the build-up of Subchapter C gain of any kind, which § 1374 would insist on taxing to ensure an *immediate* second tax.

The built-in gain tax also applies to assets acquired from C corporations (or from another S corporation subject to § 1374) in certain nonrecognition transactions.[21] Section 1374(d)(8) potentially duplicates built-in gain (or loss) if, for example, a C corporation

---

[17] Even ignoring deferral, the total tax burden under § 1374 can be higher than if no S election were made and the former C corporation sold its assets and distributed the proceeds as a dividend taxable at a maximum 20% rate in the shareholders' hands. Thus, the introduction of a preferential rate for dividends means that § 1374 no longer merely preserves the effect of a double-tax burden, its original purpose.

[18] In a highly publicized "leveraged partnership" transaction, the Tribune Company (a former C corporation that converted to S status) sought to defer reporting gain on sale of the Chicago Cubs until after the recognition period. *See Tribune Media Co. v. Comm'r*, T.C. Memo 2021–122. Since Tribune was wholly owned by an ESOP, the § 1374 built-in gain would have been exempt at both the corporate and shareholder levels. *See* I.R.C. § 512(e)(3).

[19] However, § 1374 will apply to disposition of exchanged-basis property received in a § 1031 exchange. I.R.C. § 1374(d)(6).

[20] Reg. § 1.1374–4(h).

[21] I.R.C. § 1374(d)(8).

(X) elects S status when it owns a C subsidiary (Y) that is subsequently liquidated tax free under §§ 332 and 337. The built-in gain (or loss) in Y's assets is potentially counted twice: once in the NUBIG attributable to X's assets (including the Y stock) upon X's conversion to S status and again in the NUBIG attributable to the former Y assets acquired by X in the liquidation. In this situation, the regulations provide an adjustment intended to eliminate any duplicated built-in gain (or loss) attributable to X's former Y stock that is redeemed or cancelled.[22]

¶ 5.02   S CORPORATION EFFECTS OF PASSIVE INVESTMENT INCOME—§ 1375

Now, a "pure" S corporation need not worry about having passive investment income. For this purpose, a pure S corporation is one that has never been a C corporation and has no Subchapter C earnings and profits from C years of its own or those of a predecessor corporation (or from a tax-free acquisition in which earnings and profits carry over under § 381). Thus, pure S corporations are free to have any amount of passive income without concern. Indeed, they may even act as personal holding companies with impunity under § 541.

If the S corporation *does*, in fact, have any Subchapter C earnings and profits from any source, it must worry about having too much passive investment income for too long on two counts. One concern (discussed in ¶ 2.18) is that if such income exceeds a specified limit for three consecutive years, S status will terminate. The second concern is that if net passive investment income exceeds 25% of gross receipts even for a single year, the sting tax under § 1375 may apply.[23]

Congress was concerned that shareholders of C corporations that held passive investments would be able to extract retained corporate earnings without liquidating the corporation and paying a second (shareholder-level) tax on liquidation. Actual liquidation of the corporation and transfer of its assets to a partnership would incur two levels of tax, even though formation of the partnership itself would be tax free. An S election would avoid the taxable-liquidation step, thereby affording an advantage over the partnership option. To prevent this disparity, Congress could have imposed a toll charge on corporations with investment assets making an S election. It could have treated the election as a constructive liquidation and re-incorporation. Congress instead chose to enact the special corporate-level tax of § 1375 on excess passive investment income and the functional termination rule of § 1362(d)(3).

So, a new S corporation without Subchapter C earnings and profits is free to have unlimited passive investment income *without* fear of termination or exposure to the § 1375 tax. An S corporation *with* Subchapter C earnings and profits must fear (or plan around) both undesired termination and the entity-level sting tax.

To free itself from the § 1375 limits on passive investment income, an S corporation may do well to "zero out" its Subchapter C earnings and profits. A special rule permits an S corporation, with the consent of all affected shareholders, to elect to treat distributions as attributable first to accumulated earnings and profits.[24] This election

---

[22] Reg. § 1.1374–3(b)(1). The adjustment would also be triggered if X elected QSub status for Y, triggering a deemed liquidation of Y. Reg. § 1.1374–3(c) (ex. 2).

[23] *See* I.R.C. §§ 1362(d)(3), 1375.

[24] I.R.C. § 1368(e)(3); Reg. § 1.1368–1(f). The election has the effect of bypassing the order of priorities otherwise imposed by the distribution rules of § 1368(c).

may be useful if a corporation wishes to purge itself of accumulated earnings and profits. To guard against any miscalculation of earnings and profits, or any redetermination in a later audit, it may be advisable to make a § 1368(e)(3) election annually.

¶ 5.03   SECTION 1375 TERMINATION

Under § 1362(d)(3), as mentioned in ¶ 2.18, an S election of a corporation *with* Subchapter C earnings and profits will terminate on the first day of the tax year beginning after the third consecutive taxable year during which the corporation has gross receipts more than 25% of which are passive investment income. The key terms are defined in the statute and will be considered in the following material on the § 1375 tax. A waiver of termination is authorized in innocent, inadvertent cases.[25] Once termination occurs, re-election is prohibited for five years, unless the Secretary consents to an earlier election.[26]

¶ 5.04   SECTION 1375 PENALTY TAX

The § 1375 tax is triggered if an S corporation has Subchapter C accumulated earnings and profits at the end of the year and its passive investment income (as specially defined) exceeds 25% of its gross receipts.[27] To prevent easy manipulation of the gross receipts test, only the excess of gains over losses from disposition of capital assets (other than stock and securities) is included in gross receipts; gross receipts from sales or exchanges of stock or securities are taken into account only to the extent of gains, without netting for losses.[28] The term passive investment income includes gross receipts from royalties, rents, dividends, interest, and annuities.[29]

If the § 1375 tax is incurred, the amount of passive investment income passing through to shareholders is reduced by its proportionate share of the tax.[30] The § 1375 tax is also coordinated with the § 1374 tax: built-in gain is kept out of passive investment income for purposes of calculating the § 1375 tax.[31] The result is that NRBIG is taxed only under § 1374.

The § 1375 tax may be waived if the S corporation demonstrates that it determined in good faith that it had no Subchapter C earnings and profits at the close of the year.[32] Within a reasonable time after discerning that it in fact had earnings and profits, the S corporation must distribute such profits as taxable dividends.

To trigger the § 1375 tax, total passive investment income must exceed 25% of gross receipts. The § 1375 tax is imposed, however, only on "excess net passive income" (ENPI). To determine ENPI, the total passive investment income (PII) must first be reduced by directly attributable expenses to arrive at net passive income (NPI). NPI is then multiplied by the excess of PII over 25% of gross receipts (EPII), and divided by PII for

---

[25]   I.R.C. § 1362(f).

[26]   I.R.C. § 1362(g).

[27]   I.R.C. § 1375(a). In calculating the tax, the operative terms are "excess net passive income" (§ 1375(b)(1)), "net passive income" (§ 1375(b)(2)), and "passive investment income" (§ 1375(b)(3), cross-referencing § 1362(d)(3)).

[28]   I.R.C. §§ 1375(b)(3), 1362(d)(3)(B); Reg. § 1.1362–2(c)(4)(ii).

[29]   I.R.C. § 1362(d)(3)(C)(i) (defining passive investment income for purposes of the termination rule). Note that passive investment income does not include gains from sale of stock or other capital assets.

[30]   I.R.C. § 1366(f)(3).

[31]   I.R.C. § 1375(b)(4).

[32]   I.R.C. § 1375(d). *See* Reg. § 1.1375–1(d)(1) (suggesting need for due diligence on the part of taxpayer).

the year. The result is ENPI, which can be thought of as the amount of passive income exceeding the 25% gross-receipts ceiling, reduced by its proportionate share of the expenses associated with generating such income. ENPI is then taxed at the highest corporate rate of 21% (subject to a taxable income limitation).

The formula to determine ENPI can be summarized by the following relation: ENPI is to total NPI as EPII is to PII. Expressed as a ratio,[33] this is:

$$\frac{ENPI}{NPI} = \frac{EPII}{PII}$$

From this ratio one can derive the formula for calculating ENPI:

$$ENPI = \frac{EPII}{PII} \times NPI$$

Since the base of the § 1375 tax is defined in terms of the excess of one kind of income (passive investment income) over a percentage of total *gross* receipts (rather than overall net or taxable income), this formula could yield tax liability even though the corporation operates at a loss. This result is prevented by a taxable income limitation, which provides that ENPI shall not exceed the corporation's taxable income for the year, as especially computed for this purpose.[34]

> *Example 5.4:* X Corp. is an S corporation, with gross receipts of $160,000. Of this amount, $70,000 is passive investment income consisting of rents and royalties, generated at a cost of $10,000. X Corp.'s NPI is thus $60,000. Since passive investment income exceeds 25% of gross receipts (in this case, 25% of $160,000 equals $40,000), X Corp. is potentially subject to the § 1375 tax. Here, the EPII is $30,000 ($70,000 less $40,000); only the *net* excess (ENPI) is actually taxed under § 1375. Applying the formula above, X Corp. will be taxed on ENPI of about $25,714 ($60,000 NPI × ($30,000 EPII/$70,000 PII)). Thus, X Corp. will owe tax of $5,400 ($25,714 × 21%).

Needless to say, the § 1375 tax puts stress on what kind of income will constitute passive investment income. Section 1362(d)(3)(C)(i) lists the categories of income treated as passive investment income, subject to various exceptions, and the regulations also provide helpful guidance.[35] The term passive income for these purposes is not *identical* to its use for other Code purposes, such as the passive loss rules of § 469.

In general, passive income for purposes of the § 1375 tax is the same kind of income that may trigger termination under § 1362(d)(3). Passive income for both purposes resembles but is not identical to the type of income that would invoke the personal

---

[33] This formula is a slight contraction of the one provided in Reg. § 1.1375–1(b)(1). Stated differently, ENPI = NPI × (PII – .25 x gross receipts) ÷ PII.

[34] *See* I.R.C. § 1375(b)(1)(B). The special computation of taxable income is made without regard to § 172 NOLs or certain specified corporate deductions (other than § 248 organizational expenditures). *Id.* Hence, if the corporation operates at a loss for the year or has zero taxable income under § 63(a), no § 1375 tax will be due.

[35] The exceptions are listed in § 1362(d)(3)(C)(ii)–(iv). For example, it may be difficult to determine whether rental income is passive if rents are linked to services generating part of the income. *See* Reg. § 1.1362–2(c)(5)(ii)(B)(2) (treating rental income as nonpassive if the lessor provides "significant services" or incurs "substantial costs").

holding company (PHC) tax under § 541.[36] Despite some important differences, the legislative history suggests that § 1375 is intended generally to cover the type of income that would produce tax, under § 541, to a C corporation used as a personal holding company.[37]

As a result, an S corporation with Subchapter C earnings and profits will not be a good candidate to hold personal investment assets. However, a new S corporation (without C earnings) can serve this function very well; it can avoid not only a corporate-level income tax but also the PHC tax under § 541. The only tax burden will be the individual shareholder's taxes, imposed currently at individual rates, just as if investment assets were held directly or through a partnership. Nevertheless, the shareholder will have the non-tax benefits—and costs—of incorporation.

Careful planning can sometimes help an S corporation to escape the § 1375 tax even though it has a Subchapter C history or inherited accumulated earnings and profits. For example, it may be possible to manage the passive investment income and the gross receipts of the S corporation to ensure that *excess* passive income does not arise for any particular year, or at least not for the full three years. Another strategy is methodically to zero-out all Subchapter C earnings and profits (preferably *before* the S election), perhaps by electing to have distributions treated as coming first out of accumulated earnings and profits.[38] Better yet, of course, is to use a new corporation that elects S status from the outset and never inherits accumulated earnings under § 381. In a predicament, an administrative waiver of the § 1375 tax may sought.[39]

Note, too, that some strategies that minimize the § 1375 tax (for example, accelerating a loss to invoke the taxable income limitation) will not prevent the taxable year from being counted toward the three-year disqualification period which triggers termination of the S election.

An S corporation is particularly in jeopardy under the § 1375 tax if the S corporation (or a C corporation that is contemporaneously electing S treatment) is disposing of its active business assets and holding or reinvesting the sale proceeds. Section 1375 may impose a penalty tax if the corporation has accumulated earnings and profits, even in a very small quantity (unless the Secretary mercifully waives application of the tax under § 1375(d)).

An S corporation with accumulated earnings and profits may also find its election *terminated*, under § 1362(d)(3), even if it does not have enough *net* passive investment income (passive income less related costs) to produce any or much § 1375 penalty tax. The reason is that the *termination* rule applies if *gross* passive investment income exceeds 25% of *gross* receipts.

¶ 5.05   LIFO RECAPTURE TAX

Another special tax that an S corporation faces is that imposed by § 1363(d)(1) on a LIFO-method C corporation upon conversion to S status. The special tax is intended to

---

[36] *See* Reg. § 1.1362–2(c)(5)(ii)(A)(3) (certain royalties excluded from PHC income *not* treated as royalties for purposes of the passive income test).

[37] For example, *gross* rents are passive income under § 1375, while only *net* rental income constitutes PHC income. Gains from selling stocks or securities are excluded from both PHC income and § 1375 passive income.

[38] *See* I.R.C. § 1368(e)(3). *See also* ¶ 4.04.

[39] *See* I.R.C. § 1375(d).

recapture the tax benefits enjoyed as a C corporation. It parallels the § 1374 built-in gain tax, but only as to inventory accounted for under the LIFO method during C years. The rule makes the S corporation take into income a "LIFO recapture amount" for the last taxable year as a C corporation. The tax is payable in four equal installments.[40] If § 1363(d) applies, the basis of the inventory in the corporation's hands is adjusted upward for the LIFO recapture, defined by § 1363(d)(3) as the amount by which the inventory computed using the FIFO method exceeds the inventory computed using the LIFO method. No S corporation year or passthrough item is directly affected by this recapture tax. A C corporation with a significant LIFO recapture amount should carefully consider that cost as a reason to avoid or defer an S election.

¶ 5.06　　INVESTMENT CREDIT RECAPTURE TAX

If an S corporation generates investment tax credits, the credits pass through to S shareholders.[41] The credits cannot be used against the S corporation's own tax liability, but instead the shareholders receive the benefit of the credits under the normal passthrough rule of § 1366(a)(1)(A).

Credits taken in prior years can produce a recapture tax (at the shareholder level) if the property ceases to be investment credit property or the S corporation disposes of the property prematurely; recapture can also arise when a shareholder sells her stock (which makes sense because it was the shareholder who previously claimed the credit, on a passthrough theory).[42] Although *termination* of S status does not, by itself, trigger recapture, the shareholders who originally claimed the investment credit remain liable for any future recapture.

If a C corporation elects S status, the *election* itself will not trigger investment credit recapture, since the business is continuing in a different form.[43] The new S corporation will continue to be liable, however, for any future recapture tax upon a disposition of the investment credit property.[44] If the S corporation owes recapture tax attributable to credits from previous non-S years, § 1371(d)(3) allows a reduction to accumulated earnings and profits for the recapture tax.

¶ 5.07　　ALTERNATIVE MINIMUM TAX AND § 291

In 2017, Congress repealed the alternative minimum tax ("AMT") for corporations (but not for individuals). In 2022, however, Congress imposed a minimum tax of 15% on the adjusted financial statement income of certain large C corporations.[45] For taxable years beginning after 2022, applicable corporations are required to pay the larger of the minimum tax or the regular tax. The provision excludes S corporations (and RICs and REITs) that pass though income taxed at the individual level.[46] By virtue of the general rule of § 1363(a), an S corporation itself was not subject to the AMT even under prior law. Instead, the S corporation passes through any realized AMT preference items pro

---

[40] I.R.C. § 1363(d)(2).

[41] *See* I.R.C. §§ 38, 46.

[42] *See* I.R.C. § 50(a)(1)(A).

[43] *See* I.R.C. § 1371(d)(1).

[44] I.R.C. § 1371(d)(2).

[45] I.R.C. § 55(b)(2); *see* I.R.C. § 56A (defining "adjusted financial statement income"). For the minimum tax to apply, C corporations must have $ 1 billion or more in average annual book earnings over a three-year period. I.R.C. § 59(k)(1)(B).

[46] I.R.C. § 59(k)(1)(A).

rata to its shareholders, who must then treat the items as if realized by them individually for AMT purposes.

In addition, the special rule of § 291 applies if an S corporation (or a predecessor corporation) was a C corporation for any of the three immediately preceding taxable years.[47] When applicable, § 291 reduces some specified deductions and other allowances. This cutback is apparently intended merely to prevent C corporations from avoiding § 291 recapture by converting to S status.

¶ 5.08   MIDSTREAM CONVERSION FROM C TO S

When a C corporation makes a "midstream election" of Subchapter S, the shareholders' respective bases in their shares remain unchanged. In addition, the basis of the corporate assets remains unchanged in the S corporation's hands. Any future earnings generated by these assets, however, escape the separate corporate-level tax. To be sure, the sting taxes under §§ 1374 and 1375 are designed to counter the most blatant attempts by C corporations to avoid the double-tax burden (after repeal of the *General Utilities* doctrine) upon a liquidation.

An alternative approach, in contrast to current law, would treat a C corporation making a midstream S election as undergoing a constructive liquidation. The former C corporation would be deemed to distribute its assets to shareholders, followed by a deemed recontribution by shareholders of those assets to the new S corporation. Given the substantial tax costs and likely discouraging effect on S elections by former C corporations, it is perhaps not surprising that Congress has declined to adopt this approach.[48]

---

[47]   I.R.C. § 1363(b)(4). *See Vainisi v. Comm'r*, 599 F.3d 567 (7th Cir. 2010) (negative implication for taxable years outside this period).

[48]   *See* Chapter 11.

Chapter 6

TAX CONSEQUENCES FOR S CORPORATION SHAREHOLDERS

¶ 6.01   TAX CONSEQUENCES FOR SHAREHOLDERS IN GENERAL

As earlier chapters indicate in a general way, an S election has a considerable impact on shareholders. The passthrough regime gives rise to current taxability and basis effects, utilizing individual shareholder rates and limitations. Distinctive consequences apply to actual distributions and even to sales or other transfers of shares. Chapter Six will focus on these and other implications of an S election for shareholders.

¶ 6.02   PASSTHROUGH OF INCOME AND LOSSES TO SHAREHOLDERS; IN GENERAL—§ 1366

The passthrough of corporate items of income or loss to shareholders is, of course, the most distinctive and important of Subchapter S consequences. Taxable income of the S corporation, not earnings and profits or actual distributions, is what determines the tax consequences to shareholders, at least as a first principle. If the S corporation has taxable income or loss for the year, that income or loss passes through pro rata to shareholders, whether or not distributed.[1] Each shareholder must include her share of S items in the shareholder's tax year *in* which, or *with* which, the S corporation's taxable year ends.[2]

Income passes through and increases the shareholders' ("outside") bases in their shares.[3] Losses also pass through and reduce the basis of a shareholder's shares; once stock basis is exhausted, losses reduce any basis that the shareholder has in debt of the S corporation. If the loss exceeds a shareholder's basis in both stock and debt, the excess may not be deducted currently but may be carried over to later years and deducted when positive basis in stock or debt permits.[4]

Actual distributions of cash or property reduce a shareholder's basis by the amount of cash and the fair market value of distributed property. The shareholders then take a basis in distributed property equal to its fair market value, the same amount by which their stock (and debt) basis is reduced (assuming sufficient basis). If the amount of the

---

[1]   I.R.C. § 1366; *see* ¶¶ 1.06–1.07.

[2]   I.R.C. § 1366(a), (c).

[3]   Passthrough income is reduced for entity-level taxes, if any, on built-in gains and excess passive investment income. *See* I.R.C. § 1366(f)(2), (3). *See also* ¶¶ 5.01–5.04.

[4]   For further discussion of the basis rules, see ¶¶ 6.08–6.09. A shareholder's share of the corporation's loss reduces outside stock basis even if the loss does not produce a tax benefit for the shareholder. *See Hudspeth v. Comm'r*, 914 F.2d 1207 (9th Cir. 1990). Suspended losses reduce basis in the first year in which the shareholder's basis is adequate to absorb such losses, regardless of whether the shareholder actually claims such losses. *See Barnes v. Comm'r*, 712 F.3d 581 (D.C. Cir. 2013).

distribution exceeds basis, the excess is generally taxable as gain from a sale or exchange of property.[5] Priority rules govern the order in which a shareholder's basis is reduced.[6]

¶ 6.03   CHARACTER OF PASSTHROUGH ITEMS

Income or loss retains its character as it flows through, and specific items must be separately stated to the extent that their character could affect shareholder tax liability.[7] Otherwise, the S corporation's taxable income need not be separately stated. It is the possibility that the character of any corporate item might affect the computation of any shareholder's tax liability that dictates whether the item must be separately stated. While the statute mentions some items, partly by reference to the corresponding partnership rules, this listing is not exhaustive.[8] The regulations expand the items that must be separately stated.[9]

The nature of an item of corporate income or loss (whose character is passed through) is determined as if it had been incurred in the same manner as it was incurred by the corporation, or directly from the same source.[10] In exceptional circumstances, the nature of the item realized by the corporation may be affected by its relationship to the shareholder. For example, the IRS may disallow capital gain treatment on a later sale if the shareholder contributed ordinary income property to the S corporation for purposes of converting the income to capital gain.[11]

¶ 6.04   PRORATION VERSUS INTERIM CLOSING METHOD

The general rule requires proration of S items on a per-share, per-day basis.[12] Under the proration rule, an equal portion of each item is assigned to each day of the entire tax year and then divided equally among the shares outstanding on that day.[13]

A few departures from this general rule are permitted (and sometimes required). If all "affected" shareholders consent, the S corporation may use the interim closing method to assign income (or loss) when a shareholder's *entire* interest is terminated during the year.[14] Under the interim closing method, separately stated and non-separately stated items are assigned to two short tax years, the first of which ends at the close of the day on which the shareholder's interest is completely terminated.[15]

---

[5] I.R.C. § 1368(b)(2). *See* ¶¶ 4.01–4.07.

[6] *See* Reg. § 1.1367–1(f); *see also* Reg. § 1.1368–1(e)(2). The overall result closely resembles the system for partnerships.

[7] I.R.C. § 1366(a)(1); *see also* I.R.C. § 702(a).

[8] *See* Reg. § 1.1366–1(a)(2) (separately stated items). The residual category consists of non-separately stated items. *See* Reg. § 1.1366–1(a)(3).

[9] Examples of separately stated items include short and long-term capital gains and losses (which must be separately reported, not netted at the corporate level), § 1231 gains and losses, § 165(h) casualty losses, charitable contributions, tax-exempt interest, foreign taxes, investment interest, passive activity losses, and alternative minimum tax preference items. *See* Reg. § 1.1366–1(a)(2).

[10] I.R.C. § 1366(b).

[11] *See* Reg. § 1.1366–1(b)(2). Similar rules apply for capital loss property. *See* Reg. § 1.1366–1(b)(3).

[12] I.R.C. § 1377(a)(1).

[13] *See id.*

[14] I.R.C. § 1377(a)(2). The term "affected shareholder" means the transferor (whose interest was terminated) and any shareholder to whom such shares were transferred. In the case of a redemption, the affected shareholders are all of the shareholders of the corporation during the year. *See id.*

[15] *See* Reg. § 1.1377–1(b).

The result can be to allocate (a prorated share of) gain or loss that occurred early in the entire year to the departing shareholder and (a prorated share of) later gains or losses to an incoming shareholder (or to the remaining shareholders whose interest increases when the transferor's stock is redeemed). The interim closing method applies only for purposes of determining allocations to affected shareholders. Thus, it does not affect those shareholders whose proportional ownership remains unchanged.

Another departure from strict daily proration can occur when an S election terminates during the S year, as mentioned in ¶ 2.20. The "S termination year" is divided into an S short year and a C short year; the first short year ends on the day *before* the termination date.[16] If all relevant shareholders (in both years) consent, all items of income or loss are attributed to each short tax year under normal tax accounting rules. Then, as to items attributable to the S short year, daily proration applies. By contrast, the corporation's books automatically close if 50% or more of the S corporation's stock is sold during a year in which the S election terminates. Under the automatic closure rule, all items *must* be assigned to the two short years under normal tax accounting rules.[17]

The regulations under § 1368 provide additional flexibility when there is a substantial change in ownership interests. These rules permit an elective interim closing if there is a "qualifying disposition" of the S stock.[18] For this purpose, a qualifying disposition is defined as the occurrence (during any 30-day period) of any of the following three events:

(1)   a shareholder disposes of at least 20% of the outstanding stock of the S corporation (by sale or gift);

(2)   a corporation redeems from a shareholder at least 20% of its outstanding stock in a transaction that qualifies under § 302(a) or § 303; or

(3)   a corporation issues an amount of stock to one or more *new* shareholders equal to at least 25% of the previously outstanding stock.[19]

¶ 6.05   BASIS OF SHARES: EFFECTS OF FLOWTHROUGH OF CORPORATE EARNINGS, LOSSES, AND TAXATION—§ 1367

A shareholder's basis in outstanding shares (whether in a C or S corporation) determines how much the shareholder can withdraw from the corporation before being taxed. In a C corporation, distributions out of corporate solution affect basis only if the C corporation has insufficient earnings and profits, either current or accumulated. With

---

[16]   I.R.C. § 1362(e)(3); Reg. § 1.1362–3(a) (C short year begins on termination date). If the rules under §§ 1362(e)(3) and 1377(a)(2) overlap, the former has the highest priority. Reg. § 1.1377–1(b). Such an overlap can occur, for example, if a shareholder sells her entire interest to an ineligible shareholder. In this event, an election may be made under § 1362(e)(3), but not under § 1377(a)(2).

[17]   I.R.C. § 1362(e)(6)(D). More than one sale or exchange can contribute to the required 50% change of ownership, but gifts are not counted; subsequent sales of the same stock are not counted twice. *See* Reg. § 1.1362–3(b)(3). Moreover, the pro rata method may not be employed for any item resulting from a § 338 election. I.R.C. § 1362(e)(6)(C). The tax consequences of the deemed asset sale under § 338 must be reported on a one-day C corporation tax return. *See* ¶ 7.13.

[18]   *See* Reg. § 1.1368–1(g)(2). In this case, all shareholders, not just "affected shareholders," must consent to the election. *Id.*

[19]   *Id.* (first short year ends at the close of the day on which there is a qualifying disposition of stock). The election under the § 1368 regulations has the lowest priority. Thus, if a sale of a shareholder's entire interest also constitutes a qualifying disposition, an election may be made under § 1377(a)(2), but not under the § 1368 regulations. *See* Reg. §§ 1.1377–1(b), 1.1368–1(g)(2)(iv). *See also* Reg. § 1.1368–1(g)(2)(ii) (subsequent sales of same stock not counted twice).

S corporations, however, as with partnerships, basis is a more dynamic measure. It gauges not only capital investment but also measures the shareholders' right to receive untaxed distributions and to deduct corporate losses. To the S shareholder, basis in a way represents that shareholder's share of the corporation's net (as yet undistributed) after-tax dollars. The detailed rules for basis adjustments are set forth in the Code; the regulations provide some accompanying technical rules designed to implement the flowthrough system correctly and correlate shareholder tax reporting with basis adjustments.[20]

The passthrough of an S corporation's income and loss affects a shareholder's stock basis.[21] Stock basis is adjusted only to the extent the shareholder (properly) includes required items in the shareholder's tax return.[22] As a general rule, *both* taxable and tax-exempt income increase stock basis.[23] Similarly, *both* deductible and nondeductible noncapital expenses reduce stock basis.[24] The adjustments to stock basis are normally determined at the end of the S corporation's taxable year.[25] Stock basis is first increased by items of income (including tax-exempt income) and reduced by tax-free § 1368 distributions *before* taking into account losses and other negative adjustments.[26] Thus, distributions reduce stock basis before losses. This rule is intended to maximize the amount of distributions that may be received tax free, while deferring losses if basis is inadequate.

Increases and decreases to stock basis are determined on a per-share, per-day basis.[27] If stock is acquired at different times, some shares may have positive bases even though the bases of other shares have been fully recovered. Whenever downward adjustments applicable to a particular share exceed its basis, the excess is applied to the shareholder's other shares in proportion to their bases.[28] This "spillover" rule favors taxpayers because it allows utilization of a shareholder's basis in all shares for passthrough purposes.[29] The adjustments for passthrough items may also affect the § 165(g) or § 166(d) deductions if the stock or debt becomes worthless.[30]

---

[20]   *See* I.R.C. § 1367; *see also* Reg. § 1.1367–1(f) (specifying the order of adjustments).

[21]   General tax provisions—including §§ 358, 1014 and 1015—can also affect an S shareholder's stock basis.

[22]   I.R.C. § 1367(b)(1).

[23]   *See* I.R.C. § 1367(a)(1); Reg. § 1.1367–1(b).

[24]   I.R.C. § 1367(a)(2); Reg. § 1.1367–1(c). Examples of nondeductible noncapital expenditures include federal taxes, bribes, and illegal payments.

[25]   Reg. § 1.1367–1(d)(1). Upon a sale of a shareholder's stock, however, basis adjustments are effective immediately. *See id.* The upward adjustment will reduce gain (or increase loss) recognized on the sale.

[26]   *See* I.R.C. §§ 1366(d)(1)(A), 1368(d)(1) (flush language); *see also* I.R.C. § 1367(a)(1), (2)(A). *See generally* ¶ 4.03.

[27]   I.R.C. § 1377(a)(1); Reg. § 1.1367–1(b), (c).

[28]   Reg. § 1.1367–1(c)(3). Whenever downward adjustments applicable to a particular share exceed its basis, the § 1367 regulations indicate that the excess is applied to reduce the basis of the shareholder's other shares in proportion to their remaining bases. Reg. § 1.1367–1(c)(3); Reg. § 1.1367–1(h) (ex. 3).

[29]   *See* T.D. 8508, 1994–1 C.B. 219, 220 (clarifying that the spillover rule applies to basis adjustments for distributions as well as losses). This approach resembles the "unitary basis" approach for partnership interests. *See* Rev. Rul. 84–53, 1984–1 C.B. 159. The unitary basis approach seems inconsistent, however, with the share-by-share approach of computing gain under the § 1368 regulations. *See* Reg. § 1.1368–3 (ex. 1, 2); *see also* Eustice, Kuntz & Bogdanski, Federal Income Taxation of S Corporations ¶ 8.03[2][c] (5th ed. 2015) (distribution should trigger gain only if the basis of *all* shares is reduced to zero, but this result is not "entirely certain" since the § 1368 regulations "are silent on this point").

[30]   *See* I.R.C. § 1367(b)(3).

The following examples illustrate these rules:

Example 6.1: A, an individual, contributes $10,000 to X, a newly-formed calendar-year S corporation, in exchange for all of its stock. In Year 1, X earns $5,000 of taxable income and distributes $8,000 to A on December 31. Under § 1363(a), X is not taxed; under § 1366(a), the $5,000 of income passes through and is taxed directly to A. A's original basis in her X stock ($10,000) is first increased by $5,000 under § 1367(a)(1), and then reduced by $8,000 under § 1367(a)(2)(A) to reflect the tax-free distribution to A, leaving A with a stock basis of $7,000.[31]

Example 6.2: The facts are the same as in Example 6.1 above, except that X also incurs a capital loss of $9,000 in Year 1. Since distributions reduce stock basis before losses, A's stock basis is $7,000 immediately after the tax-free distribution ($10,000 original basis increased by $5,000 of income and decreased by $8,000 distribution). A's stock basis is then reduced (but not below zero) to reflect the loss for Year 1. Thus, A may deduct $7,000 of the loss currently. The remaining $2,000 of the loss is subject to the loss limitation of § 1366(d)(1) and carried over to a subsequent year under § 1366(d)(2).[32]

Example 6.3: The facts are the same as in Example 6.2 above, except that X also incurs a $200 nondeductible noncapital expenditure in Year 1.[33] A's stock basis is reduced to reflect this item before the reduction for operating losses.[34] Thus, A would be permitted to deduct only $6,800 of the loss currently, reducing her stock basis to zero ($7,000 post-distribution stock basis less $200 nondeductible noncapital expenditure less $6,800 loss). The remaining loss of $2,200 would be suspended under § 1366(d)(1).[35]

A shareholder's stock basis is decreased by the amount of any cash and the fair market value of any other property actually distributed (and *not* includable in income under § 1368).[36] The shareholder takes distributed property with a basis equal to its fair market value. Because the passthrough of income increased the shareholder's stock basis, the distribution of the cash or property *should* entail a corresponding reduction in stock basis. The shareholder will be credited with same amount of tax-paid dollars in the cash received or basis of other property distributed.

¶ 6.06   DEBT BASIS: EFFECTS OF FLOWTHROUGH AND LOCKED-IN EARNINGS

Deductions and losses passed through first reduce the shareholder's stock basis (but not below zero).[37] Once the basis of a shareholder's stock has been reduced to zero,

---

[31] Reg. §§ 1.1367–1(f), 1.1368–1(e)(2).

[32] If losses were instead taken into account prior to distributions, A would be required to recognize $2,000 of gain on the distribution, *i.e.*, the portion of the $8,000 distribution in excess of A's pre-distribution basis of $6,000 ($10,000 original basis increased by $5,000 income and decreased by $9,000 loss).

[33] *See* I.R.C. § 1367(a)(2)(D).

[34] Reg. § 1.1367–1(f).

[35] *See* Reg. § 1.1367–1(h) (ex. 2). A may elect to reverse the order of the basis reduction to allow the loss to pass through before taking into account the nondeductible noncapital expenditure. *See* Reg. §§ 1.1367–1(g), 1.1366–2(a)(3)(i). This election is almost certain to be advantageous because it allows additional losses to pass through currently, without any offsetting detriment.

[36] I.R.C. § 1368(b) (distribution applied first against basis; excess treated as gain).

[37] I.R.C. § 1367(a)(2) (basis in stock may not be reduced below zero).

downward adjustments (other than for distributions) are applied against the basis of any indebtedness.[38] Any *net increase* in basis is applied first to restore any previous reduction in the basis of debt for post-1982 taxable years, and then to increase the shareholder's stock basis.[39] For this purpose, the net increase is equal to the excess of all upward adjustments over all downward adjustments (determined after taking distributions into account). If the net increase (before distributions) does not exceed the amount of distributions, there is no net increase. Accordingly, debt basis is restored only after stock basis has been increased to the extent necessary to maximize tax-free distributions.[40]

The following examples illustrate these principles.

Example 6.4: At the beginning of Year 1, individual shareholder A holds all of the stock of X Corp., a newly-formed S corporation, with a basis of $1,000. A also holds a note from X Corp. for $1,000. If X Corp. loses $2,500 in Year 1, A's basis in both stock and debt will be reduced to zero. A will be allowed to deduct only the $2,000 offset by basis ($1,000 stock basis and $1,000 debt basis). A will be allowed to carry over $500 to deduct in the future when A acquires additional basis. Note that A's aggregate basis ($1,000 stock basis plus $1,000 debt basis) allows tax-free receipt of only $1,000 in *distributions*. Basis in *debt* may not be used to offset (that is, render tax free) *distributions,* as distinguished from permitting loss passthrough.[41]

Example 6.5: A, an individual, contributes $2,000 to X Corp., a newly-formed S corporation, in exchange for all of its stock; simultaneously A lends $5,000 to X. In Year 1, X Corp. has an operating loss of $6,000. Under § 1367(b)(2)(A), A's basis in her stock is first reduced from $2,000 to zero, and the remaining $4,000 of loss is applied to reduce A's basis in the debt from $5,000 to $1,000. In Year 2, X Corp. has operating income of $3,000 and makes no distributions. Under § 1367(b)(2)(B), A's debt basis is increased to $4,000 ($1,000 increased by the $3,000 "net increase" for Year 2), and A's stock basis remains zero. A cannot receive any tax-free distributions until her stock basis is increased above zero.

In determining the tax consequences of distributions by an S corporation, the basis adjustment rules for stock and debt threaten to create a zero-basis trap. This occurs when a shareholder-creditor cannot receive a tax-free distribution because stock basis has been reduced to zero even though debt basis is positive. The timing problem has to do with the order in which the S corporation's income increases basis when a shareholder holds both stock and debt.

Recall that earnings of an S corporation, when passed through and taxed to a shareholder, increase the shareholder's basis in *stock* under § 1367. (This allows an actual distribution of such earnings, in the same or in a later year to be made tax free under § 1368(b).) Conversely, passthrough of losses reduces stock basis under § 1367, thereby limiting both the deductibility of later losses and the ability to receive future distributions tax free.

---

[38]   I.R.C. § 1367(b)(2)(A); Reg. § 1.1367–2(b)(1).

[39]   I.R.C. § 1367(b)(2)(B); Reg. § 1.1367–2(c)(1).

[40]   *See* Reg. § 1.1367–2(e) (ex. 4, 5).

[41]   *See* I.R.C. §§ 1367(b)(2), 1368(b)(2).

If a shareholder also holds *debt* of the S corporation, the shareholder's basis in the debt also may be affected by passthrough of losses (but not by distributions) under § 1367(b)(2). That rule states that if decreases in stock basis under § 1367(a)(2) (other than for distributions) exceed the shareholder's stock basis, then such decreases will be applied to reduce the shareholder's basis in the corporation's debt (but not below zero). Basis in the debt then is restored by any net increase ("after the application of paragraphs (1) and (2) of [§ 1367](a)") for any subsequent year *before* increasing the shareholder's stock basis.

As a consequence of these rules, a shareholder-creditor can find herself subject to tax unexpectedly or in need of careful planning.

Example 6.6: Suppose C, a shareholder-creditor of an S corporation, starts out in Year 1 (a break-even year) with a positive basis in her S corporation stock and debt. In Year 2, corporate losses reduce stock basis to zero; once stock basis is exhausted, debt basis is reduced by the amount by which losses exceeds stock basis. In Year 3, the corporation passes through just enough income to restore the debt basis to its original amount (leaving the stock basis at zero). In Year 4, when no further income is earned so as to increase stock basis, the corporation makes a *distribution* of cash equal to the income earned in Year 3. (In prior years, the corporation made no distributions or repayments of debt.) The Year 4 distribution will be taxable to C, since it exceeds C's (zero) stock basis.

If the Year 4 distribution had been used instead to pay off the debt, the payment would have been a tax-free return of capital. If the distribution had been made *in the same year* the corporation earned the income (Year 3), the distribution would have been tax free (up to the amount of the income passed through); no amount would have been applied to restore the basis of the debt. The reason is that income is "soaked up" first by any distributions; only the remaining net increase (*i.e.*, the excess of all upward adjustments over all downward adjustments, taking distributions into account) is applied to restore debt basis. Thus, a distribution made promptly in the year income is earned can come out tax free, since stock basis is increased before debt basis. But if the distribution is postponed until the next (break-even) year, the debt basis must be restored first (to the extent of any prior reductions), leaving stock basis unchanged and rendering the distribution taxable.

Consider another example involving these principles in which stock basis increases above zero.

Example 6.7: At the end of Year 1, D has a basis of $10,000 in her S corporation stock and a debt basis of $25,000 from a loan she made to the corporation. In Year 2 (a loss year), D is allocated a loss passthrough of $15,000, reducing D's stock basis to zero and reducing her debt basis from $25,000 to $20,000. If, in Year 3 (a profitable year), D is allocated income of $6,000 (and receives no distribution), D's basis in the debt first would be restored (from $20,000 to $25,000) and then the extra $1,000 would be added to her stock basis of zero, making it $1,000.

Now consider what happens if, in Year 4, the corporation just breaks even but distributes $5,000 cash to D. D's $1,000 basis in the stock will allow her to receive only $1,000 tax free and the remaining $4,000 will be taxable as a dividend.

If, instead, the distribution had occurred in Year 3, the result would be different. Then, the $5,000 distribution would have been tax free because it would not exceed D's $6,000 share of income; D's stock basis would first be increased momentarily to $5,000 and then reduced to zero by the $5,000 tax-free distribution. D's debt basis would be increased by only $1,000, the net increase for the year after taking into account the distribution ($6,000 income less $5,000 distribution).

Thus, the timing of a distribution—as well as the choice to make a distribution or to repay debt—may greatly affect the tax consequences.

¶ 6.07   OUTSIDE BASIS FOR ENTITY-LEVEL DEBT

One of the most important differences between the basis rules for S corporation shareholders and those for partners lies in the rules governing the relationship between "outside" (shareholder or partner) and "inside" (corporate or partnership) basis with respect to entity-level debt.[42] An S shareholder does not receive basis, or an increase in basis, for indebtedness of the S corporation to an outside lender (or to other shareholders), whether recourse or nonrecourse (as to the S corporation). So, if an S corporation borrows funds from a bank or other unrelated lender, the S shareholders do not receive any upward basis adjustment (to stock or debt), unlike partners whose aggregate outside basis would increase under § 752.[43] Even if the shareholder guarantees the S corporation's debt, as often will be required by the outside lender, the shareholder's basis does not increase. As a result, the shareholder cannot use additional losses (or receive additional tax-free distributions). In contrast, a partnership in which partners have low outside basis can borrow money and immediately distribute the borrowed funds tax free; the partnership liability immediately increases the partners' aggregate outside basis by the amount of the debt. If the S corporation later defaults and the shareholder is required to pay the lender under the guarantee, this economic outlay should increase the shareholder's outside basis.[44] "Economic outlay" is, in fact, the concept that courts have purported to apply in determining whether a shareholder obtains basis for entity-level debt.[45] This strict Subchapter S rule may severely limit the ability of shareholders to deduct losses.

---

[42] Presumably the reason for the rule denying outside basis for entity-level debt lies in the limited liability of shareholders as distinguished from general partners. Yet, even limited partners can increase basis for partnership nonrecourse liabilities (or recourse liabilities if they agree to bear the economic burden of such debt). *See* Reg. §§ 1.752–2(a) (recourse liabilities), 1.752–3(a) (nonrecourse liabilities).

[43] I.R.C. § 1367(a)(1). *See* I.R.C. § 752 (partner treated as having made a contribution of money to the partnership when share of partnership (entity-level) liabilities increases or partner assumes partnership liabilities).

[44] *See Phillips v. Comm'r*, T.C. Memo 2017–61 (2017), *aff'd*, 733 Fed. Appx. 514 (11th Cir. 2018); *Maloof v. Comm'r*, 456 F.3d 645 (6th Cir. 2006); *Leavitt v. Comm'r*, 875 F.2d 420 (4th Cir. 1989), *cert. denied*, 493 U.S. 958 (1989). *But see Selfe v. U.S.*, 778 F.2d 769 (11th Cir. 1985) (taxpayer may receive basis increase on showing that bank looked primarily to the taxpayer for repayment of loan to S corporation). Other courts have generally not followed *Selfe*.

[45] *See Broz v. Comm'r*, 727 F.3d 621 (6th Cir. 2013), *aff'g* 137 T.C. 46 (2011) (no economic outlay). Economic outlay is not identical to "cash outlay," since direct personal liability can give rise to a basis increase before any cash is actually "laid out." As discussed below, revised regulations substitute a bona-fide-indebtedness test in lieu of the concept of an economic outlay.

The impact of these limitations may be relieved if shareholders make additional cash contributions, which will increase stock basis, or make personal loans to the S corporation, which will entitle them to basis in the debt. If necessary and feasible, the shareholders can personally borrow funds and then lend them to the S corporation for its use. The difficulty of these solutions, apart from liquidity problems or the infeasibility of many shareholders borrowing to re-lend to the S corporation, lies in the fact that the shareholders must actually put additional funds at risk.

Example 6.8: A, B, and C are equal one-third shareholders of an S corporation. Each paid $100x for her shares, so each has outside stock basis of $100x. If the S corporation borrows $90x, the shareholders' stock basis remains unchanged for purposes of limiting loss deductions or taxing distributions.

In contrast, if A, B, and C each borrowed $30x individually and each contributed $30x to the S corporation, each shareholder would be entitled to increase stock basis from $100x to $130x.

Rather than contribute the borrowed $30x to the corporation, each shareholder could lend the borrowed funds to the corporation (in exchange for the corporation's note). Such a "back-to-back" loan would give each shareholder a $30x basis in the corporation's debt (without any change in stock basis).

If the shareholders merely guaranteed the corporation's debt of $90x, they would receive no basis increase. If the corporation later defaulted on the loan and each shareholder were required to make good on the guarantee by paying $30x to the lender, the result would be different. In this event, each shareholder would have a $30x basis in the shareholder's claim against the corporation or in the stock held.

Revised regulations seek to clarify the effect of entity-level debt on shareholder basis. Under these regulations, corporate debt creates basis in the hands of a shareholder only if it is "bona fide" and runs directly from the corporation to the shareholder.[46] Whether indebtedness is bona fide is determined under general federal tax principles. Thus, the concept of an actual economic outlay (as employed in court decisions) has been superseded by the bona-fide-indebtedness standard.[47]

The regulations also provide greater certainty concerning whether particular arrangements give rise to debt basis. For example, a shareholder who makes a loan to an S corporation through a disregarded entity obtains debt basis in the same manner as if the shareholder lent directly to the S corporation.[48] The regulations do not change the rule that a shareholder guarantee ordinarily does not give rise to basis until the shareholder actually makes payments under the guarantee (or shareholder notes are substituted for corporate notes to the lender).[49]

Under the regulations, a back-to-back loan between related parties may generate debt basis. For example, a shareholder may borrow from a related entity and then lend the proceeds back to the S corporation.[50] If an S corporation (S2) owes debt to another

---

[46]   Reg. § 1.1366–2(a)(2)(i).

[47]   *But see Meruelo v. Comm'r*, T.C. Memo 2018–16 (2018), *aff'd*, 923 F.3d 938 (11th Cir. 2019).

[48]   Reg. § 1.1366–2(a)(2)(iii) (ex. 1).

[49]   Reg. § 1.1366–2(a)(2)(ii), (iii) (ex. 4). *See* Rev. Rul. 75–144, 1975–1 C.B. 277 (substitution of shareholder note for corporate note).

[50]   Reg. § 1.1366–2(a)(2)(iii) (ex. 2).

entity (S1) owned by a shareholder, S1 can distribute the S2 note to the shareholder. Provided S2 becomes directly liable to the shareholder (and is relieved of its obligation to S1) as a result of the distribution, the note increases the shareholder's basis in S2.[51] Shareholders may also be able to obtain debt basis for loans to an S corporation directly from an entity related to the shareholder.[52]

The regulations address only a shareholder's basis in indebtedness (not stock). An advance of funds that is not a bona fide debt may nevertheless increase the shareholder's stock basis if it represents an actual investment in the S corporation.[53]

¶ 6.08   LIMITATION ON DEDUCTION OF PASSTHROUGH LOSSES

Several rules can limit the deduction by S shareholders of a corporate-level loss passed through to them. The most important of these limitations, apart from the usual limitations on deducting capital or quasi-capital (§ 1231) losses, include the § 1366(d)(1) loss limitation rules (¶ 6.09), § 469 passive loss rules (¶ 6.10), § 465 at-risk rules (¶ 6.11), limits on foreign losses (¶ 6.13), limits on interest deductions (¶ 6.14), and the § 461(*l*) limit on excess business losses (¶ 6.15). These will be discussed in the following sections.

¶ 6.09   BASIS LIMITATION FOR LOSSES

The most central Subchapter S rule limiting passthrough of losses is found in § 1366(d). Under that provision, the shareholder's aggregate basis in stock and debt sets a ceiling on the amount of losses and deductions that the shareholder may take into account for the taxable year.[54] Any excess amount may, however, be carried over to future years.

For purposes of the § 1366(d) limitation on shareholder deduction of losses, *stock* basis is initially increased by items of income passed through for the year.[55] Stock basis is then reduced by any tax-free distributions before the § 1366(d) limitation applies.[56] If the shareholder holds multiple blocks of stock, what counts for the § 1366(d) limitation is the shareholder's aggregate basis in stock.[57] The § 1366(d) limitation applies before

---

[51]   *Id.* (ex. 3).

[52]   *See Yates v. Comm'r*, T.C. Memo 2001–280 (2001) ("incorporated pocketbook" transaction). Under the regulations, such a transaction gives rise to debt basis only if it creates a bona fide debtor-creditor relationship between the shareholder and the borrowing S corporation. *See Messina v. Comm'r*, T.C. Memo 2017–213 (2017), *aff'd*, 799 Fed. Appx. 466 (9th Cir. 2019).

[53]   A shareholder who merely delivers her promissory note to the corporation receives no basis. *See* Rev. Rul. 81–187, 1981–2 CB 167 (no basis step-up from unsecured note that remained unpaid at end of year); *Oren v. Comm'r*, 357 F.3d 854 (8th Cir. 2004). *But see Lessinger v. Comm'r*, 872 F.2d 519 (2d Cir. 1989); *Peracchi v. Comm'r*, 143 F.3d 487 (9th Cir. 1998).

[54]   I.R.C. § 1366(d)(1).

[55]   I.R.C. §§ 1366(d)(1)(A), 1367(a).

[56]   I.R.C. § 1366(d)(1)(A); § 1368(d) (flush language). *See* Reg. § 1.1366–2(a)(3)(i). The § 1366(d) loss limit for S corporations operates in essentially the same manner as the § 704(d) loss limit for partnerships. *See* Reg. § 1.704–1(d)(2); Rev. Rul. 66–94, 1996–1 C.B. 166 (outside basis reduced by distributions before the § 704(d) loss limitation applies). In determining the § 1366(d) loss limit, the regulations also subtract nondeductible noncapital expenses unless the taxpayer elects to take losses into account first. *See* ¶ 6.05 n.35 *supra*.

[57]   The aggregate approach seems appropriate, since § 1366(d) refers to the "sum of" the shareholder's adjusted basis in stock and debt. *See* ¶6.05 n.29 *supra*.

any adjustments (upward or downward) to the shareholder's adjusted basis in any *indebtedness*.[58]

These loss limitation rules have the effect of allowing the shareholder to deduct losses and expenditures to the extent the shareholder has lost after-tax dollars, as measured by basis, but not to any further extent. The shareholder's basis may stem from the original cost of the shares or from previously taxed but undistributed earnings. In either event, the shareholder can take a loss deduction because the shareholder has lost dollars on which she previously was taxed.

Of course, a taxpayer may acquire basis without any expenditure of after-tax dollars. For example, a taxpayer may be entitled to a stepped-up (or stepped-down) basis under § 1014 or a carryover basis under § 1015. Section 1015 poses a peculiar problem, because it has a special rule for determining a donee's basis for loss purposes.[59] The Code does not specify whether that special rule should be used to limit S corporation losses passed through to a donee. Logically the § 1015 basis for determining loss on sale of the stock would seem to set the ceiling for loss passthrough, which is also the approach adopted by the regulations.[60]

If "losses" exceed basis, they may reflect a loss of as-yet untaxed income or a loss of dollars borrowed by the corporation. Since the S shareholder has limited liability, there is no presumption that the shareholder ultimately will have to pay for corporate losses by digging further into the shareholder's own pocket. If the shareholder does make additional contributions to the corporation or lends it additional funds (or if corporate income is taxed to the shareholder), outside basis will be increased, allowing for further deduction of losses in the same or future years.

Section 1366(d)(2) authorizes an indefinite carryover of losses or deductions disallowed under the § 1366(d)(1) loss limitation rule. It provides that a disallowed loss shall be treated as incurred by the corporation in the succeeding taxable year with respect to that shareholder. This carryover continues indefinitely until the loss has been fully allowed; special rules apply for carryover of loss when an S election terminates.[61] Disallowed losses are personal to the shareholder and generally cannot be transferred to any other person, *e.g.*, upon a gift of stock.[62] In the case of a tax-free transfer of a shareholder's stock to a spouse (or former spouse) under § 1041, however, a special rule permits the transferee to carry forward indefinitely any disallowed losses.[63]

Losses first reduce the shareholder's basis in her shares (but not below zero) and then reduce basis in debt. (Note that basis must be reduced even for a loss that is

---

[58] *See* I.R.C. § 1366(d)(1)(B) (ignoring any upward or downward adjustments to debt basis under § 1367(b)(2)); Reg. § 1.1366–2(a)(3)(ii) (preventing any reduction to debt basis for tax-free distributions under § 1367(b)(2)(A)).

[59] *See* I.R.C. § 1015(a); Reg. § 1.1366–2(a)(6).

[60] Reg. § 1.1366–2(a)(6).

[61] Any carried over loss is treated as incurred by the shareholder on the last day of any post-termination transition period (within the meaning of § 1377(b)). I.R.C. § 1366(d)(3)(A); Reg. § 1.1366–2(b)(1). Similar rules apply to losses suspended under the § 465 at-risk rules. I.R.C. § 1366(d)(3)(D). Thus, to the extent that the shareholder's stock basis increases during the post-termination transition period (*e.g.*, through additional capital contributions), the loss will be allowed currently and reduce stock basis. I.R.C. § 1366(d)(3)(B), (C). Only stock basis (not debt basis) is considered in determining whether suspended losses may be used during the post-termination transition period.

[62] *See* Reg. § 1.1366–2(a)(5).

[63] I.R.C. § 1366(d)(2)(B).

suspended under the § 465 at-risk rules or the § 469 passive loss rules.[64]) If and when any increase in basis occurs, it is assigned first to restore any reduction in the shareholder's basis in debt (but only for any post-1982 year) and then to restore the shareholder's basis in stock.[65] Once again, it bears remembering that entity-level debt to a third party lender does not increase a shareholder's stock (or debt) basis.

The purpose of the loss limitation rules is to limit the shareholder's deduction to the amount of her after-tax investment that has been lost. When an S corporation is failing, shareholders may anticipate that the passthrough deductions for the year will exceed their aggregate basis. They will want to deduct the entire loss and receive the corresponding tax benefits, but merely guaranteeing the corporate debt will not be enough. If they make contributions to capital, buy additional stock or lend funds to the corporation in the loss year, they will be able to use losses currently. This follows from the rule that basis increases are taken into account at year end before determining the loss limitation.[66] Alternatively, the shareholders can make contributions or loans to the S corporation in future years to which the excess loss is carried forward. Thus, shareholders can even "time" the contribution for the year in which a deduction will do the most good. In this way, shareholders can salvage a deduction—but only at the cost of putting more money at risk.

¶ 6.10   PASSIVE ACTIVITY LOSS RULES—§ 469

In 1986, Congress enacted the passive activity rules of § 469 to block taxpayers from sheltering earned income or portfolio income though losses incurred on "passive investments," such as those from real estate tax shelters. Under these rules, losses arising from passive trade or business activities, to the extent they exceed income from all such passive activities, may not be deducted against other non-passive (active or portfolio) income. Also, credits from such passive activities may only be used against tax attributable to net income from passive activities.

The disallowance rules of § 469 do not apply to an S corporation as an entity but rather to its shareholders individually.[67] The effect of § 469 is to disallow or "suspend" shareholder deduction of covered losses to the extent they exceed shareholder income from the same or another passive activity.[68] Covered losses (and credits) may not be applied against a shareholder's salary or other earned income or portfolio income (dividends, interest, royalties, or sale or exchange gains). Nevertheless, such disallowed losses reduce the shareholder's basis in stock or debt. The passive loss rules have become more important now that "pure" S corporations are allowed to have any amount of passive income without risking termination.

The workings of the passive loss rules suggest one reason to be cautious when electing S status. A C corporation might be able to conduct two businesses, offsetting

---

[64] *See* Prop. Reg. § 1.465–1(e); Temp. Reg. § 1.469–2T(d)(6) (order of loss limitation rules under §§ 1366(d), 465, and 469).

[65] I.R.C. § 1367(b)(2)(B). In the case of multiple indebtedness, any net increase is applied first to restore the basis of debt repaid during the year and then to restore the basis of remaining debt in proportion to outstanding prior reductions. *See* Reg. § 1.1367–2(c)(2).

[66] *See* I.R.C. § 1366(d)(1)(A).

[67] I.R.C. § 469(a)(2); Temp. Reg. § 1.469–1T(b), (g)(2).

[68] I.R.C. § 469(a)(1), (d)(1). Thus, all of the taxpayer's passive activities are aggregated for purposes of the § 469 passive loss limit, unlike the § 465 at-risk limit which generally applies on an activity-by-activity basis.

losses from one against income from another—for example, losses from a rental apartment may offset income from an active grocery business. A shareholder in an S corporation likely will not be able, however, to offset these same items of income and loss when they pass through. If the shareholder participates actively in both businesses, the proceeds of the grocery business will be active income, while those from the real estate investment will be deemed passive. The passive losses cannot be deducted against the active income.

There are three main categories of activities that constitute "passive activities" under § 469(c): rental real estate, rental activity other than real estate, and trade-or-business passive activities. Separate rules govern each category. In general, they all describe activities in which the taxpayer does not materially participate through the provision of services. In particular, income from owning S corporation stock is *not* treated as portfolio income (as *dividends* would be) but instead its character is determined at the *entity* level.

Passive activity losses include S corporation losses for activities in which the shareholder does not "materially participate."[69] Whether a shareholder participates materially is determined separately for each activity.[70] If the shareholder materially participates in a particular business activity of the S corporation, the shareholder is treated as active with respect to that activity and any losses arising from it. As a result, that shareholder would be able to deduct currently active losses passed through from the S corporation attributable to the activity. Since by its own terms § 469 applies on an activity-by-activity basis, however, the same shareholder may be passive with respect to other corporate activities in which the shareholder does not materially participate.

Rental activities (defined generally as any activity in which payments are principally for the use of tangible property) are treated as passive activities without regard to material participation.[71] Section 469(c)(7) provides limited relief for individuals who provide personal services mostly in real property trades or businesses and perform at least 750 hours of work in such activities during the taxable year.

Consider the following example of a passive activity loss in the S context.

Example 6.9: A, B and C own equal shares of S Corp., which owns and operates a grocery and a hotel. A manages the grocery, B manages the hotel, and C provides only financial backing. In 2023, the grocery experiences a $3,000 loss, while the hotel breaks even. One third of S Corp.'s loss passes through to each of the shareholders ($1,000 each). When reporting income or loss to its shareholders, S Corp. must separately state items of passive income or loss. Since A participates materially in the grocery, A may use the active loss to offset ordinary income from other sources. The loss allocated to B and C is a passive loss, however, which they can use in 2023 only to the extent that they have other passive income to offset. Under § 469(b), B and C can carry the passive loss forward to future tax years.

---

[69]   I.R.C. § 469(c). "Material participation" is a factual question. Section 469(h)(1) requires that the involvement be regular, continuous, and substantial. *See* § 469(h)(1) (participation by spouse); Temp. Reg. § 1.469–5T(a) (taxpayer must satisfy any one of seven alternative tests).

[70]   Temp. Reg. § 1.469–2T(e)(1).

[71]   I.R.C. § 469(c)(2), (j)(8).

In 2024, the grocery again loses $3,000, but the hotel earns $6,000. A may use his active loss from the grocery to offset part of his $2,000 share of passive income from the hotel business; under § 469, there is nothing to prevent an active loss from offsetting passive income. B and C each receive another $1,000 of passive losses from the grocery business, so that each now has $2,000 in accrued passive losses. In addition, B and C each must report $2,000 of income from the hotel business. Since B materially participates in the hotel business, B cannot offset his active hotel income against his share of passive losses from the grocery business; thus, B must carry forward the entire accrued passive loss of $2,000. Because C does not participate in the hotel business, C's passive income from this activity can be netted against C's accrued passive losses, leaving C with no passive loss carryforward.

As noted above, using a regular C corporation would avoid these somewhat odd results, since passive income and loss would be netted at the corporate level.[72] A closely held C corporation (other than a personal service corporation) also receives special treatment under the § 469 rules. Such a closely held corporation may deduct passive activity losses against its passive activity gross income and net business income (but not against portfolio income).[73] To qualify as a closely held corporation, 50% of the corporation's stock must be owned (during the last half of its taxable year) by (or for) five or fewer individuals directly or indirectly.[74]

For purposes of § 469, S shareholders are treated somewhat differently from limited partners. Under § 469(h)(2), a limited partner must treat all partnership losses as passive even if the limited partner actively participates, except as provided in regulations.[75] Thus, it may be easier for an S shareholder to meet the material participation test.[76]

To summarize, under the flowthrough approach, an S shareholder must report passive activity income against which passive activity losses from other investments may be deducted. Thus, an S corporation's passive activity losses must be segregated and subjected to the § 469 limitations on the shareholder's own tax return. Note again the requirement that an S corporation pay reasonable compensation for services and capital. Any adjustment of these items could affect the character of income and loss to the shareholder for purposes of the § 469 passive loss rules.[77]

Passive activity losses whose deduction is disallowed can be carried over indefinitely. They are suspended in the shareholder's hands until the shareholder has

---

[72] See Temp. Reg. § 1.469–1T(g)(1) (exempting corporations other than certain personal service corporations and closely held corporations from the passive loss rules).

[73] I.R.C. § 469(a)(2)(B), (e)(2); see Temp. Reg. § 1.469–1T(g)(2), (4).

[74] I.R.C. §§ 469(j), 542(a)(2). In St. Charles Invest. Co. v. Comm'r, 232 F.3d 773 (10th Cir. 2000), the court allowed former shareholders of a closely held C corporation that converted to S status to deduct suspended passive activity losses carried over from the former C corporation. The court considered that § 469(b) overrode the § 1371(b)(1) prohibition on carryovers from C years to S years. It noted that the shareholders were receiving a "windfall," since a different taxpayer (the former C corporation) had incurred the losses.

[75] The regulations provide limited relief. See Temp. Reg. § 1.469–5T(e)(2); see also Prop. Reg. § 1.469–5(e)(3), (f) (defining limited partnership interest).

[76] Since the § 1411 tax is coordinated with the § 469 rules for material participation, this relative advantage of the S corporation form may also matter upon a sale of business assets (or stock). See ¶¶ 6.21, 7.13.

[77] See ¶ 3.11.

offsetting passive income (or until final disposition of the taxpayer's entire interest in the activity).[78] An S corporation shareholder's basis is reduced under § 1367(a)(2) when a loss passes through, even if the loss is disallowed or suspended by the § 469 passive loss rules. The shareholder's basis is not reduced again when the loss ultimately is allowed under § 469.

Whether a loss must be suspended under the § 469 passive loss rules is determined *after* applying the § 1366(d)(1) loss limitation rules and the § 465 at-risk rules, discussed below.

¶ 6.11   AT-RISK RULES—§ 465

The at-risk rules of § 465 do not apply to the S corporation itself but rather to each shareholder individually. The effect of § 465 is to limit the deduction by each shareholder to the shareholder's amount "at risk." A loss disallowed under the at-risk rules nevertheless reduces the shareholder's basis in stock or debt. (When an amount at risk is increased, the disallowed loss may be deducted.)

The § 465 at-risk rules generally apply "activity-by-activity." Under a special rule, the various activities of an S corporation may be aggregated and treated as a single activity with respect to shareholders (with some exceptions). This special rule applies if the activities are part of one trade or business, provided at least 65% of the losses are allocated to shareholders who actively participate in the conduct of the S corporation's business.[79]

The amount at risk for a particular shareholder is initially the amount of money and the adjusted basis of other property contributed to the S corporation. Although adjustments must be made for any subsequent income, losses, and distributions, the amount at risk will not necessarily correspond to a shareholder's basis. A shareholder's amount at risk is increased by amounts borrowed by the entity for which the shareholder is personally liable.[80] Since shareholders are not personally liable for the S corporation's debts, they are generally not "at risk" for third-party entity-level debt.[81] If S shareholders become jointly and severally liable on corporate debt, however, they will be treated as at risk (though they may lack corresponding outside basis).[82]

The amount at risk is determined at the end of the S corporation's tax year, *before* taking into account allowable § 465(d) losses for that year. If losses exceed the shareholder's amount at risk, such excess losses are suspended and carried forward indefinitely until the shareholder's amount at risk is sufficient to absorb them.[83] Unlike basis, the amount "at risk" can be *negative*; any negative amount is subject to "recapture," that is, includable as ordinary income.[84] This recaptures losses previously allowed and deducted. An offset may be allowed when the shareholder's at-risk amount

---

[78] I.R.C. § 469(g)(1)(A).

[79] I.R.C. § 465(c)(3)(B)(ii).

[80] I.R.C. § 465(b). *See particularly* I.R.C. § 465(b)(3)(B)(ii).

[81] *See* Prop. Reg. § 1.465–24(a)(3).

[82] *See* I.R.C. § 465(b)(2).

[83] I.R.C. § 465(a)(2); Prop. Reg. § 1.465–2. The amount at risk is reduced even if deductions allowed under the at-risk rules are suspended under the passive loss rules.

[84] I.R.C. § 465(e)(1)(A), (B).

is restored, such as when the shareholder makes additional contributions or is allocated income from the S corporation.

¶ 6.12   COORDINATING BASIS, PASSIVE ACTIVITY LOSS, AND AT-RISK LIMITATIONS

The § 1366(d)(1) loss limitation rules, the § 465 at-risk rules, and the § 469 passive loss rules each represent independent limitations on a shareholder's ability to use losses. The § 1366(d)(1) limitation applies before the at-risk limitation, and it suspends losses if basis is insufficient.[85] The at-risk rules apply before the § 469 passive loss rules. When losses become allowable under the at-risk rules, they then become subject to the § 469 passive loss rules. Even if losses are limited under § 469, the amount at risk (and basis) must be reduced.

> *Example 6.10:* A contributes $20,000 to X, a calendar-year S corporation, in exchange for X stock. X is engaged in an at-risk activity in which A does not materially participate. In Year 1, A's share of X's operating loss is $50,000. Since the loss ($50,000) exceeds A's amount at risk ($20,000), A may deduct only $20,000 of loss currently. Even if the $20,000 loss is subject to further limitation under § 469, A's stock basis and amount at risk are reduced to zero at the end of Year 1.

Overview. Altogether, the at-risk and passive loss rules impose formidable limits on the ability of S shareholders to deduct losses passed through to them. The at-risk rules affect partners and S shareholders differently. To the extent partners are personally liable for partnership debt, they will be treated as at-risk for a pro rata share of such debt.[86] By contrast, S shareholders are generally not considered to be at-risk for third-party entity-level debt. Because limited partners are not personally liable, they are generally not treated as at-risk for partnership debt, unless they personally assume the partnership's recourse liabilities (or guarantee the partnership's nonrecourse liabilities). As a result, the ability of limited partners to deduct losses may be limited even if they have adequate outside basis under § 752 (*e.g.*, from partnership nonrecourse debt that is not guaranteed). Thus, limited partners and S shareholders are about on a par with respect to the § 465 at-risk rules (but not the § 469 passive loss rules or § 1366(d)(1) loss limitation rules).

¶ 6.13   LIMITS ON DEDUCTING FOREIGN LOSSES; RECAPTURE

A special set of problems and rules are encountered if the S corporation's losses are "foreign losses," sourced in another country. Now that S corporations may have foreign source income without jeopardizing their S status, the S form may be used much more often for foreign investment or trade. The existence of foreign losses alone does not create the problem; such losses pass through to shareholders just as do domestic losses.[87] The difficulty arises if S status terminates, or if S status is elected by a C corporation with prior foreign losses.

---

[85]   I.R.C. § 1366(d)(2), (3); *see* Reg. § 1.469–2T(d)(6)(i) (item disallowed under § 1366(d) is not treated as a passive activity deduction for the taxable year).

[86]   *See* Prop. Reg. § 1.465–24(a)(2).

[87]   *See* I.R.C. § 1373(a) (treating S corporation as partnership for purposes of foreign source income).

The making of an S election, or its termination, is treated as the equivalent of a "disposition" of a business for purposes of the foreign loss recapture rules of § 904(f).[88] As a consequence, if a C corporation which has previously incurred foreign losses elects S status, this "disposition" of its foreign property requires recapture (inclusion in income) of the amount of foreign losses not previously recaptured. If an S corporation with any history of foreign losses terminates its election, the entity is treated as having disposed of its foreign assets and the S shareholders are obliged to include in income any foreign losses previously passed through to them (and not previously recaptured).[89]

¶ 6.14   LIMITS ON INTEREST DEDUCTIONS

It is also necessary to consider the operation of the § 163(d) investment interest deduction limitation in the S corporation context. As background, remember that § 163(d) applies to individuals but not to C corporations. The passthrough system for S corporations preserves the character of any item that may affect shareholder tax. Thus, if an S corporation incurs investment interest expense, its deductibility must run the gauntlet of § 163(d) in each *shareholder's* return. The investment interest limit of § 163(d) applies only at the S shareholder level.[90] Interest on loans incurred by the S corporation to finance distributions to shareholders may be characterized by the shareholder's use of the funds.[91]

For purposes of §§ 163(d) and 469, interest expense (and interest income) of an S corporation must be allocated between business and non-business activities. Interest income of an S corporation (not derived in the ordinary course of business) will constitute portfolio income for purposes of § 469. Thus, passive activity losses cannot offset such portfolio income.[92]

The § 163(j) limit on the deductibility of business interest expense may also apply, but generally only if an S corporation has average annual gross receipts of more than $25 million for the preceding 3 years.[93] Thus, small- and medium-sized businesses are generally exempt. In the case of S corporations and partnerships, special rules are needed to ensure that the entity's owners are treated in a manner similar to sole proprietors.[94]

¶ 6.15   OTHER LOSS LIMITATIONS

In 2017, Congress enacted § 461(*l*) which disallows any "excess business loss" of individual passthrough business owners (including S shareholders), regardless of the taxpayer's activity in the business. In effect, such excess losses are deductible against only a limited amount of the taxpayer's nonbusiness income ($500,000 for joint filers,

---

[88]   *See* I.R.C. § 1373(b).

[89]   I.R.C. §§ 904(f), 1373(b). This foreign loss recapture rule is designed to prevent an undue double benefit to U.S. taxpayers in the form of a deduction for losses against U.S. taxable income and a later intact foreign tax credit. The problem arises particularly if the foreign tax is calculated during profitable years, without any reduction for NOL carryforwards from prior loss years.

[90]   I.R.C. § 163(d)(1). Perhaps somewhat surprisingly, the hobby loss rule of § 183 applies at the entity level. *See* Reg. § 1.183–1(a).

[91]   *See* IRS Notice 89–35, 1989–1 C.B. 675. The S corporation may elect to characterize the interest based on the corporation's own expenditures (rather than the shareholder's use of the proceeds). *Id.*

[92]   *See* Reg. § 1.1366–1(a)(2)(vii) (items of portfolio income or loss must be separately stated). *See also* IRS Notice 89–35, 1989–1 C.B. 675 (allocation of debt proceeds to capital contribution or stock purchase).

[93]   *See* I.R.C. §§ 163(j)(3), 448(c).

[94]   *See* I.R.C. § 163(j)(4) (limit applied at entity level).

$250,000 for other filers), even if nonbusiness income is greater than the specified amount. In the case of an S corporation, the limit on excess business losses applies at the shareholder level; each shareholder takes into account his pro rata share of all items of income, gain, deduction or loss.[95] The passive loss rules apply before the new loss limitation.[96] Any disallowed excess business loss is treated as a net operating loss carryforward under § 172.[97]

¶ 6.16   NO SPECIAL ALLOCATIONS

An S corporation cannot make special allocations of entity-level income, loss, deduction or credit among shareholders. This prohibition contrasts with partnerships which may make such special allocations, provided they have "substantial economic effect" as defined in the § 704(b) regulations.[98] Of course, the nature of a partnership and the structure of participants' relationships may lend themselves to special allocations. The Code, rather than any inherent trait of the corporate form, prevents an S corporation from specially allocating losses or deductions to high-bracket taxpayers, or from giving income preferences to some investors. C corporations can sometimes accomplish special allocations through the use of various classes of common or preferred shares or by issuing debt or hybrid securities. In contrast, an S corporation may have only one class of stock (though voting differences are permitted) and debt outstanding. In addition, as compared to a C corporation, the S corporation has less control over the timing of taxation of income to shareholders. By virtue of the passthrough regime, shareholders are taxed immediately, regardless of actual distributions. Consequently, some investors to whom the latitude for special allocations of profits or losses is important may find the partnership form preferable to incorporation with an S election.

¶ 6.17   TERMINAL LOSSES—§§ 165, 166 & 1244

If an S corporation suffers losses that render its shares or debt obligations worthless, its shareholders and/or creditors can seek a deduction under § 165(g) (worthless stock and worthless debt that is a "security") or § 166 (business and non-business debts). Section 1367(b)(3) provides a coordination rule for S corporations: the passthrough rules of § 1366 and the basis adjustments of § 1367 apply *before* §§ 165(g) and 166(d) are applied. This means that, in the year in which the security or debt becomes worthless, any corporate loss (or gain) will pass through as usual. Thus, passthrough of losses (with a corresponding reduction in stock or debt basis) takes priority. This rule can benefit shareholders if such losses are ordinary in nature. Only after these effects have been taken into account can the shareholders avail themselves of any deductions for worthlessness.

Under §§ 165 and 166, the loss will often be capital in nature, since the worthless stock or debt will be a capital asset in the hands of the shareholder.[99] If the stock is "§ 1244 stock," however, a (limited) ordinary loss deduction may be available.[100] This makes the important point that an S election does not render § 1244, which converts a

---

[95]   I.R.C. § 461(*l*)(4).

[96]   I.R.C. § 461(*l*)(6).

[97]   I.R.C. § 461(*l*)(2).

[98]   *See generally* Reg. § 1.704–1(b)(2).

[99]   *See* I.R.C. §§ 165(f), (g); 166(d)(1)(B), (e). If the investors hold indebtedness of the S corporation not evidenced by a "security," as defined in § 165(g), the loss may give rise to an ordinary loss deduction.

[100]   I.R.C. § 1244(a).

loss on small business stock from capital to ordinary, irrelevant for an S corporation's shareholders. At the end of an S corporation's life, even after the final year's corporate loss has passed through, the investor may have remaining basis in stock or debt. The leftover basis can give rise to a further loss deduction under § 165 or § 166. The lawyer who, through carelessness or sheer inadvertence, fails successfully to lay the groundwork to convert at least some portion of that loss to an ordinary loss, under § 1244, may be hard put to explain the oversight.

The effect of § 1244(d) must be carefully considered in the S corporation context. That section limits the § 1244 loss to the basis of the stock as originally issued. Any subsequent increases in stock basis are not taken into account in calculating the ordinary loss. Thus, § 1367 increases in stock basis due to passthrough of income apparently do not enhance § 1244 basis for purposes of ordinary loss deductions.[101] If stock basis has been decreased to zero and then increased by the passthrough of income, the § 1244 amount remains frozen, creating a potential trap for the unwary.

So long as use of capital losses is restricted, as compared with ordinary losses, taxpayers will have a keen interest in establishing ordinary loss treatment. Although § 1244 need not be affirmatively elected, it is important not to disregard the § 1244 requirements. In managing affairs at the formation, election, distribution or capitalization stage of an S corporation, it is essential to ensure that § 1244 ordinary loss treatment will be available to the fullest extent possible should terminal losses occur.

¶ 6.18 SHAREHOLDER LOSS DEDUCTIONS AND THE ACCUMULATED ADJUSTMENTS ACCOUNT

If an S corporation has accumulated earnings and profits from Subchapter C years, the AAA is employed to measure the amount of tax-free distributions that may be made to shareholders—before distributions out of accumulated earnings and profits become taxable (¶ 4.05). The AAA is adjusted upward or downward in a manner similar to the § 1367 basis adjustments.[102] The AAA (whether positive or negative) is also reduced for redemptions of outstanding shares.[103]

Losses (but not distributions) may reduce the AAA below zero. AAA will only become positive again when earnings have restored any deficit. Distributions while the AAA is negative will be taxable to shareholders as dividends to the extent of accumulated earnings and profits, if any.

¶ 6.19 ISSUING NEW SHARES AND THE ACCUMULATED ADJUSTMENTS ACCOUNT

When an S corporation issues more shares, presumably for additional contributions, the AAA is diluted. The dilution occurs because the AAA acts as a corporate-level account that measures the per-share ability of stockholders to receive tax-free distributions. This means that the new shareholders immediately become eligible for tax-free distributions. Correspondingly, if the S corporation has accumulated earnings and profits, pre-existing shareholders can no longer withdraw tax free their full share of previously taxed income

---

[101] *See* Reg. § 1.1244(d)–2(a).

[102] I.R.C. § 1368(e). Some technical rules negate any adjustment for tax-exempt income (and related expenses) and federal income taxes for C years, if any. *See* Reg. § 1.1368–2(a)(3)(i)(C).

[103] I.R.C. § 1368(e)(1)(B); Reg. § 1.1368–2(d)(1). The AAA is adjusted first for distributions governed by § 1368(a) and then for redemptions treated as exchanges if both occur during the same taxable year. *Id.*

before triggering the dividend rules of § 1368(c). This state of affairs should be reflected in the purchase price of newly-issued shares, or the corporation should be advised to use up its AAA before admitting new shareholders. Similarly, if distributions are made to new shareholders who have higher basis in their shares, larger distributions will be tax free to such shareholders than to the old shareholders.

In contrast, if the S corporation has significant accumulated earnings and profits, a new shareholder may be unexpectedly taxed on a distribution. Such a shareholder probably would have preferred the corporation to have "zeroed out" its accumulated earnings and profits before entering the picture, so that distributions would simply be tax free up to basis. Having no accumulated earnings and profits would have obviated the need for the AAA altogether. Before consummating a deal, buyers and sellers need to assess carefully the tax consequences of transferring S corporation stock.

¶ 6.20   TRANSACTIONS BETWEEN THE S CORPORATION AND ITS SHAREHOLDERS

An S election will affect transactions between the corporation and its participants (mainly its shareholders) in a number of ways. These interactions go beyond the rules for distributions and passthrough of earnings and losses. They also stand apart from the Subchapter C rules relating to formation, liquidation, and reorganization covered in Chapters 7 and 8. The tax planner and S corporation shareholder should always be mindful of these special consequences.

Such consequences include potential reallocation of shareholder payments between salaries and distributions (¶¶ 3.11 and 9.02) and among family members, as well as suspension (or disallowance) of certain losses or expenses (including interest) under the related-party rule of § 267 (¶ 3.07). Other constraints arise from the S corporation-shareholder relationship. These include the possibility that distribution of appreciated property to a more-than-50% owner may affect the character of the gain (¶ 4.07) and the shareholder's inability to obtain an increase in basis by guaranteeing loans to the S corporation (¶ 6.07).

¶ 6.21   SALES OR OTHER TRANSFERS OF STOCK IN AN S CORPORATION

In general, sales of stock in an S corporation involve similar tax considerations as do sales of stock in a C corporation. Thus, a sale of stock by an S shareholder will generally be treated as the sale of a capital asset.[104] The shareholder's recognized gain or loss on the sale will equal the difference between the amount realized and the stock's adjusted basis.[105]

While an S corporation is generally treated as an entity, Congress has enacted several provisions requiring look-through treatment analogous to partnerships. For example, if an S corporation holds appreciated "collectibles," a portion of the gain on sale of a shareholder's stock may be taxed at the 28% rate applicable to "collectibles gain."[106]

---

[104] A sale of stock will not be treated as the sale of a capital asset if (1) the stock is not a capital asset (within the meaning of § 1221) in the hands of the selling shareholder, or (2) the stock is sold at a loss and is § 1244 stock. In the case of certain related corporations, § 304(a) (along with § 318) may cause a sale of stock to be tested under § 302 for dividend equivalence. *See* I.R.C. § 304(a)(1), (a)(2); *see also* ¶ 7.16.

[105] I.R.C. § 1001.

[106] I.R.C. § 1(h)(5)(B); Reg. § 1.1(h)–1(b).

Look-through treatment does not apply, however, to unrecaptured § 1250 gain (taxed at a 25% rate).[107]

In the case of high-income individuals, § 1411 imposes a 3.8% tax on net investment income (NII) derived from a trade or business that is a passive activity (within the meaning of § 469). Upon disposition of certain active interests in S corporations (and partnerships), § 1411(c)(4) provides an important exception to the § 1411 tax. Proposed regulations limit the amount of net gain subject to the § 1411 tax to the *lesser of* (1) the amount of gain recognized by the seller for normal tax purposes (chapter 1 gain) and (2) the seller's share of net gain from a deemed sale of the passthrough entity's § 1411 property.[108] Similar rules apply for determining the seller's share of net losses from § 1411 property.[109]

The proposed regulations recognize that the character of property may vary among transferors. Some transferors may be "passive" with respect to the property, while other transferors are "active." The passive/active test is applied on an activity-by-activity basis under the principles of § 469.[110] Thus, the key is to determine whether a transferor is active with respect to at least one of the passthrough entity's activities, so that the § 1411(c)(4) exception is available to shelter gain from that activity. If the transferor is not active with respect to any of the passthrough entity's activities, then the entire net gain from disposition of the interest is subject to the § 1411 tax. The § 1411 tax is also coordinated with the § 1374 built-in gain tax and the S termination rules.[111]

> *Example 6.11:* A owns a 50% interest in S Corp., a calendar-year S corporation. In Year 2, A sells her interest (with an adjusted basis of $140,000) for $200,000 and recognizes a gain of $60,000 on the sale (chapter 1 gain). S Corp. is engaged in three trade-or-business activities (X, Y, Z) and also owns marketable securities. A is active only with respect to activity Z.
>
> A's 50% share of gain (or loss) with respect to each of the three activities is: X ($10,000 loss), Y ($16,000 gain) and Z ($50,000 gain). A's share of gain from the marketable securities is $4,000. A's 50% share of net gain attributable to the entity's § 1411 property is $10,000 ($10,000 loss from X plus $16,000 gain from Y plus $4,000 gain from marketable securities). Since the $10,000 net gain allocable to A on a deemed sale of the entity's § 1411 property is less than the

---

[107] By comparison, sale of a partnership interest is subject to full look-through treatment under § 751(a). Thus, a selling partner may recognize a mix of gain from ordinary income assets, collectibles, and residual capital gain. *See* ¶ 10.12.

[108] Prop. Reg. § 1.1411–7(b)(1)(i). For this purpose, § 1411(c) property is property owned by the entity that would give rise to net gain under § 1411(c)(1)(A)(iii) allocable to the S shareholder (or partner) and includable in the S shareholder's (or partner's) NII. *See* Reg. § 1.1411–7(a)(2)(iv). The seller may also qualify for an optional simplified reporting method in lieu of the calculation described in Prop. Reg. § 1.1411–7(b). *See* Prop. Reg. § 1.1411–7(c). The optional method is likely to be helpful if the gain associated with passive assets owned by the passthrough entity is relatively small. It is not available, however, for S corporations that have recently converted from C status.

[109] Prop. Reg. § 1.1411–7(b)(1)(ii).

[110] Under the passive loss rules, taxpayers are already required to allocate net gains and net losses on a disposition among an entity's activities. *See* Reg. § 1.469–2T(e)(3). Thus, the proposed regulations under § 1411 piggyback onto these existing rules under § 469. For purposes of § 1411, however, certain § 469 rules that recharacterize income as passive (rather than active) do not apply. *See* Reg. § 1.469–2T(e)(3)(iii).

[111] The transferor's gain on the deemed sale of assets is not reduced by the § 1366(f)(2) decrease for the § 1374 tax. Prop. Reg. § 1.1411–7(a)(4)(iii). Even if the stock sale causes the S election to terminate (and the date of the transfer is treated as starting a C year), the corporation will continue to be treated as an S corporation for purposes of applying the § 1411(c)(4) exception. *See id.*

gain recognized on sale of A's S stock ($60,000), only $10,000 of A's gain on the stock sale is subject to the § 1411 tax.[112] By contrast, if A were passive with respect to all of the entity's activities, A's entire gain would be subject to the § 1411 tax.

Special rules apply to the disposition of S stock owned by a QSST. Under § 1361(d)(1), the beneficiary of a QSST is treated as the deemed owner of the portion of the trust consisting of stock of the S corporation.[113] Nevertheless, the QSST (rather than income beneficiary) reports gain (or loss) from sale of the S stock.[114] Consistent with this rule, the proposed regulations under § 1411 look to the trust's activities in applying the § 1411(c)(4) exception.[115]

In addition, shareholders should consider certain aspects unique to S corporations when contemplating sale of their stock. These aspects include: (1) the potential termination of S status (¶ 2.17), (2) the normal per-share, per-day passthrough of an S corporation's income and loss[116] (¶ 6.04), and (3) the availability of a § 338 election (or a § 336(e) election) in connection with a disposition of S corporation stock (¶ 7.13). Moreover, shareholders who wish to transfer their S stock will often find that they are subject to transfer restrictions arising out of shareholder agreements or corporate charter restrictions.

¶ 6.22   TERMINATION OF S STATUS CAUSED BY TRANSFER OF SHARES

A transfer of S corporation shares, by sale or otherwise, can result in the termination of a corporation's S status in a number of ways.[117] For example, termination can result if:

(1) the shareholder sells or gives her stock to a prohibited shareholder,[118]

(2) a transfer causes the S corporation to have more than 100 shareholders,[119]

(3) a shareholder dies intestate and her shares in the S corporation pass by the laws of intestacy to a relative who is a nonresident alien or other disqualified shareholder,[120] or to too many shareholders,

(4) more than 50% of the S corporation's shares are sold and the buyers exercise their power to revoke S status (over the objections of the minority shareholders)[121] or

(5) a new current income beneficiary of a QSST affirmatively refuses to consent to an election to have the trust continue to be treated as a QSST,

---

[112] *See* Prop. Reg. § 1.1411–7(b)(2) (ex. 1); *see also id.* (ex. 2).

[113] *See* ¶ 2.08.

[114] Reg. § 1.1361–1(j)(8). Nevertheless, the disposition is treated as a disposition by the income beneficiary solely for purposes of applying §§ 465 and 469. *See* I.R.C. § 1361(d)(1)(C). This rule is favorable because it may free up suspended passive losses under § 469(g).

[115] Prop. Reg. § 1.1411–7(a)(4)(iii)(C).

[116] *But see* Reg. § 1.1377–1(b) (short-year election). *See also* ¶ 2.20.

[117] *See* ¶ 2.19 (tax consequences to the corporation and its shareholders upon termination of S status).

[118] *See* ¶ 2.08.

[119] I.R.C. § 1361(b)(1)(A); *see* ¶ 2.07.

[120] I.R.C. § 1361(b)(1)(C).

[121] I.R.C. § 1362(d)(1); *see* ¶ 2.14.

thus disqualifying the trust from holding S corporation shares and causing termination of the corporation's S status.[122]

Given the risk of termination caused by stock transfers to third parties, shareholders of an S corporation should take protective steps to preserve their corporation's S status in the future. Such protections might take the form of transfer restrictions and first refusal options in shareholder agreements or in the corporation's charter or bylaws. If lawful, perhaps shareholder agreements and restrictive charter provisions can attempt to restrict *any* type of transfer of the S corporation's stock, including transfers by sale or by gift, testamentary transfers, and transfers by operation of law.

¶ 6.23   GAIN OR LOSS AND BASIS CONSEQUENCES OF SALES, GIFTS AND DISPOSITIONS AT DEATH

As mentioned above, if an S shareholder sells or exchanges stock (or debt) in a taxable transaction, gain or loss will generally be realized and computed in the normal way. Thus, gain or loss (generally capital) will equal the difference between the amount realized and basis (adjusted for passthrough items).[123] If the S stock has become worthless (or is sold at a loss), § 1244 may convert a capital loss to an ordinary loss (¶ 6.17).

If stock is transferred by gift, no gain or loss will be realized. Under § 1015, basis will generally carry over (or, for purposes of computing loss, be reduced to fair market value if that is lower).[124] Death of an S shareholder will generally bring into play the fresh-start basis rule of § 1014 for property acquired from a decedent, but the basis step-up will not be available for amounts representing the right to receive income in respect of a decedent (IRD) under § 691.

Under the per-share, per-day allocation rule, a shareholder's share of corporate income or loss can shift every time the shareholder disposes of, or acquires, shares. The per-day amount is calculated by dividing year-end totals by the number of days in the year. Alternatively, an S corporation and all affected shareholders can elect to use the interim closing method to allocate income upon a complete termination of a shareholder's interest.[125] In this event, the S corporation's income will be allocated between the two short taxable years under normal tax accounting rules.

When an S shareholder dies, a proportionate share of both separately and non-separately stated income (or loss) attributable to the pre-death portion of the S corporation's tax year must be included in the decedent's final income tax return under § 1366(a). The post-death income (or loss) for the remainder of the corporation's tax year must be reported by the decedent's estate or heirs. Just as when an S election terminates, the pro rata portions of income (or loss) attributed to the decedent or her estate are

---

[122] I.R.C. § 1361(d)(2)(B)(ii); *see* ¶ 2.08 (permissible trusts, particularly QSSTs).

[123] A portion of the gain may be taxed at the 28% rate if the S corporation holds appreciated collectibles. *See* ¶ 6.21.

[124] *See* I.R.C. § 1015(a); Reg. § 1.1366–2(a)(6).

[125] I.R.C. § 1377(a)(2).

calculated on a per-share, per-day basis. Alternatively, the corporation and affected shareholders can elect to close the books on the date of death.[126] An example follows.

Example 6.12: A and B each own half of X Corp., a calendar-year S corporation. If B dies on September 30, 2024, B's estate will own half of X Corp. for the last quarter of 2024. No election is made to close the books. B's final return will include 37.5% (half of 75%) of each passthrough item; B's estate will report 12.5% (half of 25%). Together, B's return and that of her estate will account for B's full 50% share of the passthrough items.

This same per-share, per-day method applies when a shareholder sells or gives S stock away during the year. Dispositions of S shares in a redemption, liquidation, or tax-free reorganization exchange are covered in Chapters 7 and 8.

¶ 6.24   EFFECTS OF DEATH OF A SHAREHOLDER AND ESTATE PLANNING

When a shareholder of an S corporation dies, a layer of special Subchapter S problems arises. This section will mention the most significant topics.

First, the fresh-start basis rule of § 1014 applies to S corporation stock as "property acquired from a decedent." Thus, there will be a step-up (or step-down) in basis if fair market value differs from adjusted basis before death. Such differences are quite common because of the passthrough system and attendant basis consequences, leaving aside market and inflationary changes.[127] (Of course, under the usual rule of § 1014, an alternate valuation date or special use valuation will be used if an election is made under § 2032 or § 2032A.)

Favorable tax treatment applies to redemption of S shares from an estate in order to pay estate or inheritance taxes or administration expenses, just as in the case of C stock.[128] Other Subchapter C provisions also apply, unless otherwise specified or inconsistent with Subchapter S.

Now come the special Subchapter S aspects. Upon the shareholder's death, the estate becomes a shareholder and, as such, is a "permitted shareholder."[129] Its share of income and loss will pass through, prorated under the general rules.[130]

The § 1014 fresh-start basis may permit large distributions of cash or property tax free to the estate or heirs, when basis is the only rule limiting taxation of such distributions. If the S corporation was once a C corporation, however, the AAA and accumulated earnings and profits account also will be relevant.

Just as the S corporation could have made tax-free distributions to the shareholder before death up to her share of the AAA, distributions may be made to the estate up to the decedent's share of the AAA without tax. This is not surprising, since the AAA is a corporate-level account, not a personal account. The taxation of S corporation income to

---

[126] *See* Reg. § 1.1377–1(b)(4) (clarifying that a shareholder's interest terminates upon death for purposes of § 1377(a)(2)). A gift or § 1041 transfer may also result in a complete termination of the shareholder's interest. *Id.*

[127] Even the community property interest of a surviving spouse in S stock can enjoy a § 1014 fresh-start basis. *See* I.R.C. § 1014(b)(6).

[128] *See* I.R.C. § 303.

[129] *See* I.R.C. § 1361(b)(1)(B).

[130] *See* ¶¶ 6.02, 6.23.

one shareholder builds an account that can benefit another person who is the buyer or other transferee of S shares, upon a later distribution. In theory, this will be reflected in the market value of the shares. Unlike outside basis (in stock or debt), the AAA does not change upon the death of a shareholder.

If the S corporation distributes *more* than the estate's share of the AAA, a dividend will result—up to the corporation's accumulated earnings and profits from C corporation days (or from a C corporation predecessor). If taxation as a dividend will be *dis*advantageous, it may be possible to avoid such treatment through a stock redemption that qualifies for sale or exchange treatment under § 302 (subject to the attribution rules of § 318) or, especially, § 303 (up to death taxes and administration expenses). If either § 302 or § 303 applies, the usual rules will afford basis recovery and capital gain treatment. Since basis is stepped up at death by § 1014, little or no gain should result. (Even though the community property interest of a surviving spouse can benefit from the § 1014 basis step-up, that interest cannot be redeemed under the special rules of § 303.)

A serious problem implicated by the death of a shareholder is potential inadvertent or undesired termination of the S election. The adverse consequences of termination include double taxation of future distributions, elimination of loss passthrough, and ineligibility to re-elect S status for five years. The special rules applicable to the post-termination transition period[131] and possible "waiver" of some innocent and harmless terminations[132] can sometimes soften the blows, but may not entirely repair the damage.

Termination can occur after a shareholder's death in any of several ways.[133] The potentially adverse consequences of termination should be fended off by an advisor planning a shareholder's estate and drafting a will involving S corporation stock. In addition, buy-sell agreements and call provisions should be used to keep the stock of a deceased shareholder out of inappropriate hands. Indeed, a buy-sell agreement provides perhaps the primary safeguard.

If the S election is not revoked at the shareholder's death, corporate-level income will pass through and be taxable each year to the estate, whether or not distributed. This can even create a liquidity problem for some estates. Yet allowing the election to continue may yield overall tax savings for the beneficiaries (and others).[134]

If the estate does revoke the election, a corporate-level tax will have to be paid on future earnings. A shareholder-level tax will also be imposed on future distributions (even of previously taxed income, unless it is distributed during the post-termination transition period). The corporate-level tax will diminish the value of the stock held by the estate. Ill-will created among minority shareholders may redound to the estate's disadvantage.

It may be possible to counteract the effects of a termination due to an estate's distribution of S corporation stock to a disqualified shareholder (for example, a foreign person, a corporation, or an ineligible trust). If a buy-sell agreement is not in effect, other steps can be taken. These include postponing distributions as long as possible and

---

[131] *See* ¶ 4.06.

[132] *See* ¶ 2.24.

[133] *See* ¶ 6.22.

[134] Since shareholders may have conflicting interests, they should be advised perhaps to seek separate counsel when a shareholders' agreement or informal plan is negotiated.

keeping the estate open to continue as the shareholder.[135] Alternatively, the corporation may redeem the S stock from the estate under § 302 or § 303. The stock could also be sold to (some) S shareholders who are beneficiaries or to other persons whose stock ownership will not disqualify the S corporation. If necessary to avoid an undesired termination, it may be possible to obtain unanimous consent of all the beneficiaries to such a sale.

---

[135] Even when state law allows the estate to remain open, federal tax law may deem it closed once its probate and administration functions have been completed. Moreover, holding an estate open for too long may cause the estate's assets (including S stock) to be treated as owned by testate or intestate successors, potentially imperiling S status. *See, e.g., Old Virginia Brick Co. v. Comm'r,* 44 T.C. 724 (1965), *aff'd,* 367 F.2d 276 (4th Cir. 1966).

Chapter 7

TAX ISSUES ON FORMATION, LIQUIDATION, REDEMPTION, TAXABLE ACQUISITION OR DISPOSITION OF AN S CORPORATION

¶ 7.01   GENERALLY; INTERACTION OF SUBCHAPTERS S AND C*

Generally, *formation* of an S corporation is governed by the same rules applicable to C corporations.[1] Consequently, most of the issues are likely to be familiar ones. Nevertheless, even when no special rule applies to an S corporation, certain aspects of the transaction may implicate concerns unique to S corporations. The same holds true, in the S context, for redemptions, liquidations and taxable dispositions of stock or assets. Beginning with the topic of formation, Chapter Seven addresses particular events in the life-cycle of the S corporation in which the rules of Subchapters S and C must be coordinated. Many of the problems arising at the formation stage that deserve special emphasis involve "setting the stage" for successful operation of the future S corporation, including the eligibility and election rules discussed in earlier Chapters.

¶ 7.02   FORMING THE CORPORATION

An S corporation must first be formed as a corporate entity under state (enabling) corporation law before it can elect or attain the status of an S corporation.[2] An election *before* formation will not be valid.[3] In addition, it must be a "small business corporation," *i.e.*, a corporation that meets the eligibility requirements of § 1361(b).

Under the check-the-box regulations, an eligible entity whose default classification is a partnership or a disregarded entity may elect instead to be classified as a corporation and file an S election. To eliminate the burden of requiring an eligible entity to file two separate elections, the regulations generally deem an eligible entity that makes a timely S election and meets the S eligibility requirements to have also made an election to be classified as an association taxable as a corporation.[4] Thus, such an eligible entity will not be required to file a separate entity classification election under § 7701.

¶ 7.03   TRANSFER OF PROPERTY AND CAPITALIZATION

The corporation that will file an S election can be formed and capitalized tax free under the normal rules of § 351 of Subchapter C. By carefully observing these rules, both

---

*   Chapter 7 has a bit of a "how to do it" perspective, one that reviews many prior topics in a practical and planning mode. Some readers may want to skip or skim this chapter, although it can serve as a review and introduces some new material.

[1]   Recall the coordination rule of § 1371(a), which makes explicit that Subchapter C will apply to an S corporation unless otherwise provided in "this title" (that is, the entire Internal Revenue Code) or inconsistent with "this subchapter" (Subchapter S).

[2]   I.R.C. § 1361(b)(1).

[3]   I.R.C. § 1362(a). The election is made by "the corporation," and all shareholders must consent. The regulations specify the manner and time for making the election. *See* Reg. § 1.1362–6. *See also* ¶¶ 2.11–2.12.

[4]   Reg. § 301.7701–3(c)(1)(v)(C). The IRS has also provided a simplified method for taxpayers to request relief for a late S election and a late entity classification election. *See* Rev. Proc. 2013–30, 2013–36 I.R.B. 173.

the shareholders and the corporation can escape recognition of gain or loss, with substituted-basis consequences, if they wish.[5] Alternatively, they can arrange matters so as to recognize gain (or loss) and obtain a fair-market-value basis by falling outside of the scope of the § 351 nonrecognition rules. When they do apply, the rules of § 351 are not elective.[6]

When choosing the capital structure of a corporation intended to elect S status, organizers must be sure to comply with the one-class-of-stock requirement.[7] Without violating that broad limitation, an S corporation may have outstanding stock with differences in voting rights, may issue debt as well as stock, and may qualify all or some of the shares for ordinary loss treatment under § 1244.[8]

An S corporation may seem not to need thin capitalization, given the passthrough system and single tax. Organizers should anticipate that the S election may terminate, however, and that the use of debt held by shareholders could bring substantial tax advantages during C years. Debt basis permits repayments to be received tax free; losses may also be deducted against debt basis (like stock basis).[9] Of course, debt may also be desirable for non-tax reasons—for example, to gain creditor priority in the event of insolvency. For both tax and non-tax reasons, every effort must be made to guard against future reclassification of the debt as equity.[10]

If the shareholders borrow funds in order to purchase stock in the S corporation, or to lend funds to it, interest deductibility will depend on proper characterization of the interest as either investment or business interest under § 163.[11] The characterization of the interest expense is also important for purposes of the passive activity loss rules, potentially affecting not only the regular income tax but also the alternative minimum tax.[12]

If an S corporation's shares become entirely worthless, any loss during the corporation's final taxable year will pass through under § 1366. Thus, shareholders may deduct such "terminal" losses up to their respective bases in stock and debt, notwithstanding the limitations of § 165(g) (losses on worthless securities) and § 166 (losses on bad debts). Any residual loss, consisting of remaining basis in shares reduced by passthrough of terminal losses, will be subject to the limitations under §§ 165 and 166. Except to the extent § 1244 provides relief in the form of an ordinary loss, the capital loss limitations of §§ 1211 and 1212 will apply.

Eligibility for § 1244 stock treatment will often be possible for all or at least some of the S corporation's shares. Ensuring § 1244 treatment is quite important. The costs of

---

[5]   *See* I.R.C. §§ 351, 358. The low basis of contributed property will affect S shareholders when their corporation recognizes the built-in gain or takes depreciation deductions. Subchapter S has no counterpart to § 704(c) in the partnership context, which requires built-in gain or loss on contributed property to be allocated to the contributor. *See* ¶ 10.05.

[6]   Section 351(e) denies nonrecognition treatment on transfers to any corporation that is an investment company. I.R.C. § 351(e)(1). But § 351(e) applies only if the contributors are diversifying by transferring non-identical, readily marketable stocks or bonds. *See* Reg. § 1.351–1(c). Thus, an S corporation may often be used to hold investments without running afoul of § 351(e).

[7]   *See* I.R.C. § 1361(b)(1)(D). *See also* ¶ 2.09.

[8]   *See* ¶¶ 6.17, 11.02.

[9]   *See* ¶ 6.07.

[10]   *See* ¶ 2.09.

[11]   *See* I.R.C. § 163(d) and (j); Temp. Reg. § 1.163–8T. *See also* ¶ 6.14.

[12]   *See* I.R.C. §§ 469(b), 58(b).

qualifying are small, the disadvantages virtually non-existent, and the possible deduction against ordinary income of up to $100,000 loss ($50,000 for a single individual) upon disposition of § 1244 stock can be quite valuable. This follows from the fact that deductibility of capital losses against ordinary income is severely restricted.[13] An investor who has lost $100,000 and can only deduct $3,000 annually as a capital loss against ordinary income (with a capital loss carryover) will likely be very unhappy. Indeed, such a disgruntled investor may even consider a malpractice action against a tax advisor who failed to recommend steps to ensure that § 1244 would apply. The requirements of § 1244 (only individual or partnership shareholders,[14] stock issued only for money or other property, up to $1,000,000 worth of stock, and five years of more-than-50% active income) must be meshed with the Subchapter S requirements. If the initial capitalization would otherwise exceed the aggregate amount of stock permitted under § 1244, it may be possible to issue separately additional (non-§ 1244 stock) at a later date.[15]

The conventional Subchapter C rules also apply to formation of a corporation that will not elect S status at the outset. If and when an S election ever is made, however, the initial period of operation as a C corporation may produce *special*, different, and possibly disadvantageous Subchapter S treatment. This is because an S corporation that formerly was a C corporation will be particularly susceptible to the § 1374 built-in gain tax and the penalty provisions of §§ 1362(d)(3) and 1375 if too much passive investment income is earned.[16] Also, a C corporation may accumulate exposure to the § 531 accumulated earnings tax, exposure that will not disappear completely by virtue of an S election.[17] Personal holding company tax problems may also haunt the corporation after conversion from C to S status, a result avoided by an immediate S election. Investment credit recapture from C years also may trouble the later S electing corporation.[18]

Built-In Loss Property. If an S shareholder contributes "net built-in loss" property to an S corporation, § 362(e)(2) applies. Generally, § 362(e)(2) is intended to prevent duplication of loss by reducing the transferee corporation's basis in the contributed property by the amount of the "excess" basis, unless the shareholder elects, under § 362(e)(2)(C), to reduce stock basis instead. In the case of an S corporation, however, an election under § 362(e)(2)(C) may have the perverse effect of eliminating even a single level of loss.

Example 7.1: A contributes property with a fair market value of $90 and a basis of $100 to X Corp., a newly-formed S corporation, in exchange for all of X Corp.'s

---

[13]   *See* I.R.C. §§ 1211, 1212.

[14]   In *Rath v. Comm'r*, 101 T.C. 196 (1993), the court denied § 1244 loss treatment on shares issued by a C corporation *to* an S corporation, despite arguments that §§ 1363(b) and 1366(b) should be read to pass through the § 1244 treatment to the individual shareholders of the S corporation. While § 1244(a) specifies ordinary loss treatment for stock issued to a partnership, the legislative history is silent concerning similar treatment for stock issued to an S corporation.

[15]   *See* I.R.C. § 1244 and accompanying regulations. Since an increase in basis of § 1244 stock is not itself treated as § 1244 stock, only the stock's original basis will be converted into ordinary loss. *See* I.R.C. § 1244(d)(1)(B); Reg. § 1.1244(d)–2. Thus, contributions of new equity, at least up to the § 1244 ceiling, should always be accompanied by the issuance of new stock to hold the enhanced basis.

[16]   The corporation may also be subject to the add-back rules for corporate preferences and LIFO recapture. *See* I.R.C. §§ 291, 1363(b)(4), (d). *See also* ¶¶ 5.05, 5.07.

[17]   This problem can sometimes be solved after an S election by choosing to treat distributions as coming first out of accumulated earnings and profits (hence as the payment of dividends). *See* I.R.C. § 1368(e)(3).

[18]   *See* ¶ 5.06.

stock. Under § 362(e)(2), X Corp.'s basis in the contributed property is limited to $90 ($100 substituted basis under § 358 less $10 built-in loss). A's pre-contribution loss of $10 is preserved in the basis of A's stock ($100), which is worth $90. Under § 362(e)(2)(C), A may instead elect to reduce her stock basis to $90 to reflect the built-in loss. In this event, X Corp. would take an unreduced basis of $100 in the contributed property. If X Corp. later sells the property for $90, $10 loss would pass through to A, reducing her stock basis to $80. If A then sold her stock for $90 (its fair market value), she would recognize a gain of $10 (offsetting the earlier passthrough loss of $10). Thus, the pre-contribution built-in loss is effectively eliminated if the § 362(e)(2)(C) election is made.[19]

¶ 7.04 SELECTION OF A TAXABLE YEAR AND ACCOUNTING METHOD

Special rules apply to the selection of a taxable year by the corporation that wants to elect S treatment. To eliminate deferral at the shareholder level, § 1378 requires that an S corporation use a calendar year, unless it establishes a business purpose (other than deferral of income to shareholders) for a different fiscal year.[20] Sections 444 and 7519 provide limited relief. Under § 444, an S corporation may elect a fiscal year that results in no more than three months of deferral at the shareholder level (generally, a taxable year ending in September, October or November). The price of the election is that the entity must pay a tax under § 7519 intended to compensate for the shareholder-level deferral attributable to the § 444 election.

The S corporation can adopt its own accounting method within certain limitations. It may use the cash method, unless it is a tax shelter.[21] The choice of accounting method must be made with a full realization that making a change in method later may prove problematic.[22]

¶ 7.05 FORMATION AND CAPITALIZATION STRATEGIES AND PLANNING

At the formation and capitalization stages, the organizers of an S corporation must concentrate on two sets of concerns, defined temporally. The first is to comply with the eligibility and election requirements so that the desired S status is obtained. The second is to make sure that choices at the early stage will have the desired effects in the future, when those early decisions may come home to roost.

Stock. When transfers of property (including cash) are made for stock, the one-class-of-stock rule must not be violated. Abiding by that rule is consistent with some variations in shareholder financial interests. These variations include (1) issuing debt to some—or all—shareholders (whether or not in proportion to stock), (2) employing and compensating (even with profit sharing) some shareholders, (3) renting, leasing or licensing property from persons who also are shareholders and (4) issuing stock options to some shareholders. Furthermore, voting rights may differ without violating the one-

---

[19] *See* Reg. § 1.362–4(f), (h) (ex. 9(ii)).

[20] Reg. § 1.1378–1(b); *see* Rev. Proc. 2006–46, 2006–2 C.B. 859.

[21] I.R.C. § 448. *See* ¶ 3.07.

[22] *See* I.R.C. § 446(e) (requiring consent of the Secretary to change method).

class-of-stock rule.[23] Such differences may arise from the inherent terms of the shares or from a shareholder voting agreement or trust. Section 1244 qualification for less than all shares will not violate the one-class-of-stock rule. S corporation shares must be issued only to *permitted* shareholders, and to the allowed *number* of shareholders, to qualify for election.

If the S corporation is used to incorporate a partnership (or to acquire assets from a partnership), the form of the transaction must be scrutinized to avoid the prohibition on a partnership as a shareholder of an S corporation. Since a partnership is not a permitted shareholder, it should not receive stock of the S corporation (at least if such ownership is other than transitory). To be safe, the partnership should liquidate first, so that individual partners, not the partnership, transfer assets to the S corporation and become its shareholders. Alternatively, the partners can transfer their partnership interests to the S corporation in exchange for stock. The point is to avoid having any shareholder whose nature might jeopardize the S status (even though momentary ownership of S corporation stock during incorporation of a partnership may apparently be disregarded).[24]

A conversion of a partnership into a corporation under a state statute that does not require an actual transfer of the unincorporated entity's assets or interests (a "formless conversion" statute) is treated in the same manner as an election to be reclassified as a corporation under the check-the-box regulations.[25] A partnership that converts to corporate status, either by making a check-the-box election or under a formless conversion statute, is treated as transferring its assets to the new corporation in exchange for stock and then distributing such stock to its partners. The new corporation is eligible to make an S election for its first taxable year.[26]

Debt. The passthrough system that applies to S corporations tends to eliminate the tax-induced bias toward debt financing that is so prevalent among C corporations. Nevertheless, debt may be desirable for tax purposes if the S election were to terminate, as well as for non-tax purposes in the event of insolvency. As mentioned before, it is important to avoid reclassification of debt as equity for both tax (possible termination of the S election) and non-tax purposes.

Debt issuance, service, repayment and forgiveness can have quite different tax consequences in an S corporation. Planning techniques developed in the Subchapter C context should not unthinkingly be carried over to the S context.

When debt is to be used, planners must attend to the difference in outside basis consequences between entity-level debt to a third party and shareholder loans to the corporation. The former yields no basis in the debt to shareholders even if they guarantee it. By contrast, the latter produces shareholder basis (even if shareholders use borrowed funds to loan to the corporation).[27] "Too much" shareholder debt can be reclassified as

---

[23] *See* I.R.C. § 1361(c)(4).

[24] *See* Rev. Rul. 84–111, 1984–2 C.B. 88 (respecting form of transaction); Rev. Rul. 2009–15, 2009–21 I.R.B. 1035 (ignoring momentary ownership of S stock by terminated partnership). *See also* Rev. Rul. 99–5, 1999–1 C.B. 434 (conversion of a disregarded entity into a partnership).

[25] *See* Reg. § 301.7701–3(c)(1)(i), (g)(1)(i); Rev. Rul. 2004–59, 2004–24 I.R.B. 1050 (deemed asset transfer to state law corporation followed by liquidating distribution of stock).

[26] *See* Rev. Rul. 2009–15, 2009–21 I.R.B. 1035 (holding that new S corporation does not have an intervening C short year, since the partnership terminates on the day before the S election).

[27] *See* ¶¶ 6.06–6.07.

stock, possibly as a second class of stock; if held pro rata, however, debt will not be reclassified as an impermissible *second class* of stock.[28]

Interest deductions at the corporate level on debt to shareholders or outsiders will pass through to shareholders. At the shareholder level, deductibility may be restricted— for example, if shareholders lack sufficient basis or the limitations under § 469 or § 163 apply. Loss on nonpayment of an S corporation's *debt* to shareholders will not necessarily receive the same tax treatment as a loss on stock, particularly to the extent favorable treatment under § 1244 applies.[29]

When an S corporation repays its debt to shareholders, the principal repayment will constitute a return of capital, up to basis, and capital gain thereafter. Ordinary interest income will generally be classified as investment income, subject to possible recharacterization under the passive activity loss rules.

The chief disadvantage of *debt* as compared to *stock* in an S corporation is that, under § 1368(b)(1), the shareholder's basis in the debt cannot be used to offset (and render tax free) *distributions* with respect to S stock. Thus, basis in shareholder debt is helpful for purposes of loss passthrough but does not allow distributions to be received tax free.

The initial capital structure, particularly the use of mixed debt and equity, may be difficult to revise later.[30] Forgiveness of corporate *debt* by shareholders (or a shareholder's exchange of debt for equity) may produce cancellation of indebtedness income to the S corporation.[31] Such income will immediately pass through to the shareholders as ordinary income. Forgiveness of *interest* can raise problems as well, particularly for the shareholder who receives stock in return.

Section 351 no longer allows "securities" (namely, long-term debt instruments) to be issued for property without recognition of gain or loss. Shareholders will incur a tax cost on issuing debt for appreciated property in a § 351 exchange, since the debt will be treated as taxable "boot" rather than as nonrecognition property. For transferors who seek to recognize gain or loss on formation transfers, however, § 351 may prove more accommodating.

To ensure favorable tax and non-tax treatment, corporate debt should be evidenced by a promissory note or other instrument; a written instrument is necessary both as *evidence* of the legal debt and to constitute "debt" for technical Subchapter S provisions.[32]

Cancellation of Indebtedness. If debt of an S corporation is forgiven, the discharge income passes through ratably to the S shareholders and increases their stock basis.[33] In the case of an S corporation, § 108(d)(7) provides that the insolvency exception and reduction of tax attributes is applied at the corporate level. In *Gitlitz,*[34] the Supreme

---

[28]   *See* ¶ 2.09.

[29]   A shareholder's loss on worthless debt probably will be treated as a capital loss, as will a loss on non-§ 1244 stock.

[30]   An S corporation can engage in a tax-free recapitalization under § 368(a)(1)(E). *See* ¶ 8.07.

[31]   *See* I.R.C. § 108(e)(8), (e)(10)(A). For the special S corporation rules concerning shareholder contributions of debt, see I.R.C. § 108(e)(6), (d)(7)(C) (ignoring basis reductions under § 1367(b)(2) for purposes of determining debt cancellation income).

[32]   *See* I.R.C. §§ 1271(a)(1), 1361(c)(5).

[33]   I.R.C. §§ 1366(a)(1)(A), 1367(a)(1)(A).

[34]   *Gitlitz v. U.S.,* 531 U.S. 206 (2001). *But see Nathel v. Comm'r,* 615 F.3d 83 (2d Cir. 2010) (rejecting taxpayers' argument, based on the reasoning of *Gitlitz,* that a contribution to capital should be treated as tax-

Court treated debt discharge income as analogous to tax-exempt income; it held that S shareholders were entitled to increase their stock basis to reflect discharge income excludable at the corporate level. Under *Gitlitz*, S shareholders received an unintended windfall, since the basis step-up allowed the passthrough of suspended losses before reduction of favorable tax attributes. Congress overturned the *Gitlitz* result by amending § 108(d)(7)(A) to provide expressly that excludable discharge income does not increase an S shareholder's stock basis.

Accordingly, an S corporation must reduce its tax attributes by the amount of income excluded under § 108(a).[35] For this purpose, any losses suspended under § 1366(d)(1) for the year of the debt discharge (including suspended losses carried forward to that year) are treated as a net operating loss of the S corporation. The excluded income reduces the S corporation's "deemed NOL," *i.e.*, the amount of losses that would have been deductible by the shareholders but for the shortfall in outside basis.[36] Any remaining debt discharge is applied to reduce the basis of the S corporation's assets.[37]

Stock Options. Stock options can alter the respective interests of different groups of investors in an S corporation. One group can be mainly creditors (with a lesser share of passthrough losses) until the options held by that group are exercised. Upon exercise, the balance of shareholdings among the investor groups can be equalized (or reversed), creating the effect of a special allocation.[38]

Stock options or stock itself can be issued for services. In an S corporation, however, employee stock that is restricted and forfeitable (and hence not taxable under § 83) will not serve to make the holder a "shareholder" entitled to passthrough of income and loss.[39] Also, if the stock is to qualify for § 1244 treatment, it must be issued for "money or other property (other than stock and securities)," not for services.[40]

¶ 7.06   SHAREHOLDER AGREEMENTS

In general, the pre-formation, formation and capitalization stage is a time when shareholder agreements and article or by-law provisions must be carefully considered. The special restrictions on an S corporation, such as those found in the permitted shareholder rules, suggest the wisdom of having buy-sell restrictions on transferability of shares. Consideration should also be given to including call or similar provisions that will be triggered by a change of status of a shareholder that would jeopardize S status. The immediate passthrough of the corporation's income may create liquidity problems

---

exempt income for purposes of increasing stock basis); *Ball v. Comm'r*, 742 F.3d 552 (3d Cir. 2014) (shareholders not entitled to increase stock basis by the amount of realized but unrecognized gain on a deemed § 332 liquidation).

[35] *See* I.R.C. § 108(b)(1), (b)(2)(A), (d)(7)(B); Reg. § 1.108–7(d).

[36] If losses are not exhausted, any remaining losses must be allocated ratably based on each shareholder's "excess amount." The excess amount equals the excess, if any, of a shareholder's suspended losses (prior to the reduction) over that shareholder's share of the excluded discharge income. *See* Reg. § 1.108–7(d)(2)(ii). The regulations also preserve proportionately the character of any remaining losses. *See* Reg. § 1.108–7(d)(3), (e) (ex. 5(iii)).

[37] Under § 108, the S corporation can elect to reduce the basis of depreciable assets first. *See* I.R.C. § 108(b)(5).

[38] *See* Eustice, Kuntz & Bogdanski, Federal Income Taxation of S Corporations ¶ 6.04 (5th ed. 2015).

[39] Care must be exercised that such options do not constitute a second class of stock. *See* Reg. § 1.1361–1(*l*)(4)(i), (iii)(B)(2).

[40] *See* I.R.C. § 1244(c)(1)(B).

for shareholders who lack cash to pay the tax. Thus, some agreement about regular distributions of cash may be desirable, if valid under state law. Drafting suggestions and forms are available as models.

¶ 7.07   FORMATION PITFALLS, TRAPS FOR THE UNWARY, AND SOME PLANNING MATTERS

The discussion thus far has suggested a variety of sins (of both commission and omission) to be avoided when forming an S corporation or converting from C to S status. The advantages of having no Subchapter C earnings and profits—in other words an immediate S election—should now be evident. The sting taxes of §§ 1374 and 1375 and the risk of inadvertent termination will be avoided by the S corporation free from the earnings and profit taint (¶¶ 5.02 and 2.18). Since even one dollar of earnings and profits can trigger these adverse effects, special care should be taken to ensure that earnings and profits are definitively zeroed out. An always S corporation (without any assets acquired from a C corporation with a substituted basis) need not worry about the § 1374 built-in gain tax (¶ 5.01).

Other restrictions must also be kept firmly in mind. These include the prohibition on more than one class of stock (¶ 2.09), the risk of having debt recharacterized as equity (¶ 2.09), limitations on stock ownership (¶ 2.06) and similar restrictions discussed earlier. Those forming an S corporation must also be aware of the limits imposed by the at-risk rules (¶ 6.11) and the passive activity loss rules (¶ 6.10).

As to the election itself, timing rules must be observed. An entity cannot elect S treatment until it is a corporation. Consents are required of all shareholders and must be properly filed.[41] Finally, the importance of shareholder agreements on a variety of subjects should not be underestimated (¶ 2.10).

¶ 7.08   LIQUIDATIONS, REDEMPTIONS AND ASSET (OR STOCK) DISPOSITIONS

Subchapter S contains few provisions that explicitly relate to liquidations, redemptions, and asset (or stock) dispositions. Thus, the general rule, as usual, is that Subchapter C applies to S corporations and its shareholders except to the extent otherwise inconsistent with the provisions of Subchapter S.[42] However, even when there are no special rules applicable to S corporations, there are some aspects of these transactions unique to S corporations, stemming from their nature as a passthrough entity with special eligibility requirements.

¶ 7.09   COMPLETE LIQUIDATIONS

Sections 331 and 336 govern the tax consequences to the corporation and its shareholders of complete liquidations of an S corporation,[43] not pursuant to a plan of

---

[41] For rules on the technicalities of elections, see generally Reg. § 301.7502–1.

[42] I.R.C. § 1371(a).

[43] Sections 331 and 336 apply to any complete liquidation other than the liquidation of a subsidiary into its 80% parent. *See* I.R.C. §§ 332, 337.

reorganization.[44] In general, the Code makes little distinction between S corporations and C corporations that completely liquidate.

The S Corporation. The entity-level tax consequences to a liquidating S corporation are governed by § 336. Moreover, owing to the passthrough nature of S corporations, the corporate-level effects of liquidation have immediate effects on the shareholders. If the corporation sells its assets and then distributes the proceeds pursuant to the liquidation, any gain on the sale will be passed through to the shareholders,[45] subject to operation of the § 1374 built-in gain tax.[46] Losses will also be passed through, subject to the § 336(d) loss limitations (discussed immediately below). If the corporation distributes property *in-kind*, pursuant to a complete liquidation, gain or loss (again, subject to the § 336(d) loss limitations) will be recognized as if the property were sold to the distributee at its fair market value.[47] Such gain or loss will be passed through to shareholders, who will receive a corresponding basis adjustment. The net result is just one level of tax, unless the deemed sale triggers the § 1374 sting tax.[48]

There are two situations[49] in which recognition of losses pursuant to a complete liquidation of an S corporation will be either limited or disallowed (as with a C corporation). First, under § 336(d)(1), *no loss* may be recognized by the corporation on the distribution of property to a related person[50] if the distribution either (1) is non-prorata *or* (2) consists of property acquired by the liquidating corporation within five years of the date of distribution in a § 351 transaction (or as a contribution to capital).[51] Second, under § 336(d)(2), loss recognized on any sale, exchange or distribution will be determined by reducing the basis of the property disposed of by the excess of the property's basis over its fair market value when acquired by the liquidating corporation. This rule will apply, however, only if (1) the built-in loss property was acquired in a § 351 transaction (or as a contribution to capital) *and* (2) the acquisition of such property was part of a plan the principal purpose of which was to recognize loss with respect to such property.[52]

The loss limitation rules of § 336(d) were enacted prior to § 362(e)(2). Because the latter provision generally limits the transferee corporation's basis in built-in loss property to its fair market value, the loss limitation rules of § 336(d) will often be unnecessary. Nevertheless, § 362(e)(2) may reduce but not entirely eliminate the built-

---

[44]　In the case of a reorganization, the distribution rules of § 361(c)(4) override §§ 311 and 336. *See* I.R.C. §§ 361(c)(4), 336(c).

[45]　I.R.C. § 1366.

[46]　*See* I.R.C. § 1374; *see also* ¶ 5.01.

[47]　I.R.C. § 336(a). The fair market value will be deemed to be not less than the amount of any liability to which the distributed property is subject or which is assumed by the distributee in connection with the distribution. I.R.C. § 336(b).

[48]　I.R.C. § 1366(a). If § 1374 applies, the gain passthrough is correspondingly reduced. *See* I.R.C. § 1366(f)(2).

[49]　Loss limits other than those contained in § 336(d) are discussed elsewhere. *See* ¶¶ 6.09 (§ 1366(d) loss limitation), 6.10 (passive activity losses), 6.11 (at-risk rules), 6.15 (other loss limitations).

[50]　I.R.C. § 336(d)(1). For purposes of § 336(d)(1), "related person" has the meaning given under § 267. In the context of a liquidating S corporation, a shareholder is a related person if the shareholder owns, directly or indirectly more than 50% of the value of the S corporation's stock. I.R.C. § 267(b)(2).

[51]　I.R.C. § 336(d)(1).

[52]　I.R.C. § 336(d)(2). Any acquisition within two years of the date of adoption of the plan of liquidation is deemed to have been part of a plan to recognize losses. *Id.* Note that § 336(d)(2) applies to *any* sale, exchange or distribution of a liquidating corporation. Thus, any sale in contemplation of a liquidation would likely be subject to the "anti-stuffing" rule of § 336(d).

in loss in contributed property. For example, if the same transferor transfers both built-in loss and built-in gain property in the same § 351 transfer (or contribution to capital), § 362(e)(2) eliminates only built-in losses in excess of built-in gains. Also, § 336(d)(1) may disallow losses on a liquidating distribution to a related party even if the loss accrued subsequent to the contribution. In light of the enactment of § 362(e)(2), Congress may wish to reconsider the role of the § 336(d) loss limitations.

The Shareholders. Section 331 governs the tax treatment of *shareholders* of a liquidating corporation. In general, amounts received by shareholders in a liquidating distribution are treated as received *in exchange* for their stock.[53] Thus, assuming that such stock is a capital asset, shareholders of a liquidating S corporation will generally recognize capital gain (or loss) equal to the value of the distributed property less the basis of their shares.[54] Gain recognized by the corporation on a liquidating distribution of appreciated property will be passed through and taxed to the shareholders, increasing the basis of their stock.[55] Losses at the S corporation level that avoid the § 336(d) limitations will also flow through to the shareholders, reducing their stock basis.[56] These basis adjustments will be taken into account in determining the amount of gain (loss) recognized by the shareholders on the liquidating distribution of cash or property.

If an S corporation that is a former C corporation has accumulated earnings and profits, *nonliquidating* distributions in excess of basis and the AAA will be treated as dividend income (up to the accumulated earnings and profits), rather than as gain from a sale or exchange.[57] By contrast, accumulated earnings and profits do not affect the character of a shareholder's recognized gain on liquidation under § 331.[58] Thus, any shareholder-level gain from liquidating distributions will *not* be treated as a dividend.

The operation of these liquidation rules is illustrated below.

Example 7.2: S Corp., a calendar-year S corporation, has capital assets (worth $1,000,000) which had a basis of $500,000 when contributed six years ago in a tax-free § 351 transaction. B, the sole shareholder of S Corp., has a basis of $750,000 in her shares. If S Corp. is liquidated, it will realize $500,000 in long-term capital gain upon liquidation. That gain will be passed through and taxed to B, with a corresponding increase in B's stock basis. At the same time, B will be treated as though she exchanged her shares for assets worth $1,000,000. B will recognize a capital loss of $250,000, the excess of her stock basis of $1,250,000 ($750,000 increased by $500,000 passthrough gain) over the fair market value of the distributed assets ($1,000,000). The net result to B ($250,000 gain) would be the same if § 336 did not apply and B instead received $1,000,000 cash in redemption of her stock (with a basis of $750,000).

---

[53]   I.R.C. § 331(a).

[54]   *See* I.R.C. §§ 1(h), 1001, 1221. *But see* I.R.C. § 1244 (ordinary loss). *See also* ¶ 6.17.

[55]   *See* I.R.C. § 1367(a)(1).

[56]   I.R.C. § 1367(a)(2). Disallowed losses under § 336(d) should reduce the shareholders' stock basis, under § 1367(a)(2)(D), before determining the shareholder-level gain or loss on liquidation. *See* Reg. § 1.1367–1(c)(2). Although the cited regulation only references § 267(a)(2) disallowed losses, similar principles should apply to § 336(d) disallowed losses. *See* CCA 201421015 (disallowed losses reduce both stock basis and AAA).

[57]   I.R.C. § 1368(c). *See* ¶ 4.04.

[58]   Section 1368 determines the tax consequences of distributions by an S corporation *to which § 301 would otherwise apply.* I.R.C. §§ 1368(a), 331(b) (§ 301 not applicable to distributions in complete liquidation).

Example 7.3: Now assume that S Corp.'s assets (worth $1,000,000) had a value of $1,250,000 and a basis of $1,500,000 when contributed to the corporation six years ago. B again has a basis of $750,000 in her stock. Assume that § 362(e)(2) did not apply upon contribution and that there was no plan to recognize the built-in loss in the assets. Upon a pro rata liquidating distribution when the basis of the assets is unchanged, the corporation will recognize the entire built-in loss ($500,000) which will pass through to B. B's basis in her shares will be reduced to $250,000 ($750,000 less $500,000 passthrough loss). Now, the receipt of $1,000,000 worth of assets in liquidation will result in a $750,000 capital gain for B personally. Of this gain, $500,000 will be offset on B's tax return by the loss passed through from the corporation, and she will pay taxes on the remaining $250,000.[59] The net result would be the same even if § 336 had not applied. In that event, B's outside basis would have remained $750,000, and B would have recognized a $250,000 gain on the liquidating distribution ($1,000,000 fair market value of the property less $750,000 stock basis).

As these examples illustrate, § 336 is likely to matter only if (1) the realized gain inside the corporation is ordinary (so that the ordinary character passes through) or (2) the § 1374 built-in gain tax applies (triggering corporate-level tax). A liquidating distribution of property in exchange for stock may result in a capital loss (rather than a capital gain) to the distributee shareholder.[60] In the case of a loss, § 1244 may operate to convert a capital loss into an ordinary loss from sale or exchange of the distributee's stock.[61]

Shareholders of a liquidating S corporation, like their C counterparts, sometimes would like to be able to defer gain recognition on liquidation. For example, the S corporation may sell its assets in exchange for installment notes and then distribute the installment notes pursuant to the liquidation. If the shareholders and the S corporation qualify, the S corporation will not recognize gain on the distribution of the installment notes.[62] Thus, there will be no immediate shareholder-level gain passthrough or increase in stock basis. The shareholders will not recognize gain when the note is exchanged for their shares in the S corporation but instead will report gain only as they receive payments on the installment obligations.[63] The character of the shareholder's gain will be determined as if the corporate-level gain had been passed through to the shareholders under § 1366. In order to qualify for favorable installment sale treatment, the requirements of both §§ 453(h) and 453B(h) must be met.[64]

Any corporate-level gain or loss recognized on liquidation will pass through to shareholders, with attendant basis consequences and effects on the taxability of actual

---

[59]　On a § 331 liquidation, § 267 does not apply with respect to the distributing corporation or the distributee. I.R.C. § 267(a).

[60]　I.R.C. § 331(a).

[61]　*See* ¶ 6.17.

[62]　*See* I.R.C. § 453B(h).

[63]　I.R.C. § 453(h).

[64]　The requirements are generally that (1) the installment note must be distributed pursuant to a plan of complete liquidation to which § 331 applies, (2) the sale or exchange of the property must have occurred within 12 months after the date of the adoption of the plan and the liquidation must have been completed within that 12 months, (3) if the property is inventory, it must have been sold pursuant to a bulk sale, and (4) if the property is depreciable, the buyer and the shareholder must not be related. *See* I.R.C. § 453(h). The nonrecognition rule of § 453B(h) does not apply to entity-level taxes under §§ 1374 and 1375. *See* I.R.C. § 453B(h) ("except for purposes of any tax imposed by subchapter S").

liquidating distributions received by shareholders. Sometimes the question may arise whether an S corporation should revoke its S election before liquidating, or whether a non-electing C corporation could gain tax benefits by making an S election before liquidating. Because of the § 1374 built-in gain tax, the chances for a C corporation to benefit by a last-minute S election are quite small.

¶ 7.10   SUBSIDIARY LIQUIDATIONS

Since a corporation cannot be an S corporation if it has a corporate shareholder, the provisions governing a tax-free subsidiary liquidation (§§ 332 and 337) normally will not apply to liquidation of an S corporation. Of course, these provisions may come into play if an S corporation owns a C subsidiary and makes a QSub election for the subsidiary. As discussed earlier, a QSub election is treated as giving rise to a deemed liquidation under §§ 332 and 337.[65] Pursuant to the tax-free liquidation, the S parent is deemed to acquire the assets and liabilities of the subsidiary whose separate existence comes to an end.

Suppose X (an S corporation) acquires all of the stock of Y (a C corporation) in a taxable transaction that would otherwise meet the requirements of a "qualified stock purchase" for purposes of § 338.[66] No § 338 election is made, but X elects QSub status for Y immediately after the acquisition. In this situation, the deemed liquidation of Y (as a result of the QSub election) is treated as independent from the stock purchase, consistent with the § 338 regulations.[67] Accordingly, the deemed liquidation is governed by §§ 332 and 337, with no step-up to the basis of the QSub's assets.

Alternatively, suppose X (a C corporation) acquires all of the stock of Y (an S corporation) and makes an S election for itself and a QSub election for Y immediately after the acquisition (but no § 338 election). Since Y is momentarily owned by a C corporation, the deemed liquidation of Y into X (as a result of the QSub election) could potentially expose any appreciation in Y's assets to the § 1374 built-in gain tax. To avoid this result, the QSub regulations ignore the transitory existence of an impermissible corporate shareholder (X).[68] Under this special rule, Y is treated as liquidating into X after X's S election is effective and Y does not become a C corporation for any period.[69]

¶ 7.11   DISPOSITIONS AND ACQUISITIONS: SALE OF SHARES OR ASSETS

As an alternative to liquidation of an S corporation itself, shareholders may consider other forms of "liquidating" their investment. Two such forms are (1) a sale of all or most of the corporation's shares or (2) a sale of all or most of the corporation's assets. These two forms produce different patterns of tax issues and consequences. Further, under § 338 (or the companion provision of § 336(e)), it may be possible to treat a disposition of stock as if it were a disposition of assets for tax purposes. The next sections will take up these topics. The alternative of a tax-free reorganization involving an S corporation is addressed in Chapter 8.

---

[65] See ¶ 2.08.

[66] See ¶ 7.13.

[67] See Reg. § 1.1361–4(a)(2)(ii) (ex. 1). The § 1374 built-in gain tax may apply to the assets of the former C corporation. See I.R.C. § 1374(d)(8).

[68] See Reg. § 1.1361–4(b)(3)(ii).

[69] Id.; see Reg. § 1.1361–4(a)(5)(ii) (ex. 2).

¶ 7.12   SALE OF SHARES (AND CARRYOVER ASSET BASIS)

If the S shareholders merely sell their shares in a taxable transaction in which asset basis carries over in the purchaser's hands, the consequences should be straightforward. The selling shareholders will recognize gain or loss measured, under § 1001, by the difference between their stock basis and the amount realized. Such gain or loss will generally be capital or ordinary depending on the status of the shares in the sellers' hands.[70] The corporation will continue in existence, and the AAA and accumulated earnings and profits accounts will remain unchanged. The S election will remain in effect so long as the purchasers are not disqualified by status or number.[71] The corporation's tax year will continue unless an interim closing is elected (or required). Of course, revocation will be a possibility if, after the sale, a majority of the shares is in the hands of shareholders favoring revocation.[72]

The buyers will take a cost basis in their shares. If they liquidate the corporation, the incoming shareholders will receive the benefit or burden of the gain or loss realized by the S corporation attributable to any difference between the corporation's carryover basis in its assets and their fair market value. Subchapter S, unlike Subchapter K, does not offer any mechanism for equating inside and outside basis following a sale of a shareholder's interest to reflect gain or loss recognized by the seller.[73] Thus, the basis of the S corporation's assets will remain unchanged following a stock sale.

In contrast, if the S corporation's *assets* were sold to the outside purchasers in a taxable transaction, the purchasers would take a cost basis in the assets, presumably equal to their fair market value. The S shareholders would report passthrough gain or loss from the corporate-level asset disposition, increasing or decreasing their stock basis. If the corporation were then liquidated, the shareholders would recognize additional gain or loss attributable to any remaining discrepancy between their stock basis and the amount of the liquidating distribution.

When an S corporation's stock is sold, the basis of the shares sold will be affected by corporate income (or loss) for the year of the sale. Stock basis will not be determinable until after the year is over, unless an election is made to close the corporation's books at the time of sale.[74] Absent an interim closing, events at the corporate level after the sale may affect persons who were shareholders only prior to the sale, possibly resulting in unexpected tax consequences. Even though passthrough items are allocated on a daily basis, post-sale profits or losses still affect the annual totals that are then averaged into daily amounts and prorated. For these purposes, one must consult the passthrough rules of § 1366 and special termination rules of 1362(e).

The key lesson is that the sellers and buyers in a simple stock sale should specifically address in the stock purchase contract various Subchapter S topics, including

---

[70]   *But see* I.R.C. §§ 1244, 304. Special look-through rules apply to an S shareholder's share of collectibles gain taxed at 28%. *See* ¶ 6.21.

[71]   If the sale of stock does terminate the S election, there will be an S short year and a C short year. I.R.C. § 1362(e)(1); *see* ¶ 2.20. If the buyer is a C corporation, it cannot be an eligible shareholder, and the S status of the acquired corporation will thus terminate. If the purchaser is another S corporation and acquires 100% of the S target's stock, the acquiring S corporation may elect to treat the acquired S subsidiary as a QSub. *See* ¶ 7.10.

[72]   *See* I.R.C. § 1362(d)(1).

[73]   *See* I.R.C. §§ 743, 754; *see also* Chapter 10.

[74]   I.R.C. § 1377(a)(2); *see* ¶ 2.20.

continuation of the S election, change of accounting method, and any election to close the corporation's books on the specified effective date of the sale. If S status will or may terminate, it is necessary to specify whether an election will be made to allocate profits and losses to the two short years under normal tax accounting principles.[75] Note that, in the case of an S termination year, the interim closing method is mandatory if 50% or more of the corporation's stock is sold.[76]

Sometimes a purchase of shares of a corporation is coupled with a redemption of shares. A "boot-strap" acquisition may allow the purchaser to acquire the corporation partly for its own assets, especially if the acquired corporation has excess liquid assets.[77] For a seller of S stock, the tax effects of a redemption treated as a § 302 exchange or a § 1368 distribution must be compared with a taxable sale (and with a nontaxable disposition). If the S corporation has accumulated earnings and profits, the buyer may want to weigh the alternatives of (1) withdrawing funds tax free from the S corporation immediately after the acquisition (up to retained AAA), without triggering dividend treatment or (2) having the seller withdraw the funds first and then sell the stock for a lower price.

¶ 7.13 DISPOSITION OF SHARES TREATED AS AN ASSET ACQUISITION—§§ 338 & 336(e)

A corporate buyer of S stock may elect, under § 338, to have the stock acquisition treated as if it were an asset acquisition. A § 338 election makes it unnecessary for an acquiring corporation actually to liquidate the acquired corporation after a stock purchase, in order to obtain a step-up in the basis of the acquired corporation's assets to reflect the price paid for the stock. To so elect, the buyer must make a "qualified stock purchase," as defined in § 338(d)(3), which invokes the ownership requirement of § 1504(a)(2).[78] To elect, therefore, the acquiring corporation must possess stock representing at least 80% of both the total value and the total voting power of the acquired corporation.

The § 338 election can only be made by a purchasing corporation, including an S corporation (the election is unavailable to an individual purchaser). If the election is made, the tax consequences will be essentially the same as if the acquired corporation sold its assets and then, as a new corporation, repurchased the same assets. The actual sale of stock is ignored. If either the acquired or the acquiring corporation is an S corporation, a § 338 election produces some unique results.

If the acquired corporation has an S election in force, the acquisition will terminate the S election. (Recall ¶ 2.08: a corporation is prohibited as a shareholder of an S corporation.) The S short year ends on the day *before* the termination; the target's deemed asset sale occurs during the one-day C short year commencing and ending on the acquisition date (*i.e.*, when the C corporation acquires the requisite 80% control).[79] *Another* C short year begins on the following day. Because of the interaction of §§ 338(a)

---

[75] *See* ¶ 2.20.

[76] *See* I.R.C. § 1362(e)(6)(D).

[77] *See Zenz v. Quinlivan*, 213 F.2d 914 (6th Cir. 1954).

[78] *See* I.R.C. § 338(a)(1), (d)(3), (g), (h)(2).

[79] I.R.C. § 1362(e). The acquired corporation must file a one-day "deemed sale" return as a C corporation. *See* Reg. §§ 1.338–2(c)(8), 1.338–10(a)(3).

and 1362(e)(1), a corporation will thus experience (at least) three short years in this 365-day period.

Under § 1366(e)(6)(D), the S corporation's books will automatically close since, by definition, more than 50% of the S stock will have been sold in the S termination year.[80] The special rule of § 1362(e)(6)(C) ensures that any income resulting from the § 338 election will be taxed to the acquiring corporation on its one-day C short year and thus will not pass through to the selling S shareholders.[81] Since § 1366(e)(6)(D) accomplishes the same result, the protection afforded S shareholders by § 1362(e)(6)(C) is likely superfluous.[82]

Section 338(h)(10) Election. Rather than a regular § 338 election, the purchasing C corporation and the S shareholders may jointly make a § 338(h)(10) election.[83] The advantage of the § 338(h)(10) election is that the basis of the acquired corporation's assets will be stepped up to fair market value with only a single-level tax rather than two taxes (once to shareholders on sale of their stock and again to the acquired corporation on the deemed sale of its assets). If the § 338(h)(10) election is made, the actual sale of stock will be disregarded, and the acquired S corporation will instead be treated as selling its assets with the normal gain (or loss) passthrough and basis consequences. All of the S shareholders (including those who do not sell their stock) must consent to the election.[84] Any gain (or loss) recognized by the target (while still an S corporation) on the deemed sale of its assets passes through to its shareholders under § 1366 and increases the basis of their stock under § 1367.[85] The S corporation is deemed to distribute the sale proceeds to its shareholders in a complete liquidation governed by § 331.[86] To the extent that stock basis has already been increased to reflect previously taxed gain attributable to the deemed asset sale, the S shareholders should generally not recognize any further gain on the liquidation.[87]

If the purchaser is another S corporation and acquires 100% of the S target's stock, the acquiring S corporation may elect to treat the acquired S subsidiary as a QSub. The acquiring S corporation may also make a joint election under § 338(h)(10) with the S target's shareholders, allowing the basis of the S target's assets to be stepped up with only a single-level tax.[88] The QSub election is effective on the day after the acquisition date (after the consequences of the § 338 deemed sale are taken into account).[89]

Section 336(e) Election. Although a § 338 election is only available to a corporate purchaser, § 336(e) extends the principles of § 338(h)(10) to individual purchasers and S corporation targets.[90] Moreover, § 336(e) applies to distributions as well as sales or

---

[80] *See* ¶ 2.20.

[81] *See* I.R.C. § 1362(e)(6)(C) (requiring specific allocation of gain resulting from 338 election).

[82] *See* Eustice, Kuntz & Bogdanski, *supra*, at ¶ 13.06[9][b][ii].

[83] Reg. § 1.338(h)(10)–1(c)(1). If a § 338(h)(10) election is made, S status continues through the acquisition date (including the time of the deemed sale and deemed liquidation). Reg. § 1.338(h)(10)–1(d)(3).

[84] Reg. § 1.338(h)(10)–1(c)(3).

[85] Reg. § 1.338(h)(10)–1(d)(3).

[86] Reg. § 1.338(h)(10)–1(d)(5).

[87] *See* Reg. § 1.338(h)(10)–1(e) (ex. 10) (installment sale). For purposes of the § 1411 tax, a sale of S stock followed by a § 338(h)(10) election is treated as a fully taxable asset sale. In determining a shareholder's net investment income, any additional gain (or loss) on liquidation is ignored. *See* Prop. Reg. § 1.1411–7(a)(4)(i).

[88] *See* Reg. § 1.1361–4(d) (ex. 3).

[89] Reg. § 1.1361–4(b)(4); *see* ¶ 7.10 (consequences if QSub election and no § 338 election).

[90] *See* I.R.C. § 336(e). If both provisions overlap, § 338(h)(10) takes precedence. Reg. § 1.336–1(b)(6)(ii).

exchanges.[91] The tax consequences of a § 336(e) election mimic those of a § 338(h)(10) election. As in the case of a § 338(h)(10) election, a § 336(e) election for an S target will generally result in a stepped-up basis in the S target's assets for the benefit of the purchaser, at the cost of only a single-level tax on the S target's shareholders, who increase their stock basis for any net recognized gain.

A § 336(e) election may be made if S shareholders sell 80% or more of an S corporation's stock within a 12-month period.[92] The S target shareholders may sell their stock to other individuals. As in the case of a § 338(h)(10) election, all of the S target shareholders (not just the selling shareholders) must consent to the election.[93] The S shareholders must enter into a binding, written agreement with the target, which must be filed with the target's final return.[94]

If a § 336(e) election is made, the actual sale of the S stock is ignored, and the transaction is treated instead as a sale of the S target's assets.[95] The deemed asset sale generally triggers corporate-level gains and losses that pass through to the S target's shareholders under § 1366, with corresponding adjustments to basis under § 1367.[96] The S target is treated as distributing the proceeds to its shareholders in a complete liquidation governed by §§ 331 and 336.[97] The target's S election is terminated, but the purchasers may elect S status for the new corporation, which is deemed to acquire the S target's assets with a stepped-up basis.[98]

¶ 7.14   SALES OF ASSETS

Instead of liquidating their S corporation, shareholders may instead have the corporation sell all (or most) of its assets. The corporation may then distribute the sale proceeds in liquidation or perhaps reinvest the proceeds. The tax consequences of an asset disposition are considered here.

A sale of an S corporation's assets will, under familiar principles, produce corporate-level gain or loss and a passthrough, with character intact, to shareholders. Such a sale may be undertaken for exclusively non-tax reasons or may be driven, or colored, by tax considerations. For example, an installment sale offers the shareholders the benefit of installment reporting, when they cannot structure the deal as a sale of shares. They can even receive the installment notes from the S corporation in liquidation without accelerating gain (with the character of the gain in the corporation's hands preserved).[99] Alternatively, the S corporation may sell assets rather than liquidate in order to preserve the *ordinary* loss status inherent in corporate assets. These permutations are illustrated below.

---

[91]   Reg. § 1.336–1(b)(6)(i).

[92]   *Id.*

[93]   Reg. § 1.336–2(h)(3).

[94]   *Id.; see* Reg. § 1.336–2(h)(8) (ex. 2).

[95]   Reg. § 1.336–2(b)(1)(i)(A).

[96]   Reg. § 1.336–2(b)(1)(iii)(A).

[97]   *Id.* Under § 331, the target S shareholders may recognize gain (or loss) on the liquidating distribution, after taking into account any adjustments to their stock basis to reflect the corporate-level consequences of the § 338 deemed asset sale.

[98]   Reg. § 1.336–2(b)(1)(ii).

[99]   *See* I.R.C. §§ 453(h), 453B(h), 331. *See also* ¶ 7.09.

Example 7.4: S Corp. has assets with a basis of $500 and a fair market value of $2,000. A owns all the stock of S Corp., with a basis in her stock of $500. A wishes to sell the corporation to Mega Corp., but Mega Corp. refuses to buy stock, offering instead to purchase just the assets for $2,000. If Mega Corp. pays all cash at once, S Corp.'s gain ($1,500) will pass through and be taxed to A, increasing A's stock basis to $2,000 ($500 increased by $1,500 passthrough gain). A may now withdraw the $2,000 cash from corporate solution without paying any further tax.

Example 7.5: Suppose Mega Corp. offers to pay for the assets with a 25-year note, having a face value of $2,000 (and bearing adequate stated interest). After S Corp. sells the assets, it may either retain the note or distribute it to A in complete liquidation. If S Corp. has C earnings and profits and decides to retain the note (and has no other activity), it must be careful not to run afoul of the sting tax under § 1375 and the termination threat of § 1362(d)(3), discussed in ¶¶ 5.02–5.04. If S Corp. instead distributes the note to A, A will be taxed on the gain only as Mega Corp. makes payments on the note, provided that the requirements of §§ 453(h) and 453B(h) (discussed in ¶ 7.09) are met.

When an asset disposition is contemplated, especially one that leaves a "shell" S corporation receiving investment income in the form of interest payments, careful thought must be given to operation of the sting tax provisions, but only if the S corporation was once a C corporation (or otherwise has C attributes). If an S corporation plans to revoke its election or sees termination looming, it may choose to sell some of its assets during the S years to avoid the double-tax burden of selling or distributing assets while a C corporation.

¶ 7.15   SALE OF QSUB STOCK TREATED AS ASSET SALE

QSub status will normally end if QSub stock is sold, since the S parent will no longer own 100% of the former QSub.[100] If a termination results, a special rule treats the stock sale as a sale of a portion of the QSub's assets to the purchaser. Following the deemed asset sale, the purchaser and the former S parent are deemed to contribute all of the QSub's assets (and assumed liabilities) to a new corporation in a § 351 exchange.[101] But for this relief provision, the S parent might be taxed on the entire gain in the former QSub's assets if it lacked 80% control following the sale.

For example, assume an S parent sells 21% of the stock of a QSub to an unrelated buyer, terminating QSub status. The stock sale is ignored and the S parent is instead treated as selling an undivided interest in a portion of the QSub's assets. Although the S parent is taxable on the gain attributable to the sold portion of the assets, the formation of the new corporation is governed by § 351.[102] Thus, the new corporation is treated as acquiring its assets in a tax-free transaction, with the former S parent and buyer contributing their respective shares of the assets.

Suppose that an S parent instead sells 100% of the stock of a QSub to an unrelated buyer. In this event, the regulations simply treat the S parent as selling the QSub's

---

[100]   *See* Reg. § 1.1365–5(a)(4) (ex. 1) (sale of one share).

[101]   I.R.C. § 1361(b)(3)(C)(ii).

[102]   *See* Reg. § 1.1361–5(b)(3) (ex. 5).

assets to the buyer who then contributes the assets to a new corporation.[103] Thus, the buyer obtains the benefit of a cost basis in the assets without the need for a § 338 election (regardless of whether the buyer is a corporation). The deemed sale of assets will, of course, be fully taxable to the S parent.

¶ 7.16   REDEMPTIONS AND PARTIAL LIQUIDATIONS

An S corporation's transfer of property (including cash) to its shareholders in exchange for stock may be treated either as a redemption exchange or as a distribution with respect to the stock (possibly a dividend). In both the C and S contexts, the rules of §§ 302, 303 and 304 (discussed in Chapter Six) apply in distinguishing between redemption exchange and distribution treatment. In a redemption exchange, the shareholder will generally recognize capital gain or loss[104] equal to the difference between the fair market value of the property received and the basis allocated to the shares redeemed.[105] By contrast, if the stock redemption fails to qualify as a sale or exchange, the distribution rules of rules of § 1368 will apply.[106] Under § 1368(b)(1) and (c)(1), the distribution will be tax free to the extent of the shareholder's stock basis (up to AAA).[107] Any excess will generally be taxed as capital gain, except to the extent it is treated, under § 1368(c)(2), as a dividend out of accumulated earnings and profits.

A cash redemption (or distribution) does not trigger gain or loss to the distributing corporation. If property other than cash is distributed, gain (but not loss) is recognized at the corporate level, under § 311, equal to the excess of the fair market value of the property over its basis in the S corporation's hands. Gain recognized by the S corporation will pass through and be taxed to the shareholders.[108] (If § 1374 applies, the built-in gain will also be taxed at the corporate level and the passthrough items will be reduced by the corporate-level tax.[109])

Sale or exchange treatment will apply if the redemption satisfies the requirements of § 302(b) or § 303.[110] Under § 302, a distribution in redemption of shares is generally treated as a sale or exchange only if it is either (1) not essentially equivalent to a dividend,[111] (2) "substantially disproportionate,"[112] (3) in complete redemption of the

---

[103] *See id.* (ex. 9).

[104] Unless the corporation's books are closed, a redeemed shareholder's share of income or loss will be determined on a per-share, per-day basis. I.R.C. § 1377(a)(2); *see* ¶ 2.20.

[105] *See* I.R.C. § 302(a).

[106] Note that § 1368 applies only to distributions to which § 301 would otherwise apply (*i.e.*, distributions falling outside § 302(b) or § 303). The tax treatment of § 1368 distributions is discussed more fully in Chapter 4.

[107] If the redemption is treated as a § 1368 distribution, the AAA and accumulated earnings and profits will be adjusted accordingly. *See* I.R.C. § 1368(e)(1)(A); Reg. § 1.1368–2(a)(3)(ii); *see also* I.R.C. § 1371(c)(3).

[108] I.R.C. § 1366(a); *see* ¶ 4.07.

[109] I.R.C. §§ 1374, 1366(f)(2); *see* ¶ 5.01.

[110] As discussed below, § 303 allows exchange treatment on the redemption of shares held by the estate or beneficiaries of a deceased shareholder. I.R.C. § 303.

[111] I.R.C. § 302(b)(1); *see also U.S. v. Davis*, 397 U.S. 301, 313 (1970) (a redemption is essentially equivalent to a dividend unless it results in "a meaningful reduction of the shareholder's proportionate interest in the corporation").

[112] I.R.C. § 302(b)(2). In general, a redemption is "substantially disproportionate" if, after the redemption, the redeeming shareholder owns less than 50% of the voting power of the corporation and the percentage of voting stock owned by the shareholder after the redemption is less than 80% of the shareholder's former percentage ownership. *Id.*

shareholder's interest in the corporation,[113] or (4) in partial liquidation of the corporation.[114]

A distribution will be deemed to be in partial liquidation if (1) it is not essentially equivalent to a dividend (determined at the corporate rather than the shareholder level)[115] *and* (2) is made pursuant to a plan and occurs within the tax year the plan is adopted or the succeeding tax year.[116]

When testing a transaction under § 302, the ownership attribution rules of § 318(a) apply, unless they can be waived under § 302(c). Thus, it may be difficult to qualify for redemption exchange treatment under § 302(a) if, as will often be the case, the shareholders of an S corporation are related. In appropriate circumstances, § 304 can apply.[117]

The Code sections dealing with redemptions and partial liquidations apply to both S corporations and C corporations alike. S shareholders should carefully consider whether they want a receipt of property to be treated as a § 1368 distribution *with respect to* stock or, instead, as redemption exchange. As long as the S corporation has never been a C corporation (or otherwise acquired accumulated earnings and profits), an S shareholder will generally prefer a § 1368 distribution, which will be tax free to the extent of the basis in *all* the shareholder's stock.[118] If redemption exchange treatment applies, a shareholder's basis recovery is limited to the basis properly allocable to the shares redeemed.

If the S corporation does have accumulated earnings and profits but lacks a sizeable AAA balance, however, redemption exchange treatment may be most favorable.[119] Under such circumstances, a § 1368 distribution may be taxed almost entirely as a dividend,[120]

---

[113] I.R.C. § 302(b)(3). When applying § 302(b)(3), the family attribution rules of § 318(a) can be waived if the redeemed shareholder (1) retains no interest in the S corporation other than as a creditor, (2) does not acquire an interest (other than stock acquired by gift or inheritance) within 10 years of the distribution, and (3) agrees to notify the IRS of the acquisition of any prohibited interest within 10 years of the redemption. *See* I.R.C. § 302(c)(2).

[114] I.R.C. § 302(b)(4). In addition, the distributee shareholder must not be a corporation if the distribution is to qualify for partial liquidation treatment. Stock held by a partnership, estate or trust is treated as if actually held by the entity's partners or beneficiaries. I.R.C. § 302(e)(5). Individual S shareholders should be treated in a manner similar to partners for this purpose, although the statute may need to be amended to achieve this result.

[115] A distribution will be deemed to be not essentially equivalent to a dividend, determined at the corporate level, if (1) the distribution is attributable to the corporation ceasing to conduct, or consists of the assets of, a separate trade or business which the corporation has actively conducted for five years prior to the date of the distribution and which was not acquired in a taxable transaction within such five-year period (a "qualified trade or business"), and (2) the distributing corporation is actively engaged in a qualified trade or business immediately after the distribution. *See* I.R.C. § 302(e)(2), (3).

[116] I.R.C. § 302(e)(1)(B).

[117] *See Hurst v. Comm'r*, 124 T.C. 16 (2005) (§ 304 issue raised but not decided).

[118] I.R.C. § 1368(b)(1). A shareholder will recognize capital gain to the extent that the fair market value of the distributed property exceeds the shareholder's total stock basis. I.R.C. § 1368(b)(2). *See* Rev. Rul. 95–14, 1995–1 C.B. 169 (redemption characterized as § 301 distribution by virtue of § 301(d); entire redemption treated as a tax-free § 1368 distribution that reduced AAA).

[119] On the tax consequences to the shareholders of a § 1368 distribution, see generally Chapter 4. Under § 1368(e)(1)(B), if the redemption is treated as an exchange, the AAA and accumulated earnings and profits will be reduced proportionately. I.R.C. §§ 1368(e)(1)(B), 1371(c)(2); Reg. § 1.1368–2(d)(1).

[120] I.R.C. § 1368(c).

while a redemption exchange allows at least partial basis recovery.[121] In addition, a shareholder may be able to recognize a loss in her stock if a transfer is treated as a redemption exchange rather than as a § 1368 distribution. Shareholders in different positions may have different or inconsistent interests. Thus, it may be helpful to have an agreement or declaration in connection with a redemption, specifying among the shareholders the understood or agreed character of the transaction.

¶ 7.17   SECTION 303: REDEMPTION OF STOCK TO PAY DEATH TAXES

If certain conditions are met, § 303 provides sale or exchange treatment for a redemption of shares held by a deceased shareholder's estate (or beneficiaries).[122] A distribution in redemption of stock included in determining the gross estate of a decedent (for federal estate tax purposes) may qualify, under § 303, to the extent of the sum of: (1) the estate, legacy and succession taxes imposed because of the decedent's death, and (2) funeral and administrative expenses deductible by the estate under §§ 2053 or 2106.[123] Because the basis of the redeemed shares will be stepped up upon the shareholder's death under § 1014, there is likely to be little or no tax cost to the estate or heirs on the redemption. In order for § 303 to apply, the amounts must generally be distributed within a specified period after the decedent's death.[124] In addition, the value of the stock owned by the deceased shareholder must exceed 35% of the shareholder's gross estate less the estate's allowable deductions under § 2053 or § 2054.[125]

---

[121] *See* Rev. Rul. 77–245, 1977–2 C.B. 105. Under § 302(b)(4), partial liquidation treatment may apply even if shareholders fail to surrender any stock. *See* Rev. Rul. 90–13, 1990–1 C.B. 65 (deemed surrender of stock).

[122] I.R.C. § 303.

[123] I.R.C. § 303(a).

[124] I.R.C. § 303(b)(1). Distributions must generally occur within three years plus 90 days (with certain extensions) after the decedent's death.

[125] I.R.C. § 303(b)(2).

Chapter 8

TAX-FREE REORGANIZATIONS INVOLVING S CORPORATIONS

¶ 8.01   REORGANIZATIONS AND DIVISIONS OF S CORPORATIONS*

Because an S corporation is a corporation, not a partnership, and is generally governed by Subchapter C, it can qualify to engage in tax-free reorganizations and divisions.[1] This ability represents one of the main advantages of S corporations over partnerships and some other passthrough forms of business organization. It also suggests why thinking of an S corporation as being taxed analogously to a partnership may often be misleading.

In general, the normal rules under Subchapter C governing reorganizations apply in the S context.[2] When an S corporation is involved, however, special considerations and collateral consequences may come into play. Chapter 8 discusses tax-free reorganizations and divisions from the perspective of S corporations, as transferors or transferees or otherwise as participants in these transactions.[3]

The six basic and two hybrid forms of reorganization are defined in § 368(a). Divisive reorganizations or corporate divisions are covered by § 368(a)(1)(D) and by § 355. S corporations are most often involved in acquisitive A or C reorganizations, or in divisive D reorganizations, for reasons that will become apparent. Perhaps because S corporations have historically been relatively small, closely held businesses with simple capital structures, their use of tax-free reorganizations most often has been to engage with commonly-owned corporations or to realign ownership among them. As S corporations have grown larger in terms of assets and revenue, however, their role is no longer so limited. Indeed, a large S corporation may be an attractive target for a publicly held corporation, although such a combination would mean loss of S status.

The principal issues for S corporations when participating in tax-free reorganizations tend to cluster around the topics of qualifying to participate, potential termination of S status, the taxation of income and losses in the pre- and post-

---

*   Chapter Eight involves rather advanced materials, including complex reorganization rules as applied to S corporations. These topics go beyond the usual coverage of an introduction to Subchapter S. Some readers may wish to proceed directly to the following chapters and their comparisons of S corporations with non-electing C corporations and partnerships.

[1]   Under former § 1372(a), an S corporation in its capacity as a shareholder of another corporation was treated as an individual. Nevertheless, this rule was not viewed as blocking S corporations from participating in acquisitive or divisive reorganizations.

[2]   *See* I.R.C. §§ 368, 354, 355, 361, 358, 362. A reorganization may be undertaken by one or more C corporations in order to make an S election feasible by arranging to meet the eligibility qualifications. A reorganization requires a "business purpose," "continuity of interest," and "continuity of business enterprise." Reg. § 1.368–1(b). Whether qualifying for an S election satisfies the business-purpose requirement of *Gregory v. Helvering*, 293 U.S. 465 (1935), remains unsettled, though there will often be other valid business purposes that may suffice. Presumably, an incorporation and S election that is undertaken in contemplation of a tax-free reorganization or division would not be objectionable. *See Dover Corp. v. Comm'r*, 122 T.C. 324 (2004) (no business purpose required for check-the-box election).

[3]   Taxable acquisitions and dispositions were covered in Chapter Seven.

reorganization taxable year, eligibility to elect or re-elect Subchapter S treatment, carryover or transfer of corporate attributes or taints, tax treatment of accompanying or contemporaneous distributions, and use of suspended losses. These issues are discussed below as they apply to corporate reorganizations and divisions involving S corporations.

¶ 8.02   TYPE A REORGANIZATIONS—MERGERS AND CONSOLIDATIONS

When an S corporation is to be combined with another corporation (whether an S or C corporation), the A reorganization merger (§ 368(a)(1)(A)) offers itself as a flexible and convenient form. (Note that the C "practical merger" (§ 368(a)(1)(C)), discussed in ¶ 8.04, may serve a related function.) In an A reorganization, the type of consideration used is not limited by statute, although the continuity of interest doctrine may limit the total amount of boot or debt to be employed.[4] As a corporation under state corporate and enabling law, an S corporation can merge or consolidate without any special corporate law problems.

If an S corporation is the acquiror (surviving) corporation, its S status will normally continue. Although nothing in the tax law automatically terminates the S election, termination can result if the merger causes the S corporation to have a prohibited shareholder, to have a second class of stock, to have more than the permitted number of shareholders (100), or if more than 50% of the shareholders consent to a revocation. (These topics were discussed in ¶¶ 2.08, 2.09 and 2.16.) If the S election *does* terminate, a new election cannot be made for five years, unless permission is granted to re-elect sooner.[5] To avoid this result, prohibited shareholders may be cashed out or given only debt in the merger exchange. Careful attention should be given in advance to whether the acquiror's S election is to be revoked or continued, and new shareholder agreements may well be in order.

If the S corporation is the target (transferor) in a merger or consolidation, the corporation's S status will end because it will no longer exist as a separate entity. The acquired corporation retains its S status through the end of its existence; thus, there is no "termination" of its S election with respect to its final taxable year.[6] This lack of a termination may have important consequences for the ability of the surviving corporation to elect S status. As of the date of the reorganization, all items of income and loss will pass through to the S target's shareholders, thereby accelerating the passthrough consequences.

If an S corporation is merged into a *new* corporation, the surviving or new corporation may generally make an immediate S election. An immediate election is permitted because there was no technical termination of the target's S status, despite its disappearance as a separate entity.[7] By contrast, if a *surviving* corporation was an S

---

[4]   The regulations provide that 40% continuity is sufficient. *See* Reg. § 1.368–1(e)(2)(iv) (ex. 1).

[5]   I.R.C. § 1362(g). *See* ¶ 2.14 *et seq.*

[6]   *See* Rev. Rul. 64–94, 1964–1 C.B. 317. The event that would otherwise cause disqualification (*i.e.*, the target's ceasing to be a small business corporation) coincides with the close of its taxable year as of the date of the transfer. *See* I.R.C. §§ 1362(d)(2), 381(b)(1); *see also* Eustice, Kuntz & Bogdanski, Federal Income Taxation of S Corporations ¶ 12.02[2] (5th ed. 2015).

[7]   *See* Rev. Rul. 70–232, 1970–1 C.B. 177 (involving consolidation of two S corporations).

corporation but lost or revoked its S status, no new election would be possible for five years without special permission.[8]

If an acquiring S corporation retains its S status, as will normally be the case, special issues arise concerning allocation of income and loss. Under the normal passthrough rules, corporate income and loss for the *entire* tax year that includes the reorganization will be allocated per-day, per-share among all shareholders.[9] Absent an elective (or mandatory) interim closing of the corporation's books, it does not matter whether such items actually arose before or after the merger. There may be shifting of income (or loss) since the passthrough items will be shared among the surviving corporation's original shareholders (including any who were redeemed pursuant to the reorganization) as well as the target's former shareholders who received acquiror stock in the reorganization.

Alternatively, the acquiring S corporation may be permitted (or required) to use the interim closing method of allocating income (and loss). For example, the acquiring corporation can elect to close its books if a shareholder's interest in the acquiring corporation is completely redeemed, but only if all affected shareholders consent.[10] The acquiring corporation may also take advantage of the interim closing rules under the § 1368 regulations. In particular, these rules permit an election to close the books if the acquiror issues stock to new shareholders equal to at least 25% of the previously outstanding stock.[11]

When two S corporations merge (and the surviving corporation retains its S status), the target's positive or negative AAA carries over.[12] Thus, former target shareholders may receive the benefit of tax-free distributions from the combined AAA, even though the earnings arose before they were shareholders in the acquiring corporation. Conversely, the original shareholders of the surviving corporation may find that the benefit of the AAA is diluted, since it must now be shared with the new shareholders. Here is an illustration:

Example 8.1: On January 1, 2023, two calendar-year S corporations (S1 and S2) merge: S1 (with five shareholders and no AAA) merges into S2 (with five shareholders and an AAA of $1,000). Neither corporation has accumulated earnings and profits from C years. Although S1 ceases to exist, some important tax attributes carry over to S2. Prior to the merger, each of the five original shareholders of S2 could have received up to $200 in tax-free distributions from the AAA. Following the merger, their proportionate share of the AAA has been reduced by half. (There are now twice as many shareholders to claim a piece of the pie.) Now, a post-reorganization distribution of $200 to each of S2's original shareholders will likely be treated partially as a § 1368(b)(1) tax-free distribution out of the AAA ($100) and partially as basis recovery or gain from sale or exchange ($100).[13]

---

[8]   I.R.C. § 1362(g). This assumes the new corporation qualifies as a "successor corporation." *See* Reg. § 1.1362–5(b).

[9]   I.R.C. §§ 1366, 1377(a)(1).

[10]   I.R.C. § 1377(a)(2).

[11]   Reg. § 1.1368–1(g)(2)(i)(C); *see* ¶¶ 2.20, 6.04.

[12]   Reg. § 1.1368–2(d)(2) (referring to transactions to which § 381(a)(2) applies).

[13]   To avoid a disproportionate distribution, each of S1's former shareholders should also receive a $200 distribution, half of which would be covered by S2's AAA.

If S1 were instead a C corporation (with $1,000 of accumulated earnings and profits), S2's AAA would again be diluted but now S2 would also inherit S1's accumulated earnings and profits.[14] Thus, a post-reorganization distribution of $200 to each of S2's original shareholders would be treated partially as a tax-free § 1368(b)(1) distribution out of the AAA ($100) and partially as a taxable § 1368(c)(2) distribution ($100) out of former S1's accumulated earnings and profits.

As indicated above, an acquiring S corporation may inherit earnings and profits of an acquired C corporation, adversely affecting the tax treatment of subsequent distributions. The acquiring S corporation may also become exposed to the penalty provisions of §§ 1362(d)(3) and 1375 relating to excess passive investment income. In addition, an S corporation that acquires appreciated assets from a C corporation may become subject to the § 1374 built-in gain tax. Generally, an acquiring S corporation will not be allowed to use NOLs of an acquired C corporation,[15] though it can carry forward the NOLs for use in the event the S election terminates. An inherited NOL may, however, be used against the § 1374 tax on built-in gain attributable to assets of the acquired corporation.[16]

Of course, an acquired S corporation will never have generated NOLs, since the losses will have passed through to its shareholders. Provided the acquiring corporation is an S corporation, the regulations permit carryover of any suspended losses of a target shareholder (as a shareholder of the acquiring corporation) for the benefit only of that shareholder.[17] If a target shareholder does not receive any stock of the acquiring corporation, the loss carryover simply disappears.[18] A shareholder with suspended losses may consider increasing stock basis prior to the merger to ensure deduction of any suspended losses.

If the merger *terminates* the acquiring corporation's S status (*e.g.*, because a prohibited shareholder acquires stock), the normal termination rules apply for purposes of allocating passthrough items. There will be an S short year, ending on the day before the merger, and a C short year, beginning on the day of the merger.[19] Shareholders will have the chance to elect the interim closing method rather than the per-share, per-day method for attributing items to each of the two years. Only persons who were S shareholders during the S short year and any who were shareholders on the first day of the C short year need consent to the election. Because the S election is terminating, the interim closing method is mandatory upon a sale or exchange of 50% or more of the S stock.[20]

---

[14]   *See* I.R.C. § 381(c)(2).

[15]   I.R.C. § 1371(b)(1).

[16]   *See* I.R.C. § 1374(d)(8); Reg. § 1.1374–1(c), 1.1374–8(a); *see also* ¶ 5.01. Under § 361(a), no gain or loss will generally be recognized on a transfer of assets to a corporation which is a party to the reorganization. Nevertheless, the § 1374 tax may be triggered under the provision governing distribution of boot. *See* I.R.C. § 361(c)(2)(A).

[17]   *See* Reg. § 1.1366–2(c)(1). If two S corporations merge, there is no post-termination transition period. By contrast, if the acquiror is a C corporation, a post-termination transition period commences. Suspended losses can be carried over only by shareholders who owned stock of the target S corporation at the time of the S termination. *See* Reg. § 1.1377–2(b).

[18]   Reg. § 1.1366–2(a)(5).

[19]   I.R.C. § 1362(e)(1).

[20]   *See* I.R.C. § 1362(e)(6)(D).

¶ 8.03   TYPE B REORGANIZATIONS—STOCK FOR STOCK

The two-sided survival prospects in a B reorganization contrast with the one-sided survival prospects in an A reorganization. If an S corporation participates in a B reorganization (under § 368(a)(1)(B)), it will usually survive, either as a parent of the acquired corporation or as a subsidiary of the acquiring corporation. Either possibility may, however, raise problems for continued S status.

If an S corporation acquires a subsidiary in a B reorganization, the S status of the acquiring corporation generally continues. By contrast, if an S corporation is acquired in a B reorganization, its S status will terminate because it has a prohibited corporate shareholder.[21] The termination occurs, under § 1362(d)(2)(B), as of the date of the reorganization. Thereafter, S status cannot be re-elected, without special dispensation, for five years.[22]

If the acquiring corporation's S status terminates (e.g., because of a prohibited corporate shareholder), it will have two short tax years. The normal per-share, per-day allocation rules will apply unless the interim closing method is elected (or required).[23] If the acquiring corporation's S election survives, the passthrough items for the *entire* year (without regard to whether they arose before or after the reorganization) will flow through to the shareholders (including any departing or new shareholders). The new shareholders will also be able to take advantage of the acquiring corporation's AAA. This "unfair" dilution of the AAA can be countered by making pre-reorganization distributions, so as to avoid sharing the AAA with the new shareholders.

In the case of an acquired corporation whose S status terminates, the post-termination transition period (PTTP) will last at least one year.[24] Normally, suspended losses may be deducted until the end of the PTTP if the shareholders have sufficient stock basis. But if the former target shareholders own only stock of the acquiring corporation, § 1363(d)(3) may literally disallow any loss deduction.[25] Thus, such shareholders would be well-advised to ensure use of those losses prior to the reorganization through additional capital contributions or other means.

If some minority shareholders continue to own target stock, they may be able to obtain tax-free distributions, under § 1371(e), from the target's AAA.[26] Pre-reorganization distributions by the target to its shareholders should not adversely affect qualification as a B reorganization, as long as such distributions are not funded by the acquiring corporation. Since a B reorganization involves an exchange of stock *solely* for stock, cash distributions during the reorganization should be avoided.

---

[21] *See* I.R.C. §§ 1361(b)(1)(B), 1362(d)(2). If the acquiring S corporation makes a prompt QSub election for the target, the transaction may be treated under the step-transaction doctrine as an asset acquisition. As such, it may qualify as a C or D reorganization, but not as a B reorganization. *See* Reg. § 1.1361–4(a)(2)(ii) (ex. 2, 3).

[22] I.R.C. § 1362(g); *see* ¶ 2.21.

[23] I.R.C. § 1362(e)(2); *see* ¶ 2.20.

[24] I.R.C. § 1377(b)(1).

[25] Literally, § 1366(d)(3) requires that the distribution be with respect to the shareholder's stock in the *acquired* corporation. *See* I.R.C. § 1366(d)(3) (referring to "stock in the corporation"); Eustice, Kuntz & Bogdanski, *supra*, at ¶ 12.03[6] (recommending that the regulations be revised to permit target shareholders to use suspended losses against the *acquiring* corporation's stock).

[26] *See* I.R.C. § 1371(e); Reg. § 1.1377–2(b) (last sentence).

Any NOLs of an acquired C corporation would continue to be lodged with the C subsidiary, which survives intact. If an S corporation involved in a B exchange has attributes from a prior C year of its own, those C attributes may again become operative if its S status terminates.

¶ 8.04   TYPE C REORGANIZATIONS AND PRACTICAL MERGERS

Whereas the B reorganization imposes a solely stock-for-stock requirement, the C reorganization (under § 368(a)(1)(C)) involves a stock-for-assets exchange in which a limited amount of cash (boot) consideration is permitted. If an S corporation is the acquiring corporation and transfers stock in exchange for substantially all the assets of a target corporation, it might appear that the acquiring corporation's S status should terminate. Momentarily at least, a prohibited corporate shareholder (the acquired corporation) will own stock of the acquiring S corporation. Alternatively, the reorganization could be structured so that the acquiring S corporation issues its stock only to eligible individual shareholders of the acquired corporation. In this event, the acquiring S corporation would never formally issue stock to a prohibited corporate shareholder.[27]

Under § 368(a)(2)(G), the target in a C reorganization must distribute all its property, including shares acquired in the exchange, in liquidation.[28] Because a prompt liquidation of the acquired corporation would render the prohibited corporate shareholder a transitory one, there is thus a strong case for non-termination of the acquiror's S status.[29] If an S corporation transfers substantially all of its assets to another corporation in a C reorganization, the target's S status normally should continue.[30] As a result of the required liquidation under § 368(a)(2)(G), however, the target's separate existence will end. The liquidation is governed by the rules for distributions pursuant to a reorganization.[31]

If the S corporation is the *acquiring* corporation and its S election terminates, the familiar Subchapter S rules and choices for short taxable years and income allocation come into play.[32] A post-termination transition period will ensue, allowing tax-free distributions from the AAA even as to new shareholders. Following the reorganization, the target's AAA will be blended with the acquiring corporation's AAA.[33]

A target S corporation's taxable year ends, under § 381(b), on transfer of its assets to the acquiror. Under the normal year-end allocation rules, the reorganization may thus accelerate income (or loss) passthrough for the target's short taxable year. Any suspended losses at the shareholder level are carried forward for the benefit of the

---

[27]   Nevertheless, the step-transaction doctrine may treat the transaction as a constructive receipt of stock at the corporate level followed by a distribution of such stock to the acquired corporation's shareholders. *See* Rev. Rul. 69–6, 1969–1 C.B. 104.

[28]   *See* I.R.C. § 368(a)(2)(G). If the case of an overlap, the D reorganization rules trump those of C. *See* I.R.C. § 368(a)(2)(A).

[29]   Eustice, Kuntz & Bogdanski, *supra*, at ¶ 12.04[2].

[30]   *See* Rev. Rul. 71–266, 1971–2 C.B. 262. A reorganization terminates the target corporation's taxable year but does not standing alone terminate the S election. *See* I.R.C. § 381(b).

[31]   *See* I.R.C. § 336(c); *see also* I.R.C. § 361(c)(4) (reorganization distribution rules trump § 311).

[32]   *See* ¶¶ 2.20, 2.22.

[33]   Reg. § 1.1368–2(d)(2) (regardless of whether AAA is positive or negative); § 312(h)(2) (proper allocation of earnings and profits).

particular shareholder.[34] As in the case of an A merger, target shareholders may wish to increase their basis to allow passthrough of losses prior to the reorganization.

Also, target shareholders should generally attempt to take distributions prior to the reorganization (up to AAA) rather than receive cash (boot) in the reorganization. While pre-reorganization distributions will be governed by the favorable rules of § 1368, the potentially harsher rules of § 356 may apply to any boot received in the reorganization.[35] Care must be exercised, though, to ensure that pre-reorganization distributions do not jeopardize the "substantially-all-of-the properties" requirement for purposes of qualifying as a C reorganization.

¶ 8.05   FORWARD AND REVERSE TRIANGULAR MERGERS

The forward and reverse triangular mergers expand the A merger but contain their own specific requirements. In a forward triangular merger (§ 368(a)(2)(D)), a subsidiary uses the stock of its parent (previously transferred to the subsidiary) as consideration in a merger with the target corporation. Formerly, an S corporation could not be the parent (controlling corporation) because it was not permitted to own 80% of the stock of another corporation. Now, an S corporation can have a C corporation or, alternatively, a QSub as a controlled subsidiary.[36] An S corporation cannot be the controlled subsidiary because it would have a prohibited corporate shareholder. If an S corporation is the target whose assets are acquired in a forward triangular merger, the target's tax consequences should parallel those of an A merger.

In a reverse triangular merger (§ 368(a)(2)(E)), the acquiring corporation's controlled subsidiary is merged into the acquired corporation which survives the merger. An S corporation cannot be the merged controlled subsidiary because of the prohibition on a corporate shareholder. An S corporation may be the acquired (surviving) corporation, but its S election would terminate when it is becomes a subsidiary of the controlling corporation. As to the acquired S corporation, the transaction resembles a B reorganization.

To sum up, an S corporation can be the target in either a forward or reverse triangular merger. However, because the target (or, in a reverse triangular merger, the entity into which the target is merged) becomes a subsidiary of another corporation, the target's S status will be lost as a result of the reorganization. If an S corporation is the acquiring parent, the controlled subsidiary must be either a C corporation or a QSub.

¶ 8.06   NONDIVISIVE D REORGANIZATIONS

S corporations may also participate in D reorganizations (§ 368(a)(1)(D)). This section will cover nondivisive D reorganizations in which no substantial division of assets occurs (*i.e.*, at the corporate level). Divisive D reorganizations are considered later in ¶ 8.09. The hallmark of a nondivisive D reorganization is that it involves two corporations (a transferor and a controlled transferee), of which only one (the controlled transferee) survives following the asset transfers.[37]

---

[34]   Reg. § 1.1366–2(c); *see* Reg. § 1.1377–2(b) (§ 368(a)(1)(C) reorganization involving two S corporations does not start a post-termination-transition period).

[35]   *See* Rev. Rul. 71–266, 1971–1 C.B. 262.

[36]   The special rules applicable to reorganizations involving QSubs are discussed at ¶ 8.10.

[37]   *See* I.R.C. §§ 354(b)(1)(B) (required liquidation of transferor), 368(a)(2)(H) (control requirement).

In a nondivisive D reorganization, two conditions must be met: (1) the transferor corporation must transfer substantially all its assets to the transferee, and (2) the transferor corporation, its shareholders, or a combination of both must "control" the transferee corporation immediately after the transfer. In a D reorganization, an S corporation can be the transferor; it cannot be the transferee, since it cannot have a corporate shareholder. The tax consequences to S participants in a nondivisive D reorganization should resemble those of an A (or C) reorganization.

A nondivisive D reorganization may take two forms: merger or nonmerger. A merger-type D reorganization may overlap with an A reorganization (but will be respected as a D reorganization even if it fails to qualify as an A reorganization). A nonmerger-type D reorganization cannot be an A reorganization, though it can fit the description of a C reorganization. In the case of a C overlap, the more stringent rules governing D reorganizations apply.[38]

¶ 8.07   OTHER NONDIVISIVE FORMS— E AND F REORGANIZATIONS

An E reorganization is a recapitalization involving an exchange of common stock, preferred stock, or debt of a corporation for different kinds of stock or debt. Because of the one-class-of-stock rule, S corporations do not often engage in recapitalizations. But with voting and nonvoting common stock and debt permissible, there are occasions when an S corporation may want to recapitalize tax free under § 368(a)(1)(E).[39]

S shareholders also holding debt may wish to exchange *debt for stock* to avoid income on repayment of low-basis debt. A recapitalization may also avoid concerns about reclassification of the debt as a second class of stock. Under § 368(a)(1)(E), such a debt-for-equity exchange will be tax free to the shareholders only if the debt qualifies as a "security" under § 354. By contrast, if the basis of the debt exceeds its fair market value, a taxable exchange of a non-security debt may allow the holder to recognize a loss, even though it may be a capital loss. Stock issued in exchange for debt must not constitute a second class of stock, and the number and status of shareholders must remain within permitted limits. Although the S corporation generally does not recognize gain on issuing its own stock, it may recognize debt cancellation income if the debt is satisfied for less than its face amount.[40]

If *debt is exchanged for debt*, the safe harbor rule of § 1361(c)(5) for straight debt may apply.[41] If the debt qualifies as a "security," it can be exchanged for new debt under § 368(a)(1)(E) tax free.[42] If S shareholders exchange *stock for debt*, nonrecognition

---

[38]   I.R.C. § 368(a)(2)(A).

[39]   For example, a sole shareholder of an S corporation may desire to transfer control to a younger member of the family as part of an estate plan. In a recapitalization, the shareholder could exchange all of the outstanding common stock for two classes of common stock, one voting and one nonvoting, and thereafter make gifts of the stock to the children. The child active in the business could receive voting and nonvoting stock while the inactive children could receive nonvoting stock. Because the two classes of stock differ only with respect to voting rights, the recapitalization should not result in a termination of S status. *See* I.R.C. § 1361(c)(4).

[40]   *See* I.R.C. § 108(e)(8), (10).

[41]   I.R.C. § 1361(c)(5). *See* ¶ 2.09.

[42]   But a tax-free recapitalization will not prevent recognition of gain (possibly ordinary in character) if there is no written evidence of indebtedness, since such a debt is clearly not a security. *See* I.R.C. §§ 354(a)(1), 1271.

treatment will not apply, as such an exchange constitutes bailing out of earnings in a form that § 368(a)(1)(E) does not insulate from tax.

S shareholders may exchange *stock for stock* tax free, perhaps to take advantage of the liberal treatment of nonvoting stock in S corporations. Such equity exchanges may be useful in estate planning, but the one-class-of-stock requirement must be strictly observed. Thus, an exchange of common for preferred stock, or for another (a second) class of common stock, will terminate the S election (¶ 2.09).

Alternatively, a C corporation with preferred stock or a second class of common stock may undertake an E recapitalization, prior to making an S election, to conform its capital structure to the eligibility requirements of § 1361. Pursuant to a recapitalization, preferred shareholders could exchange their preferred stock for common stock, thereby satisfying the one-class-of-stock rule. Such a recapitalization may also be used to reduce the number of shareholders to 100 or fewer, in order to qualify for an S election.

An *F reorganization* is a mere change in identity, form, or place of organization of a corporation. It is now limited to transactions involving a single operating corporation.[43] An S corporation may engage in an F reorganization, so long as it otherwise remains eligible. For example, an F reorganization may be employed to change an S corporation's state of incorporation. If an S corporation is merged into a new corporation created in another state (owned by the same shareholders), the F reorganization does not terminate the S election or the corporation's taxable year.[44] Thus, there is no acceleration or bunching of income. The AAA account carries over to the successor corporation, so tax-free distributions may be made under § 1368 following the reorganization.[45]

¶ 8.08   SUMMARY OF NONDIVISIVE REORGANIZATIONS

If an S corporation is involved in an acquisitive reorganization, its existence or its S status may be placed in jeopardy. If an S corporation is acquired in an A or C reorganization, it will cease to exist (at least in its old form). Similarly, if an S corporation is acquired in a B reorganization, it will have an impermissible corporate shareholder, causing its S status to terminate. For purposes of the five-year waiting period for re-electing S status, it should be noted that a reorganization does not itself cause a termination of S status, even though the acquired corporation may cease to exist as a separate entity.

If appropriate precautions are taken, an S corporation can be the *acquiring* corporation in an A or C reorganization, and may acquire either a C corporation or another S corporation pursuant to the reorganization. Because of the 100 shareholder limit, the acquiring S corporation usually will acquire another corporation that has relatively few shareholders. (Sometimes the acquiring and target corporations will have been commonly-owned, in whole or in part.) If the acquiring S corporation assumes debt of the acquired corporation, it must exercise caution to ensure that such debt does not give rise to a second class of stock, thereby leading to disqualification of its S status.

---

[43] I.R.C. § 368(a)(1)(F) (new corporation treated as a continuation of the merged corporation). An F reorganization can occur as a discrete part of a larger transaction. *See* Reg. § 1.368–2(m)(3); Rev. Rul. 96–29, 1996–1 C.B. 50.

[44] *See* Rev. Rul. 2004–85, 2004–2 C.B. 189. *See also* ¶ 8.10

[45] *See* Reg. § 1.1368–2(d)(2).

In the case of an S corporation, choosing among the forms of acquisitive reorganizations depends not only on the usual tax and business considerations but also on the collateral consequences peculiar to S corporations, including potential termination of S status and transfers of tax attributes. If the S corporation is to be the acquiring corporation, it may engage in an A reorganization easily, since it is acquiring assets and liabilities by operation of law, so long as the end result does not violate the S eligibility rules. In a C reorganization, the momentary presence of a corporate shareholder (the transferor or acquired corporation) should not jeopardize the continued S status of the acquiring corporation. Because the transferor must promptly liquidate, under § 368(a)(2)(G), the transitory ownership should be disregarded.

Likewise, S corporations may also participate in type E and F reorganizations. They may even participate in a specialized, seventh type of reorganization involving insolvent corporations (§ 368(a)(1)(G)), although loss of S status is likely depending on how the reorganization is structured.

¶ 8.09   DIVISIVE D REORGANIZATIONS AND CORPORATE DIVISIONS

An S corporation can divide by engaging in a formal D reorganization pursuant to § 368(a)(1)(D). Alternatively, it can engage in a spin-off, split-off or split-up under § 355, without undertaking an initial D reorganization. The D reorganization involves a transfer by a corporation of part or all of its assets to another (controlled) corporation for stock, followed by a distribution of such stock that qualifies for tax-free treatment. A § 355 division can omit the first step only if there is a pre-existing controlled subsidiary (or more than one). In the S context, a D reorganization will generally precede the division.

An S corporation may be the "controlling" ("distributing") corporation in a § 355 division.[46] An S corporation may own a controlled subsidiary that is a C corporation (or a QSub).[47] Unless transitory ownership by the controlling corporation is disregarded, however, an S corporation cannot itself be the controlled subsidiary because it would have an impermissible corporate shareholder.

A D reorganization generally will not terminate the distributing corporation's taxable year.[48] Thus, the normal year-end rules for passthrough of income (or loss) for the *entire* year will apply. Passthrough items will be allocated among continuing shareholders as well as shareholders whose interests are terminated or redeemed. (If the transaction qualifies as a tax-free D reorganization, the nonrecognition provisions of § 361(c)(1) should generally prevent recognition of gain at the corporate level, notwithstanding the rules of §§ 311 and 336.[49]) Allocation of income (or loss) will be affected depending on whether the interim closing method is available. A non-prorata "split-off" (in which some shareholders exchange their interest in the distributing

---

[46]   Under prior law, there was a head-on collision between the "control" requirements of §§ 368(a)(1)(D) and 355, since an S corporation could not be a member of an affiliated group. *See* I.R.C. §§ 368(c) (control), 1504 (affiliation). Now, an S corporation may own any amount of subsidiary stock without endangering its S status.

[47]   For divisive reorganizations involving QSubs, see ¶ 8.10.

[48]   In a split-up, however, the taxable year of the distributing corporation will terminate when it is completely liquidated.

[49]   In the case of a qualifying § 355 division (with no first-step D reorganization), § 355(c) generally affords nonrecognition treatment to the distributing corporation. *See* I.R.C. § 355(c).

corporation for all or part of the stock of the controlled corporation) will alter the composition of the distributing corporation's shareholders and may also affect the ability to revoke the S election.[50]

With respect to transfer of corporate attributes, a portion of the dividing (distributing) S corporation's accumulated earnings and profits from a prior C history will be transferred to the controlled corporation.[51] In this situation, the regulations also allocate the AAA between the distributing and controlled corporations.[52] Apart from this special rule, however, the treatment of the old S corporation's AAA is unclear. If the old S corporation was always an S corporation (with no accumulated earnings and profits), its AAA may remain intact, permitting tax-free cash distributions to shareholders under § 1368 up to the entire balance of the AAA.[53] The parties should consider making pre-reorganization distributions or larding boot in the reorganization, so as to use up the AAA. In the case of a shareholder with suspended losses, such losses must be allocated in a reasonable manner between the distributing and controlled corporations.[54]

If a § 355 distribution consists of cash boot (as well as stock), the Subchapter C rules would normally tax such boot (to the extent of the recognized gain) as a dividend under § 301 (if it has a dividend-equivalent effect).[55] Since dividend treatment may conflict with the elaborate distribution regime of § 1368, the issue is whether § 356(a)(2) should bow to § 1368.[56] A similar but thornier problem arises if, under § 356(a)(1), exchange treatment would otherwise apply.[57] The uncertainty concerning the dominance of § 1368 could possibly be side-stepped by arranging to have distributions occur prior to (and separate from) the § 355 transaction, but the step-transaction doctrine may impose a high hurdle. As a policy matter, the most sensible solution would be to allow the Subchapter S regime to trump by giving primacy to § 1368(c).

If otherwise qualified, a participant in a D reorganization generally is free to elect S treatment, subject to a five-year waiting rule for an S corporation (or successor corporation) whose election terminated. Moreover, if the prospective electing corporation had a corporate shareholder at any time within the same taxable year, its S election generally cannot become effective until the next tax year.[58] Nevertheless, the IRS has ruled that it will ignore the distributing corporation's transitory ownership, thus permitting an immediate S election by the former subsidiary.[59] Ownership will not be

---

[50] *See* I.R.C. § 1362(d)(1)(B).

[51] I.R.C. §§ 312(h)(1), 1371(c)(2). Nothing in the Code directs or allows an adjustment in, or transfer of, the AAA. *See* Eustice, Kuntz & Bogdanski, *supra*, at ¶ 12.10[6][c] (noting that the AAA is the "antidote" to the "poison" of accumulated earnings and profits; thus, the regulations should "provide that the antidote follows the poison").

[52] *See* Reg. § 1.1368–2(d)(3).

[53] *See* I.R.C. §§ 1368(c)(1), 1371(e)(1). If the old S corporation liquidates (as in a split-off), its tax attributes may simply disappear.

[54] *See* Reg. § 1.1366–2(c); *see also* Reg. § 1.1361–5(b)(2) (applying a similar rule if stock of a QSub is distributed).

[55] I.R.C. § 356(b). *See Comm'r v. Clark*, 489 U.S. 726 (1989) (dividend-equivalent test).

[56] *See* I.R.C. § 1371(a) (giving primacy to Subchapter S rules if Subchapter C rules would be inconsistent).

[57] In the case of an exchange under § 356(a)(1), the technical rationale for allowing § 1368 to trump may be more difficult. *See* Eustice, Kuntz & Bogdanski, *supra*, at ¶ 12.10[6][b].

[58] I.R.C. § 1362(b)(2)(B)(i).

[59] *See* Reg. § 1.1361–5(b)(3) (ex. 4); P.L.R. 2014–26–004 (Feb. 26, 2014) (controlled corporation did not have an ineligible shareholder under § 1362(b)(1)(B)).

considered transitory, however, if the distributing corporation has owned the subsidiary for more than a brief period. Thus, use of a newly-formed subsidiary is advisable, if possible.

If a C corporation would like to gain the benefit of S corporation treatment but cannot make an S election, it may consider splitting off some of its assets or businesses by placing them in a separate corporation. The controlled subsidiary's stock may then be distributed to some or all of the C parents' shareholders tax free under § 355. The split-off corporation could then seek to elect S treatment. This plan obviously presents several potential problems, since taxpayers ought not to be allowed to escape the burdens of Subchapter C so easily.[60] At a minimum, any built-in gain would be subject to the § 1374 tax in the hands of the split-off corporation.[61]

As the regulations clarify, the goal of electing S treatment will not constitute a "business purpose" for qualifying a transaction under § 355.[62] A desire to reduce state taxes also will not suffice, at least if the federal-tax reduction is coextensive with the state-tax reduction. Thus, to obtain tax-free treatment under § 355, the participants will need to document some significant business purpose other than avoiding federal taxes under Subchapter S.

¶ 8.10   REORGANIZATIONS INVOLVING QSUBs

For purposes of the reorganization provisions, a QSub is treated as a disregarded entity, just like a single-member LLC that does not elect to be classified as a corporation.[63] Under the § 368 regulations, a merger of a "regarded" entity into a disregarded entity (including a QSub) may qualify as a tax-free reorganization under § 368(a)(1)(A). For example, assume that a C corporation (Z) merges into a QSub (X) owned by an S corporation (Y). Reorganization treatment is appropriate since Z's assets and liabilities become the assets and liabilities of X and Y (the "transferee unit") and Z's separate legal existence ends.[64] The result is the same as if Z merged into Y, since disregarded X is treated as a branch or division of its owner.

Suppose that X (an S corporation) acquires all of the stock of Y (another S corporation) in a tax-free "stock-for-stock" reorganization under § 368(a)(1)(B), and X then promptly makes a QSub election for Y. Under step-transaction principles, the transaction cannot qualify as a B reorganization, since X is acquiring Y's assets (in the deemed liquidation resulting from the QSub election). The transaction must be tested as an asset acquisition, potentially qualifying as a C or perhaps a D reorganization.[65]

---

[60] *See* Reg. § 1.355–2(b)(2) (avoidance of federal taxes taken into account in weighing business-purpose requirement).

[61] *See* I.R.C. § 1374(d)(8), (e). If the requirements of § 355 are not met, the distributing corporation will recognize gain, under § 311(b), on distribution of the controlled subsidiary's stock; the gain will pass through to the S shareholders under § 1368. *See McLaulin v. Comm'r*, 115 T.C. 255 (2000), *aff'd*, 276 F.3d 1279 (11th Cir. 2001) (five-year active business test not satisfied).

[62] *See* Reg. § 1.355–2(b)(2), (b)(5) (ex. 6).

[63] *See* Reg. § 1.368–2(b)(1)(i)(A) (defining disregarded entities).

[64] *See* Reg. § 1.368–2(b)(1)(iii) (ex. 2, 3). A merger of a disregarded entity into a regarded entity cannot qualify as a reorganization under § 368(a)(1)(A), since the transaction is divisive in nature. *See id.* (ex. 6). Such a transaction may potentially qualify as a C (or perhaps a D) reorganization. Similarly, a merger of an S corporation into a disregarded entity owned by an LLC (taxed as a partnership) cannot qualify as a tax-free reorganization. *See* Reg. § 1.368–2(b)(1)(iii) (ex. 5).

[65] *See* Reg. § 1.1361–4(a)(2)(ii) (ex. 2, 3).

Although QSub stock is generally ignored, the regulations permit a parent S corporation to distribute QSub stock in a transaction qualifying under § 355.[66] At the moment of distribution, the QSub is treated as a regarded entity (a C corporation), whose stock can satisfy the distribution requirement of § 355. Thus, a § 355 transaction can be used to accomplish a tax-free division of a QSub and its former S parent. After the distribution, shareholders with suspended losses may continue to use them.[67]

If a parent S corporation transfers 100% of a QSub's stock (whether by sale or in an A, C, or D reorganization), the QSub's status terminates.[68] If the transaction qualifies as an F reorganization, a surviving corporation that qualifies as an S corporation is treated as a continuation of the old S parent. In this instance, the parent's S election does not terminate but instead carries over to the surviving corporation.[69]

As this brief survey illustrates, a QSub can play an important function in reorganization transactions. While QSubs provide added flexibility, the threat of a QSub termination (and the possibility of even momentary C status) suggest the need to exercise extreme caution to avoid unintended consequences.

¶ 8.11 THE LIQUIDATION-REINCORPORATION DOCTRINE AND S CORPORATIONS

If an S corporation liquidates and distributes its assets to shareholders who then contribute all (or a substantial portion) of those assets to a new corporation (S or C), the liquidation-reincorporation doctrine may apply. Under that doctrine, the series of events may be collapsed or telescoped, resulting in a tax-free reorganization, most likely a D reorganization. Although originating in the C context, the liquidation-reincorporation doctrine seems to apply equally to S corporations. An argument can be made, though, that it is less necessary in the S context.

The doctrine may produce unwanted or unintended results. For example, taxpayers may intend a taxable transaction in order to recognize ordinary losses or obtain a stepped-up basis at the cost of recognizing capital gain. Reorganization treatment may deny such favorable consequences and may cause boot to be taxable at ordinary income rates. If § 1368 applies to minimize the tax burden, the purported dividend treatment may not matter so much. But an S corporation will not wish to inherit undesirable tax attributes such as C earnings and profits.

The IRS may challenge a purported liquidation of a C corporation if the assets wind up in an electing S corporation owned by the same shareholders. Unless the steps cannot be integrated or the transaction otherwise flunks the reorganization requirements, the IRS may invoke D reorganization treatment.

---

[66] *See* Reg. § 1.1361–5(b)(3) (ex. 4).

[67] *See* Reg. § 1.1361–5(b)(2) (referring to Reg. § 1.1366–2(c)(2)).

[68] *See* Rev. Rul. 2004–85, 2004–2 C.B. 189. If the acquiring corporation is an S corporation, a QSub election may be made immediately for the wholly-owned subsidiary. *See id.*

[69] *Id.; see* Rev. Rul. 2008–18, 2008–1 C.B. 674. A merger of a parent S corporation into its QSub can also qualify as an F (but not an A) reorganization. *See* Reg. § 1.1361–5(b)(3) (ex. 8).

¶ 8.12   SUMMARY OF TAX-FREE REORGANIZATIONS INVOLVING S CORPORATIONS

As Chapter 8 demonstrates, an S corporation is free to participate in § 368 tax-free reorganizations of the kind often thought of as reserved for C corporations. This ability to obtain tax-advantageous nonrecognition treatment under § 368 (or § 355 as it applies to corporate divisions) distinguishes an S corporation from a partnership. Indeed, this distinction may often drive choice-of-entity decisions.

Chapters 9 and 10 explore more systematically the tax advantages, disadvantages and pitfalls of S corporations versus C corporations and partnerships.

Chapter 9

CHOICE OF FORM: S CORPORATIONS COMPARED WITH C CORPORATIONS

¶ 9.01 ADVISING AND PLANNING—ADVANTAGES AND DISADVANTAGES OF THE S CORPORATION FORM

One useful way of evaluating the S corporation form, and of assessing the advantages and disadvantages of employing it, is to compare its main tax features with those of the C corporation and partnership forms, and then to consider its utility in some particular applications. This will be the organizing principle of Chapters 9 and 10.

As discussed in detail in Chapter 1, one of the most common types of advice requested of tax practitioners is advice regarding the choice of entity for business ventures. Today, the S corporation is a very attractive vehicle for many business operations, offering the same limited liability for shareholders as any other corporation organized under state law. From a tax perspective, the S corporation offers several major advantages. Most important, the S corporation avoids the double tax potentially applicable to C corporations. Moreover, for businesses in which losses may be anticipated, an S corporation offers the further benefit of passing through losses to shareholders, subject to other limitations on the shareholders' deduction of those losses.

Nevertheless, there are some limitations, costs, and disadvantages of an S election that restrict its use in certain circumstances. The most prominent of these is the significant restriction on eligibility for an S election, particularly the limitations on the number and type of shareholders. These limitations will often make it inconvenient or impossible to use the S corporation form, particularly when investors desire to raise large amounts of capital or when other corporations desire to participate as shareholders. Moreover, the one-class-of-stock requirement removes much of the flexibility in differentiating between classes of investors, a flexibility available both for non-electing corporations (through different classes of stock) and for partnerships (through special allocations). Finally, an S election for an existing C corporation may generate some significant complexities in calculating the corporation's future income tax liability, as well as that of its shareholders.

Moreover, the burden of the two-level corporate tax under Subchapter C is quite sensitive to changes in the rate relationship between individual and corporate taxes, as well as differences in the treatment of dividends and capital gains. These rate relationships thus play an important role in determining the relative advantage or disadvantage of the passthrough form (whether an S corporation or partnership) versus a C corporation. Indeed, even relatively modest changes in these rate relationships can have a significant impact on the choice-of-entity decision.

¶ 9.02 COMPARISON WITH NON-ELECTING C CORPORATIONS

It always bears remembering that, as a corporate entity under state law, an S corporation carries the non-tax characteristics of a non-electing C corporation. Instead of the double-tax regime, of course, the S corporation enjoys the passthrough system of Subchapter S but also is subject to the rest of Subchapter C (except when "otherwise provided" by law or inconsistent with Subchapter S). These are the sources of both the relative strengths and weaknesses of the S corporation form, as compared with non-electing C corporations and also with partnerships.

Single Tax. An S election avoids the double tax on distributed corporate earnings to which the C corporation and its shareholders are subject, once at the corporate level and again at the shareholder level. It also generally avoids the corporate-level tax, under §§ 311(b) and 336, when a C corporation distributes appreciated assets, a particularly valuable feature after repeal of the *General Utilities* rule.[1] On complete liquidation, a C corporation and its shareholders usually will experience a two-level tax. In contrast, an S corporation can be liquidated with only a single shareholder-level tax (assuming no § 1374 built-in gain problems), whether it sells assets or distributes assets in kind. Similarly, on a partial liquidation, an S corporation can sell some assets and the owners will pay only a single tax.

This elimination of the double tax on corporate income stands as the most conspicuous and distinctive feature of the S corporation, and for a profitable business it probably is the most advantageous feature. For a risky or loss-corporation, the passthrough of losses provides a matching and equally fundamental advantage of electing the S form.[2] Of course, this system may pose liquidity problems for the S shareholder who is taxed on income in the year the corporation receives it, whether or not funds are actually distributed. This helps explain why unanimous shareholder consent to the Subchapter S election must be obtained at the outset.

Many closely held C corporations escape the double tax on ordinary corporate earnings by paying out all gross income over other costs as wages, salary, bonuses, other compensation or deductible fringe benefits to shareholder-employees. If the corporation is thinly capitalized, such "profits" are distributed as deductible interest, rent or royalties to shareholder-lenders, tenants and licensors. In fact, a high percentage of closely held C corporations have historically paid no corporate income tax, not because they are failing businesses but because they are "zeroing out" taxable income by paying compensation to shareholders, either appropriately (as if at arm's length) or by disguising the distribution of profits as payment of deductible costs.[3]

An attempt to "zero out" a C corporation's income will be successful only if the business consistently has sufficient gross income to pay these expenses but not so much gross income as to exceed properly allowable deductions. When the business is unsuccessful, no double tax will have been avoided (and losses may go unused), and if it becomes *too* profitable it may cease to be able to treat all its distributions as deductible (nondividend) payments. The "reasonableness" of compensation for labor or capital may

---

[1]   Assuming § 1374 does not apply, any gain realized by the S corporation under §§ 311(b) and 336 will be taxed only once (at the shareholder level). Even before repeal of the *General Utilities* rule, an S corporation was required to recognize gain on a *liquidating* distribution of appreciated assets. The purpose of this stricter rule for S corporations was to prevent shareholders from obtaining a fair-market-value basis in the distributed assets without payment of tax at either the corporate level or the shareholder level. Thus, at least a single-level tax was imposed.

[2]   Moreover, S corporations are immune from § 382, which may reduce or eliminate C corporation losses.

[3]   This strategy may be less attractive under the 2017 Act because paying compensation may entail a higher overall tax burden than distributing dividends. *See* ¶ 9.03.

haunt the C corporation; on audit, distributions may be recharacterized as non-deductible dividends and produce two levels of tax. Under current law, the low tax rate for dividends lessens the disadvantage of dividend recharacterization.

A solely-owned S corporation may be tempted to pay no salary to its shareholder-employee and instead pass through earnings free of tax up to outside basis in stock or debt. By arranging compensation for services in the form of distributions rather than salaries, S shareholders potentially avoid employment taxes. (¶ 3.11). In these situations, the IRS is likely to argue that shareholder-employees of S corporations have received unreasonably low compensation. The stakes have increased as a result of the § 1411 tax on net passive investment income and the § 199A deduction for qualified business income. If the S shareholder-employee actively participates in the business, understating compensation potentially avoids *both* employment taxes and the 3.8% tax under § 1411. Understating compensation also potentially increases the § 199A deduction by increasing the amount of qualified business income eligible for the 20% deduction. (¶ 3.12).

The reasonableness of compensation can also become an issue in an S corporation, if it has accumulated earnings and profits and makes distributions in excess of AAA. An S corporation may also pay insufficient or excessive compensation to some employees or other shareholders in order to split income within a family. Section 1366(e) authorizes reallocation of salary or other income and corresponding adjustments to passthrough of income or loss.[4] The "kiddie tax" under § 1(g) has lessened the incentive for family income-splitting. Of course, as with shares in any corporation, S corporation stock may be given to children or other beneficiaries who will thereafter be taxable on their share of corporate income.[5]

Issuance of debt to shareholders and thin capitalization may be desirable in an S corporation for non-tax reasons: to protect assets, to equalize or legitimately to manipulate shareholder contributions and distributions, or to maximize basis (by shareholder loans, rather than entity borrowing) so as to deduct losses. Unlike in a C corporation, however, thin capitalization will not be necessary to provide larger corporate-level deductions for the cost of capital in order to eliminate corporate-level tax, so long as the S status does not terminate.

¶ 9.03   TAX RATE RELATIONSHIPS

Prior to the 1986 Act, it often proved advantageous for a business to retain and accumulate profits taxable at C corporate rates and shelter undistributed earnings from much higher individual rates. The net present value of a (lower) entity-level rate on corporate earnings and a later (and even lower) capital gains tax on distributed earnings often turned out to be *less* than the present value of an immediate tax at (higher) individual rates as in an S corporation (or partnership) investment.

---

[4]   The roles of the taxpayer and IRS are likely to be reversed, with the IRS arguing that the taxpayer's services were more valuable than the compensation received. *See Davis v. Comm'r*, 64 T.C. 1034 (1975) (no attribution or reallocation of income from two S corporations to radiologist who gave shares to his children and for whom the corporations performed services). Section 482 may authorize broader reallocation even in non-family situations.

[5]   Unlike § 704(e)(1) in the partnership context, § 1366(e) applies independently of whether shares were transferred among family members.

The 1986 Act inverted the traditional rate structure by temporarily reducing the maximum individual tax rate below the maximum corporate tax rate. Under the new rate relationship, a single tax to shareholders on income passed through by an S corporation (or partnership) was often less than the rate a C corporation alone would pay. Thus, even if the business retained most of its funds for reinvestment, an S corporation (or partnership) often entailed a lower annual tax burden than would a C corporation. The changes in tax rates wrought by the 1986 Act eliminated much of the traditional tax incentive for using C corporations, prompting a massive exodus away from C corporations.

Although the post-1986 rate structure favored passthrough taxation, it is the relationship between the corporate and the individual tax rate that matters. Since 2003, qualified dividends have been taxed at the same rate as capital gains. Parity between taxation of dividends and capital gains greatly reduces the burden of the double-tax system. It also lessens the significance of whether distributions from a C corporation are treated as a redemption of stock under § 302(a) (allowing basis recovery) or a dividend taxed at 20%. In addition, high-income individuals are subject to the 3.8% tax under § 1411 on net investment income. Accordingly, the overall rate for qualified dividends and capital gains is 23.8% (20% plus 3.8%) for such individuals.

The shareholder-level tax may be deferred (or sometimes even entirely avoided) if a C corporation retains accumulated earnings and reinvests them. Deferring distributions is advantageous because the after-tax return on retained corporate earnings will be higher than the after-tax return on amounts invested outside the corporation. While there is no advantage to deferring the distribution tax on the initial corporate earnings, the ability to earn a higher after-tax return on retained corporate earnings represents a permanent benefit that increases the longer amounts remain invested within the corporation.[6]

The 2017 Act eliminated the graduated rate structure for corporations. Under the 2017 Act, the flat 21% corporate tax rate provides an incentive to shelter income within a C corporation, as under the pre-1986 rate relationships. High-income individuals may again use corporations as tax shelters, exploiting higher corporate after-tax returns while deferring the shareholder-level tax on distributions. Nevertheless, the § 199A deduction preserves much of the tax advantage for S corporations (and partnerships) by reducing the single tax on passthrough income.

Of course, if an S corporation's shares are held until the shareholder's death, the decedent's heirs generally receive the same basis step-up, under § 1014, that they would obtain if they held shares in a C corporation. The higher basis will allow them either to sell the shares without further tax or to receive larger distributions from the S corporation without a shareholder-level tax. In a C corporation, the basis step-up at death may eliminate the bite of the shareholder-level tax if distributions and sales of stock can be deferred long enough.

¶ 9.04   ELIGIBILITY REQUIREMENT

Not every corporation can elect S treatment, as Chapters 1 and 2 revealed. Limits on the number and character of shareholders, prohibitions against certain kinds of

---

[6]   *See* Halperin, Mitigating the Potential Inequity of Reducing Corporate Tax Rates, 126 Tax Notes 641, 647–648 (2010).

shareholders and multiple classes of stock, and other eligibility requirements[7] may make it inconvenient or impossible for some businesses to qualify to make an S election. Also, the danger of inadvertent or strategic termination or revocation of S status is an uncertainty that does not beset a C corporation.

Midstream Elections. When a corporation that has been a C corporation makes a "midstream" election to convert to S status, its tax advisors should keep in mind that such a corporation may be treated differently because of its C corporation history. One difference is that the converted corporation may have accumulated earnings and profits that arose during its C years and have not been fully "zeroed out" by distributions. Having even small amounts of accumulated earnings and profits can have serious consequences for taxability of S corporation distributions under § 1368(c). Another danger is that the § 1374 built-in gain tax will apply to the former C corporation's assets or to assets acquired from a C corporation in a substituted-basis transaction.[8] The § 1375 penalty tax or § 1362(d)(3) termination rule may also come into play. Also, a special recapture rule will apply if the C corporation used the LIFO method for computing its cost of goods sold for inventory purposes.[9]

Under the guise of simplification, it has been proposed that a midstream election of S status by a C corporation should be treated as a constructive (but fully taxable) liquidation of the C corporation, followed by a deemed distribution of assets to shareholders and a deemed recontribution of the assets by the shareholders to a "new" and pure S corporation.[10] Such treatment could involve a heavy "toll charge" on an S election by a C corporation, one that would deter many such elections. The proposal would, however, permit simplification. For example, it would be possible to repeal the § 1374 built-in gain tax and the § 1375 tax on passive investment income (and the § 1362(d)(3) termination threat), the special distribution rules for S corporations with accumulated earnings and profits (except when inherited by tax-free reorganization), and the LIFO inventory recapture rules.

¶ 9.05   LOSS OF S STATUS

Having its S status in jeopardy constitutes a burden for the S corporation and its shareholders, especially in precarious situations. To protect against unplanned or unwanted loss of S status, by termination or revocation, it is always desirable to construct protective shareholder agreements, buy-sell provisions, and similar contractual or structural protections.[11] Similar arrangements, in separate instruments and/or in the corporate charter, articles, by-laws or regulations, are common and usually advisable for any closely held corporation. Thus, the only added costs and efforts are for those provisions particularly geared to Subchapter S worries, such as sales to too many shareholders or the wrong categories of persons. Care must be taken to draft these provisions in light of applicable state corporation law so as not to invalidate any of their terms.

---

[7]   I.R.C. § 1361(b)(1), (2).

[8]   I.R.C. § 1374(d)(8); *see* ¶¶ 5.01, 9.08.

[9]   I.R.C. § 1363(d); *see* ¶ 5.05.

[10]   *See* ¶ 11.04.

[11]   *See* ¶ 2.10.

¶ 9.06   ABILITY TO RAISE CAPITAL

In some contexts, an S corporation may be somewhat at a disadvantage in raising capital, because it must not have nonresident alien shareholders, corporate shareholders, more than 100 individual shareholders (given the special definition of family members in § 1361(c)(1), the total can go much higher) or multiple classes of stock (except for voting and nonvoting shares). Often, however, these limitations will not bite, and sometimes there is enough latitude or a solution can be found for the difficulty. Debt as well as stock can be used, including safe harbor non-prorata debt or pro rata debt that will not be reclassified as a second class of stock. Shareholder interest on debt whose proceeds are used to capitalize the S corporation may be subject to more flexible tracing rules than in a C corporation.[12]

¶ 9.07   OTHER DIFFERENCES OR ADVANTAGES

The S corporation, unlike its C counterpart, will be free from the accumulated earnings and personal holding company taxes.[13] Start-up losses will be deductible up to stock basis (with suspended losses carried forward), and passive losses may be usable by shareholders against passive income from other sources.

If the S corporation has a checkered past (as a C corporation) and has not fully distributed accumulated earnings and profits from C years (or inherited from a C predecessor), dangers may lurk in the form of the sting taxes under §§ 1374 and 1375 (and possible termination). But a pure (or purified) S corporation can realize gain on asset appreciation or passive investment income without fear of these sting provisions. It may also have foreign source income without adverse consequences.

Furthermore, as discussed in ¶ 6.24, the S corporation form is fairly amenable to estate planning within the limit of permitted shareholders, the single-class-of-stock rule and the § 1366(e) limit on family income-splitting.

¶ 9.08   PENALTY TAXES

Although the S corporation enjoys immunity from the accumulated earnings and personal holding company taxes, it will be subject to the § 1374 built-in gain tax and the § 1375 tax on excess passive investment income. C corporations need not concern themselves with these sting taxes. Of course, an S corporation with no C accumulated earnings and profits is also immune from these sting taxes.

¶ 9.09   SUBCHAPTER C APPLICATION TO AN S CORPORATION

An S corporation, like a C corporation (but unlike a partnership), is subject to Subchapter C when Subchapter S does not remove it from Subchapter C's jurisdiction. This means that the S and C corporations are in many respects equal, especially vis-à-vis formation, liquidation, redemption, tax-free reorganization and similar organic changes. However, as a participant in a restructuring governed by Subchapter C, an S corporation may be at a disadvantage because it must guard against undesired loss of its S status in, or as a consequence of, the restructuring. If it is to survive and to maintain

---

[12]   *See* IRS Notice 89–35, 1989–1 C.B. 675.
[13]   *See* I.R.C. §§ 531, 541.

its S status, the S corporation must not acquire a prohibited shareholder or a second class of stock. Before allowing S status to terminate, a planner needs to carefully consider the consequences of such a termination, including the five-year bar against re-election. When participating in tax-free restructurings, the S corporation must also worry about any carryovers of tax attributes from a C corporation (or an S corporation with a C history).

The point remains that the S corporation, unlike a partnership, can take part in Subchapter C tax-free reorganizations and divisions on much the same terms as C corporations.

¶ 9.10   COMPENSATION

S corporations stand on just about the same footing as C corporations when it comes to qualified deferred compensation plans.[14] As to excludable statutory fringe benefits, such as meals and lodging, medical and death benefits and group-term life insurance, non-electing C corporations enjoy an advantage over S corporations, which are subject to partnership rules for "2% shareholders."[15] The IRS may also challenge an S corporation's failure to pay adequate compensation to shareholder-employees seeking to minimize employment taxes (or to shift income to family members). S corporations are less likely than C corporations to be subject to constructive dividend challenges for payment of unreasonably high salary.

¶ 9.11   STATE INCOME TAXES

An electing S corporation may find itself paying a separate corporate income tax under state law if that law does not have a counterpart to Subchapter S. In contrast, in a state that has no parallel to Subchapter S but does not tax individual income, there may be *no* tax on either the S corporation or on its shareholders.

State taxation of S corporations becomes quite complicated when interstate business or investment occurs, and a "host" state faces the problem of how to tax nonresident shareholders. There is no constitutional bar against a state taxing nonresident shareholders on income sourced in the taxing state or attributable to a corporation domiciled in the taxing state. To ensure collection of such taxes, some states condition S corporation treatment (and exemption from state corporate income tax) on shareholders consenting to such taxation, or require the S corporation to pay the tax if the nonresident fails to do so. Innocent shareholders can therefore be hurt by the failure of another shareholder to pay or consent. Accordingly, a shareholder agreement should probably include such consents and related protections. Some states require the S corporation to withhold and pay an appropriate percentage of every nonresident's pro rata share of S corporation income, whether or not distributed. Alternatively, they may tax the S corporation directly, or even prohibit S treatment if there are nonresident shareholders. (This latter rule parallels the federal S prohibition against any foreign shareholder.)

Basis problems also bedevil treatment of nonresident S shareholders. A shareholder's basis in S shares will be reduced by losses passed through. The lower basis will result in increased gain realized upon sale of S stock, which will be taxed by the

---

[14] *See* ¶ 3.09. *See also* Eustice, Kuntz & Bogdanski, Federal Income Taxation of S Corporations ¶ 11.06[1] (5th ed. 2015).

[15] *See* I.R.C. § 1372(a).

resident or domicile state, not the host state (of incorporation). The Model S Corporation Income Tax Act, adopted by some states, is intended to address these and similar problems.[16] It includes automatic state recognition of federal S elections, allows for taxation of nonresident shareholders, and requires agreements by nonresident shareholders to report and pay tax with back-up responsibility on the corporation if such agreements are not filed. It requires a nonresident shareholder to start with a zero basis increased or decreased for income or loss attributable to the host state, and requires suspended losses to be carried forward.

Under the 2017 Act, an individual's itemized deduction for all state or local taxes is capped (for years 2018 through 2025) at $10,000.[17] Thus, passthrough owners (partners, S corporation shareholders, and sole proprietors) potentially stand to lose a substantial portion of the benefit from deducting state income taxes on their share of business profits. In response to these concerns, several states have restructured their state income tax regimes by enacting an elective passthrough entity tax. The entity-level tax allows state income taxes to be deducted at the entity level, circumventing the limitation on itemized deductions passed through to the individual owners.[18] This work-around for the $10,000 cap provides an additional incentive for sole proprietors (and individual owners of disregarded entities) to convert to S corporation status.

¶ 9.12   OVERALL ASSESSMENT

Under the substantive law of Subchapters S and C, the S corporation generally remains a very attractive mode of doing business. Nevertheless, the 2017 Act makes the choice between an S corporation and a C corporation much closer. The S corporation offers many advantages over the C corporation, whether for the closely held start-up or high-risk enterprise or for the profitable one (whether earnings are to be retained or distributed). The S corporation always deserves careful consideration when choosing the form of business entity or making the tax election itself. As Chapter 10 points out, S corporations also compare favorably with entities taxable as partnerships (including LLCs), though not in every instance.

---

[16] *See* Am. Bar Ass'n Sec. of Taxation, Comm. on S Corporations, Subcomm. on State Tax'n of S Corporations, Report [on] State Taxation of S Corporations: Model S Corporation Income Tax Act and Commentary, 42 Tax Law. 1001 (1989). *See also* Maule, The Model Act: Overview, 2 S Corps. 339 (1989).

[17] *See* I.R.C. § 164(b)(6). By contrast, C corporations may deduct as § 162 ordinary and necessary business expenses any state or local income, property or sales taxes incurred in connection with business operations.

[18] Entity-level state income taxes will reduce the passthrough owners' share of non-separately-stated items (but will not be subject to the § 164(b)(6) limitation at the individual level as separately-stated items). *See* IRS Notice 2020–75, 2020–49 I.R.B. 1453.

Chapter 10

CHOICE OF FORM: S CORPORATIONS COMPARED WITH PARTNERSHIPS (AND LLCs)

¶ 10.01   COMPARISON OF S CORPORATIONS WITH PARTNERSHIPS (AND LLCs)

The advantages and disadvantages of the S corporation form are revealed even more starkly by comparing it with the general or limited partnership form (including LLPs and LLLPs). In non-tax respects, the differences are greater simply because the S corporation does constitute a separate corporate entity for non-tax purposes. In this sense, the S corporation is quite similar to an LLC, which may elect to be taxed as either a partnership or a corporation. Since LLCs will nearly always elect to be treated as partnerships for federal tax purposes, the comparison with partnerships will be relevant for LLCs as well.[1]

The S corporation's main characteristics and governing principles are determined by specific corporation law and modified, as permitted, by terms in its constitutive documents and side agreements. By contrast, the partnership form is shaped less by the non-tax law; instead, more scope is left to contractual invention and agreement among the partners and with outsiders. The S corporation rules contemplate an entity with passthrough of most items of income and loss, whereas the partnership system approaches an aggregate of individuals with resulting freedom and complexity.

Although the Subchapter S regime resembles the system for taxing partnerships, important differences remain between Subchapters K and S. Sometimes these differences are so important as to dictate the choice-of-form decision for particular businesses. The following sections will emphasize these differences, in order to assess the relative merits and future prospects of each form of business organization.[2]

¶ 10.02   DOUBLE-TAX AVOIDANCE

Both the S corporation and the partnership (or LLC taxed as a partnership) share the characteristic of passthrough taxation and avoidance of the classical unintegrated "double-tax" treatment applicable to a non-electing corporation under Subchapter C. Both regimes pass through items which retain their entity-level character for whatever significance that may have in the individual tax returns of their owners. Section 1366(a) provides a passthrough system closely resembling § 702, and the basis adjustments and

---

[1]   Even if S corporation status is desired, it may sometimes be advantageous for non-tax reasons (such as access to LLC governance rules) to form an entity as an LLC under state law and elect corporate status (with a separate S election). *See, e.g.,* Looney & Levitt, Operating an S Corporation Through a State Law Limited Liability Company, 66 N.Y.U. Ann. Inst. Fed. Tax'n § 17.01 (2008).

[2]   For a thoroughgoing review and analysis of the similarities and differences between Subchapter S and the partnership tax regime of Subchapter K, see McMahon & Simmons, When Subchapter S Meets Subchapter C, 67 Tax Law. 231 (2014). *See also* Am. Bar Ass'n Sec. of Taxation, Comm. on S Corporations, Report on the Comparison of S Corporations and Partnerships, Part I, 44 Tax Law. 483 (1991); *id.,* Part II, 44 Tax Law. 813 (1991).

timing rules parallel each other.[3] Thus, both passthrough systems permit their owners to take advantage of a single-tax regime.

¶ 10.03   LOSSES

The two passthrough systems allow owners to use entity-level losses immediately on their individual tax returns. This gives S corporations, like partnerships, considerable advantage over the non-electing C corporation form if losses are experienced.[4] The deductibility of losses may be limited, however, at the owner level. Allowable losses cannot exceed the S shareholder's stock (and debt) basis and the partner's "outside" basis (the basis of the partnership interest). The computation of basis for the two kinds of owners differs, since third-party entity-level indebtedness increases a partner's outside basis but not an S shareholder's stock basis.[5] As a result, losses attributable to entity-level borrowing are much more likely to be suspended in the case of an S owner due to lack of outside basis. To increase outside basis and allow passthrough of additional losses, S shareholders must borrow funds and relend them or contribute them to the S corporation. These differences can be crucial for some investors who will prefer the partnership form. Other limitations on losses generally apply to S shareholders and partners alike.[6]

¶ 10.04   FORMATION AND CAPITALIZATION

Although the procedures for forming a corporation that will make an S election differ from those for forming a partnership, these differences should be familiar and are not likely to be influential in the choice of form.[7]

The eligibility requirements and election technicalities may have greater significance. For example, a partnership with impunity can have more than 100 participants, can differentiate the interests of those participants in almost any desired fashion, and can have corporate partners. Similarly, the partnership need not fear revocation or termination in quite the same way as does an S corporation, notwithstanding the power of a partner to dissolve the partnership under certain circumstances. Also, the danger exists that a widely held partnership may be treated as an association taxable as a corporation under § 7704.

With respect to capitalization and contribution of assets, there is little to choose between the S corporation and partnership forms. Investors can contribute appreciated assets to either entity without recognition of gain,[8] and the entity itself does not

---

[3]   Likewise, apart from the § 1374 tax, gain on the sale (or distribution) of appreciated assets is taxed only once. *See* ¶ 7.09.

[4]   A C corporation can only carry over a net operating loss, subject to the limitations of § 382.

[5]   I.R.C. §§ 751(a), 722; *see* ¶ 6.07. As noted earlier, the basis adjustment rules for losses and distributions have been largely harmonized for S corporations and partnerships. *See* ¶¶ 6.05, 6.09.

[6]   *See* ¶¶ 6.12, 6.15.

[7]   It often is less costly in legal fees to set up a simple corporation than to draft a high-quality partnership agreement that is well tailored to the situation. Nevertheless, elaborate close corporation arrangements can sometimes end up costing nearly as much.

[8]   *See* I.R.C. §§ 351, 721. Unlike § 351, § 721 does not contain a control requirement. Moreover, if liabilities exceed the basis of contributed property, § 357(c) may hit harder than §§ 731 and 752. Section 357(c) triggers gain recognition if liabilities assumed by the corporation exceed the shareholder's basis in contributed property. I.R.C. § 357(c), (d) (definition of assumption). Under § 351, debt issued in the exchange is treated as "securities" boot and hence taxable.

recognize gain upon exchanging an ownership interest for contributed assets.[9] If an investor prefers, a taxable exchange often can be arranged by constructing a truly separate sale or exchange or a loan, lease or license. When ownership interests are exchanged for services, § 83 applies to both partnerships and S corporations, although §§ 721 and 1032 may produce different results.[10] Under an aggregate approach, a partnership may be required to recognize gain upon transfer of a partnership interest for services.[11] Proposed regulations would, however, provide tax-free § 1032-type treatment at the partnership level.[12]

The differing control requirements for S corporations and partnerships can create problems for subsequent transfers of property to the entity in exchange for an ownership interest. Section 351 requires that the transferor own and control stock possessing at least 80% of *both* the total combined voting power *and* the total nonvoting shares to receive nonrecognition treatment. Section 721, the partnership counterpart to § 351, contains no similar control requirement. Although this distinction may have little effect on initial transfers to an S corporation, subsequent transfers to an existing S corporation could require the new transferors (who lack control) to recognize gain on the exchange. In contrast, subsequent transfers to a partnership will generally be tax free.

Boot received in transfers to the entity is also treated differently. Under § 351(b), realized gain is recognized to the extent of cash and other boot received, while only cash in excess of outside basis triggers gain recognition under § 731(a). Debt shifted from the transferor to the entity is also treated differently.[13]

This similarity (and ease) of formation and contribution must not lead the tax advisor to view lightly the choice-of-form decision. It is far easier (in tax terms) to enter one of these two forms than it is to exit (although both forms are easier to exit than is the non-electing C corporation.[14] (For more on liquidations and reorganizations, see Chapters 7 and 8).

---

[9]　*See* I.R.C. §§ 1032, 721.

[10]　An important difference exists with respect to the tax treatment of the entity upon issuance of an ownership interest for services. Section 1032 specifically provides that a corporation will not recognize gain or loss upon the issuance of its stock in exchange for property. Although the definition of property generally does not include services, the regulations extend this nonrecognition treatment to the corporation that issues stock in exchange for services. Reg. § 1.1032–1(a).

[11]　In the partnership context, there is no provision analogous to § 1032. Under an aggregate approach, a partnership that issues a partnership interest to a service partner is deemed to engage in a two-step transaction: (1) the partnership is deemed to transfer to the service provider assets equal in value to the services rendered, and (2) the service provider is then deemed to re-transfer these assets to the partnership in exchange for a partnership interest. Upon a transfer of appreciated property in satisfaction of a service obligation, the aggregate approach requires the partnership to recognize gain (and the partnership receives a fair-market-value basis in the assets deemed re-contributed by the service partner). *See McDougal v. Comm'r*, 62 T.C. 720 (1974).

[12]　*See* Prop. Reg. § 1.721–1(b)(1) (rejecting the deemed sale approach as inconsistent with the broad nonrecognition policies underlying § 721). Receipt of a partnership profits interest may also be tax free to the recipient. Under a safe harbor rule, a profits interest is deemed to have a zero value provided that the recipient would not be entitled to any distribution upon an immediate liquidation of the partnership. *See* Rev. Proc. 93–27, 1993–2 C.B. 343.

[13]　*See* I.R.C. §§ 357, 752.

[14]　The S corporation will not be easier to unwind if it should lose its S status and revert to a non-electing C corporation.

¶ 10.05   FLEXIBILITY IN ALLOCATIONS OF ITEMS OF SPECIAL TAX CONSEQUENCE

Items of Income or Loss. One respect in which the partnership form is conceded to enjoy a significant edge over the S corporation has to do with the special allocations of passthrough items that can be made in a partnership. Compared to the flexible "distributive share" concept in a partnership, the Subchapter S one-class-of-stock rule results in a more rigid allocation system.

By statute, items of income and loss in an S corporation must be allocated to shareholders pro rata; an S corporation cannot make "item allocations." For example, pre-formation gain or loss inherent in an asset contributed to the business cannot be allocated to the contributing shareholder, as it must be to a contributing partner.[15] In an S corporation, it is possible to make some form of special allocation by holding out some assets and compensating for their use by interest, wages, stock options, rent or royalties. Different classes of stock having differing rights in corporate profits or assets cannot be used, however. Unlike a C corporation, an S corporation cannot freeze future appreciation in corporate value by issuing preferred stock, or by giving some shareholders dividend or liquidation preferences. Only differences in voting rights may be used to discriminate among S shareholders.

In contrast, subject only to the § 704(b) requirement of "substantial economic effect,"[16] a partnership agreement can flexibly allocate income, loss and post-contribution appreciation among various partners or classes of partners. For example, depreciation can be allocated to high-bracket partners with outside income to shelter, or taxable income can be allocated to low-bracket partners and tax-exempt income to high-bracket partners, provided the allocations have substantial economic effect and the partners' capital accounts are properly maintained. Allocations may switch or "flip-flop" at key points, again so long as the § 704(b) test is satisfied. The partnership anti-abuse rule and other common law and statutory rules against improper shifting of income among related parties may further restrain flexibility; similar anti-income-shifting rules also apply to S corporations.[17]

As to management and governance, even though an S corporation can issue nonvoting and voting stock, the partnership agreement offers a wider variety of control-sharing arrangements. Under many state laws, it is now possible for limited partners to participate in management and control activities without jeopardizing their limited liability status. Of course, LLC members may typically participate in governance with impunity, narrowing the advantage of S corporations.

¶ 10.06   TAXABLE YEAR

An S corporation must use a "permitted year,"[18] which means a calendar year unless the IRS approves use of a different year, such as a natural business year, or unless a

---

[15] *See* I.R.C. § 704(c). This provision adds considerable complexity, especially if the partnership has multiple assets and undergoes frequent revaluations.

[16] *See* I.R.C. § 704(b).

[17] *See* I.R.C. § 1366(e). Under the partnership anti-abuse rules, a transaction may be recharacterized even if it complies with the literal language of the statute and regulations. *See* Reg. § 1.701–2.

[18] I.R.C. § 1378.

special tax is paid to offset the benefit of tax deferral.[19] Even then, income deferral is quite limited, and permission to change the entity's taxable year is hard to obtain. A partnership must generally use the same calendar year as its individual partners, unless a business purpose can be established for a different year.[20] Like an S corporation, a partnership can obtain ready approval for a taxable year ending in September, October or November if the owners use calendar years, but the special tax under § 7519 must be paid if this option is elected. Again, not much deferral is permitted, though tax return preparers may be able to spread out their workload more conveniently.

¶ 10.07   TAXATION OF DISTRIBUTIONS

In both the partnership and S corporation form, the passthrough system implies that actual distributions of previously taxed income must not be taxed again when distributed. Cash distributions up to outside basis (or the AAA in an S corporation with accumulated earnings and profits) can be made tax free by either the S corporation or the partnership.

Distributions in *kind* raise more problems. Nevertheless, such distributions are likely to entail a lower tax cost in an S corporation (or a partnership) than in a C corporation. Because § 1371(a)(1) makes Subchapter C rules generally applicable, an S corporation that distributes property in kind must recognize gain under § 311 or § 336. This corporate-level gain will pass through and be taxed to shareholders, increasing their outside bases. Consequently, S shareholders will often owe little or no second tax upon receipt of the distributed property, unlike on a C corporation distribution.

A partnership can generally distribute property tax free, unless it makes a disproportionate distribution of § 751 assets.[21] When applicable, § 751 may tax both the partnership and the partners on the deemed exchange of § 751 assets for non-§ 751 assets. No similarly complex rule haunts the S corporation. If the partnership has only appreciated non-§ 751 assets, such "cold assets" can be distributed in kind without incurring a tax cost, unlike a C or S corporation.

The starting point for the rules governing partnership distributions is no tax at the entity or owner level, though *some* distributions (including cash distributions in excess of basis) do prove taxable at the owner level.[22] By contrast, an S corporation distribution is much more likely to trigger gain recognition at the entity level, under § 311 or § 336. The recognized corporate-level gain passes through and is taxed to the shareholders. (If it has assets with a prior C history, the S corporation may also be subject to the § 1374 tax on built-in gain, with a corresponding reduction in the gain passed through to shareholders.)

Partly because an S corporation's distribution of property other than cash will usually trigger entity-level recognition, there is less need for a rule permitting inside basis adjustments in the S context. Thus, there is no Subchapter S rule allowing the

---

[19] *See* I.R.C. §§ 444, 7519; *see also* ¶ 3.08.

[20] *See* I.R.C. § 706(b)(1).

[21] *See* I.R.C. § 751(b). Section 751 assets consist of so-called hot assets (inventory and unrealized receivables, including § 1245 recapture) and lukewarm assets (collectibles gain and unrecaptured § 1250 gain).

[22] Since partnership-level gain is not recognized on a distribution, the distributee partner must generally take a basis in the distributed property equal to its basis in the partnership's hands. *See* I.R.C. § 732(a)(1) (nonliquidating distributions). A different rule applies for liquidating distributions, since the basis of the distributed property in the distributee's hands must be adjusted (upward or downward) to match the distributee's outside basis immediately before the distribution. *See* I.R.C. § 732(b).

entity to adjust the inside basis of undistributed assets to compensate for changes in the bases of distributed assets in the hands of the distributee (or for the distributee's recognition of gain or loss). These inside basis adjustments, as discussed below, can create considerable complexity in the case of partnerships and represent a cost of the substituted-basis rules generally applicable to partnership distributions.

Subchapter S lacks a parallel to § 707(c) governing so-called "guaranteed payments" to a partner for services or use of capital. A salary is deductible by an S or C corporation so long as it represents reasonable compensation. Fringe benefits are taxed to "2% shareholders" as if they were partners. Subchapter S has no counterpart to § 736, the rule governing payments to retiring partners.[23] Instead, S shareholders or employees are taxed under simpler, general principles applying to sales of ownership interests or retirement payments.

¶ 10.08   LIQUIDATIONS OF S CORPORATIONS AND PARTNERSHIPS

The tax cost of liquidating an S corporation may well turn out to be greater than that of liquidating a partnership with comparable assets. At the entity level, liquidation of the S corporation will be governed by § 336(a). Thus, gain (and sometimes loss) *will* be recognized by the S corporation on the distribution of property in complete liquidation, as if such property had been sold to the distributee at fair market value. This gain is passed through and taxed to the shareholders, entitling them to increase their outside basis in stock. (Also, the § 1374 tax on built-in gain may apply to the S corporation.)

At the shareholder level, § 331 will cause the individual owners to recognize gain (or loss) equal to the difference between the fair market value of the property received and their stock basis. Each shareholder's stock basis will be increased to reflect the corporate-level gain, under § 336(a), included in the shareholder's income. Additional gain (or loss) may have to be recognized at the shareholder level under § 331, because outside basis rarely corresponds exactly to the fair market value of property and cash distributed. Any such congruence would be only coincidental.

In contrast, the liquidating partnership "entity" will normally avoid recognition of gain unless there is something special going on, such as a § 751(b) deemed exchange of hot assets for cold assets.[24] At the partner level, no gain or loss will generally be recognized unless money distributed exceeds a partner's outside basis (or § 751(b) applies).[25] On a liquidating distribution, the distributee partner generally takes a basis in the distributed property equal to the distributee's outside basis in the partnership interest, reduced by any money received.[26] Nonrecognition of gain upon liquidation merely defers the tax burden, which will be triggered subsequently when the distributee disposes of the distributed asset.

Although this is only a cursory comparison, it supports the generalization that it is often easier and cheaper to get out of partnership form than out of corporate form, *particularly* if no S election is in effect. The tax burden at both the entity level and the

---

[23]   *See* I.R.C. § 736. Section 736 may also involve complexities that rival those under § 751(b).

[24]   *See* I.R.C. §§ 731(b), 751(b).

[25]   I.R.C. § 731(a)(1), (c). Gain may also be triggered upon a distribution of contributed property (other than to the partner who contributed such property) within seven years of the original contribution. *See* I.R.C. §§ 704(c)(1)(B), 737.

[26]   I.R.C. § 732(b).

owner level must be taken into account in the choice of entity. Of course, if there are inherent *losses* to be recognized, the corporate form may sometimes produce "better" results, by allowing two levels of loss recognition.[27] Not only will corporate-level loss recognition be more likely (particularly in a liquidating distribution), but the nature of the loss can be ordinary if stock in the S corporation qualifies for § 1244 treatment. Nevertheless, Congress has tightened the rules to prevent duplication of loss for partnerships as well as S and C corporations.

Congress permanently repealed the so-called "collapsible corporation" provision of former § 341, the Subchapter C counterpart of § 751. Thus, S corporations arguably enjoy an advantage over partnerships, since gain to shareholders on liquidation will generally be capital gain. Of course, the S corporation itself may recognize ordinary income on a deemed sale of its assets which will pass through to the S shareholders, with its character intact. If Congress were to repeal the collapsible partnership provision of § 751(b), it would eliminate one major disparity between partnerships and S corporations.[28]

¶ 10.09   TAX CONSEQUENCES OF PARTIAL LIQUIDATIONS AND REDEMPTIONS

A cash redemption of outstanding stock by an S corporation will be treated as a § 1368 distribution (potential dividend) if it does not qualify as a sale or exchange under § 302. Failing to qualify for sale of exchange treatment under § 302 can actually prove favorable in the S corporation setting. If the S corporation does not have accumulated earnings and profits, a § 1368 distribution will be treated as a return of capital (up to basis), and then as gain from a sale or exchange. If it does have accumulated earnings and profits, the § 1368 distribution will be treated as tax free up to the AAA, then as a dividend up to accumulated earnings and profits, then as return of basis, and finally as gain from a sale or exchange. If property other than cash is distributed, the distribution rules of § 1368 will continue to govern the tax consequences to the shareholders. The corporation will have to recognize gain under § 311, however, as a price of the distributee taking a fair-market-value basis.

If a redemption by the S corporation *does* qualify as a sale or exchange of stock under § 302, the distribution rules of § 1368 are displaced by the normal sale or exchange rules. Consequently, the results parallel those of a C corporation, with corresponding adjustments to stock basis and AAA.[29] In the case of a redemption or partial liquidation taxable under § 302, the shareholder is allowed to offset only the basis of *particular* shares redeemed against the redemption proceeds to determine recognized gain or loss.

In the case of a partnership, there is no concept of a partial liquidation of a partner's interest.[30] Unless the partner's interest is completely redeemed, the normal rules for nonliquidating distributions apply. Thus, a partial liquidation will not trigger gain to the distributee unless the amount of cash distributed exceeds the distributee's *entire*

---

[27] But § 362(e)(2) generally eliminates loss duplication when the basis of contributed property exceeds its fair market value. *See* I.R.C. § 362(e)(2); *see also* ¶ 7.03.

[28] Arguably, more consistency between the tax treatment of liquidations of S corporations and partnerships would be desirable. Until that is achieved, the differences must be acknowledged and foreseen.

[29] *See* I.R.C. § 1368(e)(1)(B); *see also* ¶ 7.16.

[30] A distribution is considered a nonliquidating distribution unless it results in a complete termination of the distributee's interest (or the partnership). I.R.C. § 761(d).

outside basis. Any property distributed to the redeemed partner who retains a reduced partnership interest will generally take the same basis in the distributee's hands as in the partnership's hands. Thus, a partial liquidation of a partner's interest is treated more favorably than a comparable partial liquidation (or redemption) of an S shareholder's stock. Not only is gain not recognized at the partnership level but the distributee is not required to allocate basis between the redeemed and nonredeemed interests.

If a partner's interest is *completely* liquidated, yet a different set of rules comes into play. Again, the partnership generally treats any liquidating distribution as a nonrecognition event, whether cash or appreciated property is distributed. Because the distributee no longer has any interest in the partnership, however, the basis of the distributed property will be a substituted basis determined by reference to the distributee's former outside basis. Under the rules of § 732(b), any cash distributed is first applied against the partner's outside basis; the partner's remaining outside basis is then assigned to the distributed property, so that such property may take a higher (or lower) basis in the distributee's hands than in the partnership's hands. Special rules then apply to determine whether the partnership will be permitted (or required) to adjust the inside basis of its property to reflect any change in the basis of the distributed property (or any gain or loss recognized by the distributee).[31] Partnership payments to a retiring or deceased partner are further complicated by the specialized regime of § 736, for which there is no Subchapter S analogue.

In spite of these complexities, one can still discern that the separate-entity approach differentiates the S corporation from the partnership. The differences generally favor the partnership, where a redemption or partial liquidation will often entail a lower tax burden, measured in present value terms. Other benefits or detriments resulting from these differences may be less clear cut. In general, recognition or nonrecognition treatment under the distribution rules of both Subchapters K and S is well correlated with the basis rules. This correlation is essential to ensure that any deferral of tax will be only temporary, although such deferral may prove especially beneficial in the case of partnership distributions.

¶ 10.10   RECAPITALIZATIONS

Because of the one-class-of-stock rule, an S corporation can undertake only a very limited recapitalization if it wishes to retain its S eligibility. It can exchange stock for debt, or voting stock for nonvoting stock.[32] In addition, a C corporation sometimes may recapitalize in order to qualify to make an S election, or an S corporation may recapitalize and willingly lose its S status. Despite these restrictions, eligibility for a Subchapter C-type tax-free recapitalization may nevertheless prove quite valuable in the S context.

By contrast, a partnership can construct ownership interests virtually without constraint. At least among existing partners, it is often possible to alter or realign the partnership's capital structure and the partners' interests without a tax burden. Sometimes, changes in sharing of partnership liabilities will trigger a taxable constructive distribution under § 752.

---

[31] *See* I.R.C. §§ 734(b), 754.

[32] *See* I.R.C. §§ 354, 368(a)(1)(E); *see also* ¶ 8.07.

¶ 10.11   REORGANIZATIONS AND DIVISIONS

As discussed in ¶ 9.09, the S corporation is governed by the general rules of Subchapter C when reorganizing or dividing. Thus, an S corporation benefits from the stability and predictability (and elaborate, complex technical rules) of the body of law accompanying §§ 368 and 355. Careful compliance with these rules permits tax-free exchanges of stock and assets to combine, divide or realign corporate entities. Any "boot" in the exchange may trigger recognition of gain (or possibly dividend income); generally, no loss will be recognized. The S corporation, of course, faces a special concern in the form of possible termination of S status through disqualification, and hence must keep an eye on both Subchapter C and Subchapter S. The increase in the number of permissible shareholders and use of nonvoting stock and safe harbor debt mean that S corporations are more likely to engage in tax-free reorganizations. Indeed, the enhanced popularity of S corporations in general is likely to produce much more frequent use of, and stress on, the tax-free reorganization rules in the S context.

Tax-free exchanges of partnership interests (or assets) do not have the benefit of a special comprehensive and articulated body of rules such as those of Subchapter C that govern an S corporation. While two partnerships can merge, or a single partnership may divide, a partnership cannot take part in a corporate reorganization.[33] Congress has limited § 1031 nonrecognition treatment to exchanges of real property. Interests in partnerships that have elected out of Subchapter K under § 761(a) are treated as interests in the partnership's underlying assets, rather than interests in a partnership.[34] Thus, like-kind exchange treatment may still be available for the assets of an electing partnership.

¶ 10.12   SALES OR EXCHANGES OF EQUITY INTERESTS

The tax treatment of a sale or exchange of equity interests in an S corporation has been discussed in earlier Chapters and compared with tax-free reorganizations and with taxable and tax-deferred dispositions of partnership and C corporation investments.[35] The usual income tax regime for determining gain or loss on sale or exchange of an asset governs transfers of S corporation shares. Under the prevailing entity approach, the character of the gain or loss is normally determined by the character of the stock and its relationship to the seller, not by the nature of the underlying assets of the S corporation. Since an S shareholder's stock and debt are independent investments, debt does not affect the seller's amount realized on a stock sale, unlike under the § 752(d) rule for partnership interests. By comparison to transfer of a partnership interest, a sale of stock (in an S or C corporation) seems relatively simple (and safe).

Subchapter K adopts a "modified entity" approach with respect to the tax treatment of transfers of partnership interests. A partnership interest is treated as separate property, not merely as evidence of ownership in the partnership's aggregate assets. Transfer of a partnership interest is generally treated as a sale or exchange of a capital asset (except to the extent § 751(a) applies) with a separate basis.[36] Taxable gain (or loss) must be recognized and will be computed under conventional principles. Assumption of

[33] See I.R.C. § 708(b)(2).
[34] See I.R.C. § 1031(e).
[35] See ¶¶ 6.21, 7.11, 8.12.
[36] See I.R.C. §§ 741, 751(a).

partnership liabilities is taken into account as part of the seller's amount realized (and the buyer's cost basis in the acquired partnership interest). The outside basis of the seller's partnership interest will be adjusted for the seller's share of undistributed income or loss for the portion of the partnership's taxable year prior to disposition.[37] Under § 741, the transferee obtains a cost basis in the acquired partnership interest, which includes the transferee's share of liabilities.[38]

For partnerships, special rules may override the general rule that the transfer of a partnership interest is treated as a sale of an interest in an entity. The entity approach of § 741 is substantially modified (and complicated) by the hot-asset rules of § 751. Under § 751(a), sale of a partnership interest is subject to full look-through treatment as if each partner owned that partner's fractional interest in the partnership's hot or lukewarm assets. A selling partner's gain from sale of a partnership interest is characterized as ordinary income to the extent attributable to hot assets (inventory and unrealized receivables, including § 1245 recapture). Similar rules apply to a selling partner's share of lukewarm gain (unrecaptured § 1250 gain and collectibles gain) taxed at a 25% or 28% rate. By contrast, no such bifurcation is generally needed to determine the character of an S shareholder's gain on sale of an interest, since Subchapter S lacks any analogue to the hot-asset rules of § 751. Under § 1(h), however, partial look-through treatment does apply to a selling S shareholder's share of any net collectibles gain taxed at the 28% rate.[39]

One very important difference between a partnership and an S corporation involves the entity's basis in its assets when an entity interest is transferred. If shares in an S corporation are transferred by sale, by gift or at death, the new owner's basis in those shares has no effect on the entity's basis in the underlying assets. For example, if shares are sold at a gain, resulting in a higher (cost) basis to the new owner, the underlying assets retain the basis they had in the hands of the S corporation. Thus, there is no way to step up the basis of the S corporation's assets for the benefit of the purchaser, since the S corporation lacks the equivalent of a § 743(b) adjustment to inside basis available to partnerships.[40]

While the general rule (no adjustment to inside basis) is the same for partnerships, the partnership may change this result by making a "§ 754 election." If a § 754 election is made (or required), the partnership is entitled, under § 743(b), to step up (or down) the basis of the purchasing partner's share of partnership assets to reflect the higher (or

---

[37] Allocation of profit and loss between seller and buyer is determined under § 706. *See* I.R.C. § 706.

[38] Installment sale reporting is generally available, except for recapture income. *See* Rev. Rul. 89–108, 1989–2 C.B. 100; *Mingo v. Comm'r*, 773 F.3d 629 (5th Cir. 2014). The holding period of a partnership interest is determined by reference to the partner's holding period for contributed property (a "tacked" holding period), provided the property is capital gain property (*i.e.*, capital assets or § 1231 property). I.R.C. § 1223(1); Reg. § 1.1223–3(a) (split holding period if partnership interest acquired at different times or in exchange for multiple assets with different holding periods). Even if the partnership interest has a split holding period, a partner has a single unitary basis in a partnership interest. *See* Rev. Rul. 84–53, 1984–1 C.B. 159.

[39] I.R.C. § 1(h)(5)(B); Reg. § 1.1(h)–1(b). Look-through treatment does not apply, however, to a selling S shareholder's share of unrecaptured § 1250 gain. In the case of both S corporations and partnerships, the § 1411 tax may apply on sale of an interest in the entity, depending on the level of the transferor's activity. *See* ¶ 6.21.

[40] In the partnership context, the § 743(b) adjustment gives the purchasing partner the equivalent of a cost basis in the partnership's assets. The inside basis adjustment avoids (temporary) double taxation (once to the seller and again to the purchaser) when the partnership later sells appreciated assets. While Subchapter S lacks a § 743(b) counterpart, inside basis may be stepped up if § 338 or § 336(e) applies (or QSub stock is sold). *See* ¶¶ 7.13, 7.15.

lower) outside basis in the acquired interest. These basis adjustments are intended to give the purchasing partner the equivalent of a cost basis in that partner's share of the partnership's assets. Following a sale of a partnership interest, only the purchasing partner (not the other partners) benefits from the § 743(b) basis adjustment. To prevent duplication of a substantial loss, the partnership may be required to adjust inside basis following sale of a partnership interest.[41]

A transfer of stock in an S corporation generally does not implicate any special income allocation rules for the year of ownership change.[42] Under the default rule, income is allocated among the shareholders using the per-share, per-day calculation for the entire year even though stock is transferred during the year. The S corporation may use the interim closing method under specified circumstances, such as a complete termination of a shareholder's interest if all affected shareholders agree. In this event, amounts are allocated between the separate periods before and after the termination under normal tax accounting rules. By contrast, the interim closing method applies by default upon sale of a partnership interest, unless the partners agree to use the proration method.[43]

A comparison between the consequences of the death of an S shareholder or partner reveals some important differences. When an S shareholder dies, the S shares will pass to successors with a basis equal to their fair market value at death, under § 1014. No inside basis adjustment can be made to the S corporation's assets. By contrast, if a partnership has a § 754 election in effect, the deceased partner's successor will be entitled to an increase to that partner's share of the partnership's inside basis in its assets to reflect pre-death appreciation. Consequently, a successor who continues to hold the partnership interest will obtain tax benefits from a higher inside basis attributable to the deceased partner's interest.

Even though treatment of an S corporation as a separate entity is firmly entrenched, § 1367(b)(4) denies a full basis step-up under § 1014 to the extent that the value of such stock is attributable to "income in respect of a decedent" (IRD).[44] Similarly, the IRD rules may come into play in the case of a partnership. To the extent of IRD items, the successor's basis for the partnership interest will be less than its death-time fair market value.[45] Thus, the IRD rules for partnerships and S corporations are similar, though not quite identical.

A deceased shareholder's pro rata share of income is includable on the return for the decedent's final taxable year, accelerating reporting of income (or loss). The decedent's estate or beneficiary reports its pro rata share of income (or loss) for the post-death period. Rather than using the per-share, per-day method of allocation, an election may be made to close the corporation's books as of the date of death.[46] In the case of a partnership, the partnership's taxable year automatically closes on the date of death with respect to the deceased partner.[47] One peculiarity of S corporations is the

[41] *See* I.R.C. § 743(d) (substantial built-in loss); *see also* I.R.C. § 734(d) (substantial basis reduction).

[42] *See* I.R.C. § 1377(a); ¶ 6.21.

[43] *See* Reg. § 1.706–4(a)(1) (allocations to reflect partners' varying interests).

[44] *See* I.R.C. § 691(c) (allowing a deduction for estate tax attributable to IRD items).

[45] In the partnership context, the IRD concept is broader, since it also includes certain § 736(a) payments. *See* I.R.C. § 753.

[46] I.R.C. § 1377(a)(2); Reg. § 1.1377–1(b)(4).

[47] I.R.C. § 706(c)(2)(A); Reg. § 1.706–1(c)(2).

termination risk if the deceased shareholder's S stock passes to an ineligible shareholder or into the hands of too many new shareholders.

A transfer of stock of an S corporation can have other special ramifications, including eligibility for, or termination of, S status, compliance with or violation of share transfer restrictions, and basis effects that have special significance as to the passthrough of losses or taxability of distributions. While a sale of more than 50% of an S corporation's stock can threaten its continued S status, a partnership is treated as continuing to exist until a termination occurs.[48] A termination occurs only if no part of the partnership's business continues to be conducted in partnership form.[49] Thus, a sale of partnership interests does not trigger a termination of the partnership.

¶ 10.13   ABILITY TO RAISE CAPITAL

An S corporation will be subject to some legal and practical limits on its ability to raise capital that do not hamper a partnership. In particular, the numerical shareholder limit, the prohibitions against corporate or foreign shareholders, and the rule against multiple classes of stock may inhibit the S corporation's access to capital. A partnership is not similarly constrained in its ability to access capital, although it may face reluctance on the part of some potential investors to invest in partnership interests rather than the familiar and convenient vehicle of corporate stock. A partnership may also face a risk of reclassification as a corporation, under § 7704, if its interests are too widely held or traded over an exchange. Outside basis from entity-level borrowing under § 752 will provide a tax benefit for partnerships that is not available in an S corporation. This difference may indirectly affect capital-raising efforts and favors the partnership form.

¶ 10.14   INVESTMENT RESTRICTIONS

Section 1361(b)(2) places various restrictions on the type of business in which an S corporation can engage. For example, an insurance company or a bank that uses the reserve method of accounting for bad debts cannot be an S corporation. The Code does not restrict the S corporation from owning shares in such businesses, however. An S corporation may own any amount of stock in another corporation, though it may not be included in a consolidated group.

¶ 10.15   INCOME SPLITTING AND ESTATE PLANNING

In some ways, a corporation and corporate stock lend themselves to income splitting and estate planning more readily than do a partnership and partnership interests. This holds true even for an S corporation and S stock, despite all the limitations on capital structure and shareholder eligibility. Shares of S stock can be given to minor dependents, who will thereafter be taxable (subject to the § 1(g) "kiddie tax") on a pro rata share of passthrough income, subject to the income-shifting and reasonable compensation rules of § 1366(e). General rules restricting anticipatory assignments of income may also apply. A partnership interest also may be given to children, allowing future partnership income to be shifted to them. This technique is limited by the family partnership rules of § 704(e), which parallel 1366(e).

---

[48] I.R.C. § 708(a).

[49] I.R.C. § 708(b)(1).

To be sure, the use of trusts owning stock in an S corporation is narrowly circumscribed by the permitted shareholder rules of § 1361. In contrast, partnership interests may be held by trusts without any such limits. S corporation stock may not be held by a *foreign* trust, and a permitted trust must fit the strict categories of trusts described in § 1361(c)(2), as discussed in ¶ 2.08.

Unlike a partnership or a C corporation, an S corporation cannot issue ownership interests with different preferences or rights in income or assets. Thus, the S corporation cannot so easily be used to accomplish an estate "freeze" or otherwise separate growth potential from income security.[50] But use of debt, voting and nonvoting common shares, and loans, leases or licenses of assets may often accomplish much the same result. A tax-free recapitalization of an S corporation may serve to realign interests for estate planning purposes.

Because of the prohibited shareholder rules of § 1361(b), S corporation stock held by a decedent must be treated with caution if it goes into a testamentary trust. Also, it must not be held by an estate for too long. Fortunately, permitted shareholders include the estate of an individual in bankruptcy.[51] Other tax effects of the death of an S shareholder can be important, as mentioned in ¶ 6.24.

¶ 10.16   FOREIGN AND INTERNATIONAL APPLICATIONS

A partnership may have foreign partners as well as foreign income. An S corporation may not have foreign shareholders, though it may have any amount of foreign income. The prohibition against foreign (nonresident alien) shareholders can cause problems for an S corporation with a resident-alien shareholder who changes residence. Similarly, difficulties may arise if a citizen residing abroad expatriates or a shareholder marries a foreign national. Shareholder buy-sell agreements should be carefully drafted to deal with these possibilities.[52]

Since S corporations are permitted to have foreign income, their use in international or foreign operations has increased. An S corporation's operations outside the United States may be conducted in branch form (or through an entity that is disregarded under the check-the-box regulations).[53] For foreign tax purposes, the S corporation may be characterized by the other nation as a separate taxable entity (an association taxable as a corporation) or as a conduit like a partnership. Even if it is not accorded conduit treatment by the foreign country's tax law, for U.S. purposes it can pass through to its shareholders the § 901 direct foreign tax credit for payment of a foreign corporate income

---

[50] Most preferred-equity estate freezes are blocked by § 2701.

[51] I.R.C. § 1361(c)(3); *see* ¶ 2.08.

[52] The prohibition against foreign shareholders probably stems from a notion that the U.S. Treasury should collect at least some tax from a U.S. corporation or its shareholders. As a legal or as a practical matter, it might be more difficult to collect such tax in the case of a nonresident alien shareholder of an S corporation. This reason should perhaps give way to the enhanced need for, and utility of, S corporations and increased internationalization of business and investment. As discussed in ¶ 2.08, a nonresident alien can be a potential current beneficiary of an ESBT.

[53] Use of a foreign subsidiary treated as a corporation for U.S. tax purposes is likely to be disadvantageous because the S corporation and its shareholders cannot avail themselves of the § 902 indirect foreign tax credit for taxes actually paid by the foreign corporation. *See* I.R.C. § 1373(a) (treating an S corporation as a partnership for this purpose). The result is double taxation of the foreign income: once by the foreign country as income is earned, and again at the U.S. shareholder level (with a credit for any withholding taxes levied by the foreign country).

tax.[54] A second S corporation can be formed by the same (or overlapping) shareholders to conduct operations in another country or to insulate assets of one business from risks and liabilities of another. Two S corporations can form a partnership or joint venture. Alternatively, an S corporation can join with a C corporation or foreign corporation or an individual so long as the prohibited shareholder rule is not violated. Liquidation or reorganization of an S corporation that invests or does business abroad requires careful planning. Special problems may be encountered, including recapture of foreign losses and foreign tax credit issues.

¶ 10.17   FRINGE BENEFITS AND RETIREMENT COMPENSATION

For fringe-benefit purposes, § 1372(a) explicitly subjects an S corporation and its "2% shareholders" to partnership and partner treatment, putting the two forms of business organization on a par.[55] Both S corporations and partnerships may now generally use the same types of qualified-plan arrangements that were formerly available only to C corporations.[56]

An S corporation can use *nonqualified* deferred compensation plans in the same way that a non-electing C corporation can. Unlike a partnership, an S corporation can utilize phantom stock and incentive stock options. Use of nonqualified deferred compensation by an S corporation may be an advantage over the partnership form. Nevertheless, a partnership may be able to achieve an even more tax-advantageous result. For example, a service provider may receive a partnership profits interest tax free and thereby convert ordinary income into capital gain.[57]

¶ 10.18   SPECIAL APPLICATIONS: REAL ESTATE; TAX SHELTERS; PORTFOLIO INVESTMENTS

For tax shelters and real estate investments, the ability to pass through losses makes the partnership or S corporation especially appealing compared to the C corporation. Nevertheless, some characteristics of, or special limitations placed upon, S corporations may argue in favor of the partnership form in these situations. For example, the inability to make partnership-type special allocations may render the S corporation form less suitable for real estate investments, whether or not they are designed particularly as tax shelters. Of course, it may make sense to use an S corporation (or an LLC) as the vehicle for the general partner's interest in a real estate (or other) limited partnership.

Probably two factors most decisively favor the partnership form for leveraged or tax-shelter real estate investments. First, partners have the ability to obtain increases in outside basis for entity-level debt, unlike S shareholders. Under § 752, even debt for which no partner has any personal liability (*e.g.*, debt that is nonrecourse at the entity level) generates outside basis. Second, a partnership, unlike an S corporation, can distribute appreciated assets in kind without recognition of entity-level gain.

---

[54]   *See* I.R.C. § 1373(a).

[55]   *See* ¶ 3.10.

[56]   *See* ¶ 3.09.

[57]   *But see* I.R.C. § 1061 (taxing long-term capital gain attributable to an "applicable partnership interest" as short-term capital gain unless a 3-year holding period is satisfied).

An S corporation that has never been a C corporation can serve as a personal holding company, since it avoids both the personal holding company tax of § 541 and the accumulated earnings tax of § 531. Thus, it can have unlimited passive investment income and foreign source income without triggering these taxes. If the S corporation has or inherits accumulated earnings and profits, however, the results could be disastrous. In this situation, the § 1375 sting tax and § 1362(d)(3) involuntary termination loom large. The obvious solution is to use a fresh-start S corporation, with no subchapter C attributes, and carefully to preserve its untainted Subchapter S status.

¶ 10.19   OTHER CONSIDERATIONS

Applicable state law may include a corporate income tax as well as an individual income tax but may not allow an S election. If so, it may be advantageous to use the partnership form to achieve full conduit treatment—a single tax on firm profits and a full passthrough of losses—for state as well as federal income tax purposes. (¶ 9.11.) When comparing the partnership and S corporation forms, it is essential to consider any state tax on partnerships and their partners or on conduit corporations and their owners. In addition, an S corporation may be useful to minimize employment taxes; the § 1411 tax on net investment income and the § 199A deduction also need to be taken into account. (¶¶ 3.11–3.12.)

Repayment of shareholder loans made to the S corporation can produce adverse tax consequences, in the form of basis reductions. These consequences should be understood and gauged when choosing the S form over a partnership, or when capitalizing the entity with shareholder loans (rather than third-party loans) in order to obtain outside basis for S shareholders.

Of course, the non-tax differences between a partnership and a corporation that elects Subchapter S treatment for federal income tax purposes may strongly influence the choice-of-form analysis. These non-tax differences must never be underestimated. On the whole it is not surprising that the tax perspective alone may not be determinative. Subchapter S was originally conceived, after all, to take tax considerations out of the choice-of-entity decision to the extent possible. Indeed, some may argue that S corporations have outlived their usefulness, now that LLCs combine the flexibility of partnership taxation and the non-tax advantages of limited liability.

In any event, the tax advisor's best judgment and analysis should be memorialized, probably in a letter to the client, who should have a full opportunity to study the reasoning and react to it. Such an approach may help to minimize the possibility of later misunderstandings, particularly in the event that the client does not follow the advice given and the course actually taken proves costly in tax or other terms. The tax advisor may also wish to emphasize the need for subsequent monitoring of the S corporation's eligibility and its potential vulnerability to sting taxes or involuntary termination.

¶ 10.20   PROBLEM AREAS; INVENTIVE STRUCTURES

As a full-fledged corporation, a "person" in law, an S corporation can enter into partnership with other legal persons, including other S corporations. It can also make taxable or tax-free acquisitions and dispositions much like those made by a C corporation.

Some planning problems can be solved by structures that combine several related entities, with one or more S corporations participating in the structure. In doing so, the creative tax planner must exercise care to ensure that use of multiple S corporations does not violate the prohibited shareholder rule or run afoul of other constraints under Subchapters K and S.[58]

---

[58] Unless used primarily to avoid the 100-shareholder limit, a partnership arrangement can allow special allocations to be made to the S corporation partners. *See* Rev. Rul. 94–43, 1994–2 C.B. 198; Reg. § 1.701–2(d) (ex. 2).

Chapter 11

COMPLIANCE, AFTERTHOUGHTS, FORETHOUGHTS AND LEGISLATIVE POLICY

¶ 11.01   INTRODUCTION

Chapter 11 considers briefly several topics, ranging from compliance and administration to legislative and reform proposals. It begins with an important practical reminder.

¶ 11.02   COMBINING SUBCHAPTER S WITH § 1244

When capitalizing a corporation that will make an S election, it is important not to overlook the favorable rules of § 1244 concerning losses on small business stock. In anticipation of potential losses on termination, precautions *should* be taken to qualify as much stock of an S corporation as possible for ordinary loss treatment under § 1244.[1]

¶ 11.03   COMPLIANCE AND PROCEDURE; FORMS; REPORTING REQUIREMENTS AND AUDIT

An S corporation must file an income tax return, Form 1120S, even though it usually does not have to pay any tax.[2] In addition to the basic Form 1120S, additional forms may be needed for certain purposes. Every S corporation must file a Schedule K-1 (for its form 1120S) for each shareholder, in order to show each shareholder's annual share of passthrough items. A copy of the K-1 goes to each shareholder and another copy must accompany the 1120S filed by the corporation. Further forms or schedules are available, such as Schedule M to compute and record the S corporation's AAA. For more instruction on compliance and reporting, one should consult these IRS forms and other IRS instructions and filing materials. Reference should also be made to professional manuals or guide books, as well as state filing information for state-level income taxes (and possible S elections or parallel treatment).

In 1996, Congress repealed the so-called "unified audit rules" applicable to S corporations (former §§ 6241–6245) that allowed the IRS to make audit adjustments at the entity level. These determinations were then binding on S shareholders (except as modified in a unified proceeding). In repealing the unified audit rules for S corporations, Congress indicated that they were not needed for entities with only a limited number of shareholders.[3] Under the consistency rule of § 6037, S shareholders must treat "subchapter S items" on their individual returns in a manner consistent with their

---

[1]   These measures are outlined in ¶ 6.17.

[2]   *See* I.R.C. § 6037; Reg. §§ 1.6037–1, 1.6012–2.

[3]   Even under prior law, the unified audit rules did not apply to S corporations with five or fewer shareholders, unless the corporation elected to have them apply. If an S corporation is a partner in a partnership, the S shareholders will count toward the 100-partner threshold under the centralized partnership audit rules. *See* I.R.C. § 6221(b)(2).

treatment on the S corporation's return.[4] The consistency rule is intended to prevent whipsawing of the government.

As to state income taxation, special problems of income allocation often arise because states are not consistent in their taxation of an electing S corporation.[5] Consequently, if the S corporation has multi-state *operations*, corporate income and expenses must be allocated between and among the states involved. Multi-state *shareholders* also present special complications at the state tax level.

Other administrative and procedural concerns include applicable statutes of limitations[6] and estimated tax reporting and payments.[7] Formalities must be observed concerning the S election itself, other corporate or shareholder elections, and changes of taxable year.

¶ 11.04   A GLIMPSE INTO THE FUTURE?

As suggested in Chapter 1, Subchapter S has been perceived by some as a model toward which all corporate taxation may one day evolve.[8] Although proposals for corporate-shareholder integration currently seem to have little political support, the dividing line between corporations subject to the double-tax regime and passthrough entities is widely viewed as unsatisfactory. A more sensible dividing line would be between publicly traded and nonpublicly traded corporations. By eliminating the linkage between organizational form and tax status, the check-the-box regulations undermine the traditional justification for multiple passthrough regimes. Indeed, some may question whether Subchapter S is still needed, since it is now possible to combine limited liability and single-level taxation by forming an LLC taxed as a partnership.

Proposals for legislative change often implicitly or explicitly involve issues concerning whether they would merely simplify (or improve) Subchapter S or further expand its availability. In the near future, revenue considerations are likely to rule out any dramatic expansion of Subchapter S. Consequently, simplification proposals are most likely to stand a chance for success if they are directed at easing the mechanics of the Subchapter S rules and eliminating unintended pitfalls, rather than expanding S eligibility or utility in new ways.

Unified Passthrough System. The fundamental issue is whether a unified system of passthrough taxation would be preferable to a two-track regime which preserves some version of existing Subchapters K and S. In the late 1990s, a study by the American Law Institute concluded that a unified passthrough system would be too complex and unwieldy.[9] The study recommended a simpler set of rules (modelled on Subchapter S)

---

[4]   *See* I.R.C. § 6037(c)(1). A "subchapter S item" is any item of an S corporation that, pursuant to regulations, is more appropriately determined at the corporate level than at the shareholder level. *See* I.R.C. § 6037(c)(4).

[5]   *See* ¶ 9.11

[6]   For purposes of determining a deficiency, the relevant statute of limitations relates to the date on which the particular shareholder filed a return (not the date on which the S corporation filed its return). *See Bufferd v. Comm'r*, 506 U.S. 523 (1993).

[7]   If an S corporation is required to pay a corporate-level tax, it must make estimated tax payments. *See* I.R.C. § 6655(g)(4).

[8]   *See* Eustice, Subchapter S Corporations and Partnerships: A Search for the Pass-Through Paradigm (Some Preliminary Proposals), 39 Tax L. Rev. 345 (1984).

[9]   *See* Am. Law Inst. Reporters' Study, Taxation of Private Business Enterprises 102–103 (1999) (Yin & Shakow, reporters).

for relatively simple businesses with a single class of residual ownership interests and a more complex set of rules (modelled on Subchapter K) for businesses with more complex sharing arrangements.

Various legislative proposals have been suggested to reform taxation of passthrough entities. One proposal would repeal Subchapters K and S, and create a single set of rules for all nonpublicly traded passthrough entities (and those publicly traded entities qualifying for an exception under § 7704).[10] For S corporations, the unified passthrough regime would offer many advantages, including elimination of the one class-of-stock rule, lifting of limitations on eligible shareholders, and inclusion of entity-level debt in outside basis. These benefits would be coupled, however, with substantial new compliance burdens applicable to all passthrough corporations.

Under the proposed unified system, all passthrough entities would be subject to new rules (1) requiring recognition of gain on distributions of appreciated property (similar to the existing S rules), (2) limiting special allocations to three categories consisting of ordinary income, capital gains (including qualified dividends taxed at 20%) and tax credits, (3) imposing mandatory basis adjustments in connection with sales of interests and distributions of property, (4) expanding the hot-asset rules of § 751(b), and (5) introducing entity-level withholding (with a credit at the owner level).

Thus far, the consensus seems to be that the complexity and disadvantages of the proposed unified regime would likely outweigh its benefits and the substantial transition costs. Indeed, subjecting all passthrough entities to a modified version of existing Subchapter K could produce the worst of all possible worlds: increased complexity for less sophisticated taxpayers, without adequate safeguards to prevent sophisticated taxpayers from exploiting imprecise and flexible rules. Given the lukewarm reception accorded the unified passthrough proposal, the most likely outcome is that Congress will continue to follow the trend of restricting the flexibility of Subchapter K while further loosening some of the restrictions of Subchapter S.

Even if a single set of unified rules proves infeasible, it would still be desirable to eliminate differences in the existing two-track system to the extent that such disparities are unrelated to simplification or compliance concerns. One of the major discontinuities between Subchapters K and S relates to nonrecognition upon a partnership distribution of appreciated property. Despite recent measures chipping away at Subchapter K's general nonrecognition rule, applying rules similar to §§ 311(b) and 336 to partnership distributions of appreciated property may be a long overdue reform. It would harmonize the partnership rules with those of Subchapter S. Moreover, a general recognition rule for partnership distributions could allow significant simplification by reducing or eliminating the need for some of the most complex provisions of Subchapter K.[11] By contrast, it seems extremely unlikely that Congress would allow carryover-basis treatment on property distributions by S corporations, given the potential for income-shifting and other abuses.

---

[10] *See* Technical Explanation of the Ways and Means Committee Discussion Draft Provisions to Reform the Taxation of Small Businesses and Passthrough Entities (Mar. 12, 2013). A less ambitious reform proposal would retain both Subchapters K and S but would modify the rules of Subchapter K to address abuses and liberalize the rules of Subchapter S. *See* Taylor, Subchapter S Out the Window? What's Going On?, 139 Tax Notes 1051 (2013).

[11] For example, it might be possible to repeal the hot-asset rules of § 751(b), although an anti-abuse rule might still be needed to prevent shifting of ordinary income.

Another significant difference between Subchapters K and S relates to the ability of partnerships to adjust inside basis following a sale of a partnership interest or a distribution of partnership property. Until recently, one of the curious features of Subchapter K was that inside-basis adjustments were entirely elective, so that taxpayers would make the adjustments only when they proved advantageous. Extending inside-basis adjustments to Subchapter S might be viewed as inconsistent with the need to preserve simplicity.[12] In the case of a major shift of ownership of an S corporation, however, a § 338 election (or a § 336(e) election) makes possible an adjustment to the inside basis of S assets, coupled with a single level of tax.[13]

Another major difference in the treatment of partnerships and S corporations relates to the inclusion of entity-level debt in outside basis. While partners are permitted to include nonrecourse debt in outside basis, an S shareholder may be denied a basis increase even for entity-level debt that the shareholder personally guarantees. But for Congress' perennial concerns about tax shelters, it might seem sensible to extend rules similar to § 752 to Subchapter S, although it would entail considerable complexity. Revised regulations concerning bona-fide debt held by S shareholders may help somewhat to ease continuing frictions.[14]

In the reorganization area, the advantage of S corporations over partnerships seems likely to persist. The Subchapter K provisions concerning partnership mergers, divisions, and other restructurings are quite primitive compared to the elaborate reorganization rules of Subchapter C. Rather than attempt to craft a similarly elaborate body of law under Subchapter K, it would seem better to focus attention on the ongoing work of rationalizing and modernizing the Subchapter C rules governing reorganizations. As a policy matter, it is not clear that partnerships should be permitted to engage in tax-free reorganizations with C or S corporations. Permitting such cross-species tax-free restructurings would also raise difficult technical issues (analogous to those under Subchapter S) concerning how adequately to preserve C attributes when a former C corporation wishes to migrate out of the double-tax system.

As a practical matter, choice-of-entity decisions are often motivated less by considerations of administrative simplicity than by desire to exploit particular loopholes, such as the employment-tax loophole enjoyed by S shareholders. Under current law, S corporation shareholders who materially participate in the business can avoid both self-employment taxes and the 3.8% tax under § 1411 by disguising salary as distributions with respect to stock.[15] Given the purpose of the § 1411 "mirror" tax, it seems illogical that income passed through and distributed to an S shareholder should be treated as neither employment income nor investment income. With respect to employment taxes, there is no policy reason why S shareholders should be treated more favorably than partners or LLC members who materially participate in the business.[16] While

---

[12] Nevertheless, such inside basis adjustments might actually prove less complex for S corporations because a redemption of a portion of an S shareholder's interest is already treated as a partial liquidation. Adoption of the § 302 redemption model would also allow elimination of the anachronistic rules of § 736.

[13] See ¶ 7.13.

[14] See ¶ 6.07.

[15] See ¶ 3.11; see also GAO, Tax Gap: Actions Needed To Address Noncompliance With S Corporation Tax Rules 25 (2009) (estimating that, in 2003 and 2004, S shareholders underreported compensation by roughly $23.6 billion, reducing collection of self-employment taxes by roughly $3 billion).

[16] In 1997, Treasury proposed regulations that attempt to distinguish between active and inactive passthrough participants, but Congress imposed a one-year moratorium on enforcement of the regulations. See

eliminating the S employment-tax loophole would level the playing field for different types of entities, such a proposal is certain to encounter strong political opposition.

C to S Conversions. In the choice-of-entity area, one of the most vexing issues is the appropriate "toll charge" to be imposed when an entity migrates from C corporation status to passthrough status. Although conversion from a C corporation to a partnership (or LLC) triggers two full levels of tax—one at the corporate level and one at the shareholder level—migration from a C corporation to an S corporation (or RIC or REIT) triggers neither an immediate corporate-level nor shareholder-level tax on built-in gain attributable to a prior C history.[17] In the case of S corporations, § 1374 is intended to preserve the corporate-level tax on such built-in gain. Similarly, the termination threat of § 1362(d) and the § 1375 tax on excess passive investment income apply only if an S corporation has a prior C history (or inherits accumulated earnings and profits from a C corporation).

To harmonize choice-of-entity differences, it would be possible, of course, to treat conversion of a C corporation to S status as a constructive liquidation in which the corporation distributed assets to its shareholders who then immediately re-contributed those assets to a new S corporation.[18] While such a toll charge might practically eliminate conversions—given the cost of two full levels of tax—it would undoubtedly eliminate much complexity under Subchapter S. It would allow repeal of the sting taxes under §§ 1374 and 1375, and the threat of disqualification under § 1362(d)(3).[19] There would no longer be a need for an AAA system and different rules for taxing distributions by S corporations that once were C corporations, the election of dividend treatment to zero-out earnings and profits, recapture of LIFO inventory, and special carryover rules for NOLs.

The theory behind the deemed-liquidation approach is to put converting C corporations on a par with those that actually liquidate and with nonconverting C corporations whose assets will generate future income subject to the corporate-level tax. Conversion by a C corporation to S corporation status may be regarded as the functional equivalent of withdrawing assets from corporate solution, as upon on a liquidation. Particularly if the corporation's basis in its assets exceeds the shareholders' bases in their shares, the conversion to S status offers the shareholders some of the benefits of the higher "inside" basis of the corporate assets, without any immediate shareholder-level tax to justify that basis increase. To be sure, a shareholder tax may later be collected, but the deferral will be advantageous. Extracting assets from corporate solution, or out from under the usual corporate income tax, allows their future yields to be received at a lower overall tax rate. Arguably, the concept of a deemed liquidation and reincorporation is consistent with the theory underlying *General Utilities* repeal.

Prop. Reg. § 1.1402(a)–2; Joint Comm. on Tax'n, Options to Improve Tax Compliance and Reform Tax Expenditures 97–99 (JCS–02–05) (2005).

[17]   Although there is no parallel statutory provision, the regulations apply § 1374 principles to RICs and REITs to prevent circumvention of *General Utilities* repeal. *See* Reg. § 1.337(d)–7.

[18]   *See* Nunnallee, The S Conversion: Tax Free or Constructive Liquidation (A Case for Compromise), 48 Tax Notes 1659 (1990).

[19]   It would also be possible to repeal the § 1366(f) passthrough reduction for these penalty taxes. Abolishing the § 1375 tax on excess passive investment income may also raise the policy issue of whether, by electing S status, a former C corporation should be able to avoid the personal holding company tax under § 541, without liquidating or purging its accumulated earnings and profits.

Nevertheless, the deterrent effect of the deemed liquidation and toll charge would need to be considered very seriously.

Indeed, Congress moved recently in precisely the opposite direction by permanently shortening the § 1374 recognition period for built-in gain. As a policy matter, a five-year recognition period does not seem justified. It may be possible to avoid corporate-level tax simply by electing S status and waiting to sell built-in gain assets. As the experience with the partnership disguised sale rules suggests, a longer waiting period may be needed to police strategic S elections.

Operation of the § 1374 built-in gain tax is arguably flawed because it imposes tax *immediately* at both the corporate and shareholder level when built-in gain assets are sold. By contrast, if the corporate-level gain were taxed while the assets remained in C solution, the shareholder-level tax could be deferred until a distribution. One possible compromise solution would be to impose the § 1374 tax at the corporate level (at the maximum corporate tax rate), while deferring the shareholder-level tax (by denying any shareholder-level basis adjustment for built-in gain recognized and taxed at the corporate level) until an actual distribution.[20] Under this compromise approach, there would be a strong argument for removing *any* limit on the built-in gain recognition period. Alternatively, a C corporation could be allowed electively to recognize gain (or loss) upon a conversion (or acquisition) as if it had sold all of its assets to an unrelated party, analogous to a § 338 election.[21]

Congress should also reexamine proposals permitting (or requiring) a former C corporation to purge its earnings and profits to gain access to Subchapter S. The current low tax rate on qualified dividends would allow tax-efficient purging of retained C earnings through a deemed dividend distribution. Such treatment would help to harmonize the rules for S corporations, on the one hand, and those for RICs and REITs, on the other hand. In the case of a passthrough entity that qualifies as a RIC or REIT, conversion from C status effectively ends deferral of shareholder-level taxation on undistributed C earnings and profits.[22] If partnerships, S corporations, and other passthrough entities are viewed simply as alternative integration models, the rules governing movement into (and out of) these different regime should be parallel, to the extent possible.

Continued Expansion of Passthroughs. The future direction of business taxation is highly uncertain. While the 21% corporate tax rate is permanent under the 2017 Act, the individual tax provisions (including the § 199A deduction) are scheduled to expire after 2025. Higher individual rates and elimination of the § 199A deduction would render passthrough taxation less beneficial, while C corporations would offer increased tax-shelter opportunities. Indeed, the continued expansion of passthrough entities might be halted, potentially reversing the post-1986 "disincorporation" phenomenon. Given the

---

[20] *See* Yin, Comments on Taxation of Passthrough Entities, 140 Tax Notes 358 (2013); *see also* Ginsburg, Subchapter S and Accumulated E&P: A Different View, 17 Tax Notes 571 (1982).

[21] Reg. § 1.337(d)–7(c)(5) (permitting a RIC or REIT to elect deemed sale treatment and to adjust the basis of assets to fair market value).

[22] A RIC or REIT is not permitted to have any accumulated C earnings and profits. I.R.C. §§ 852(a)(2)(B), 857(a)(2)(B). In the case of a former C corporation, any distributions to shareholders for purposes of qualifying as a RIC or REIT are treated as made first from Subchapter C earnings and profits. *See* I.R.C. §§ 852(c)(3), 857(d)(3).

importance of the passthrough sector, however, Congress would likely face strong pressure to hold harmless passthrough entities and their owners.

Alternatively, Congress may increase the corporate tax rate to 25% or even higher.[23] In addition to increasing the corporate tax rate, Congress could increase the tax rates on dividends and capital gains. If the maximum corporate tax rate were increased to 25% and dividends were taxed at ordinary income rates of 25%, the combined corporate-shareholder tax burden on distributed earnings would be identical to a single 43.75% tax at the individual level.[24] Under this set of rate relationships, C corporations would no longer be attractive as tax shelters, assuming the corporation distributed dividends. Passthrough entities would remain the default organizational choice, particularly if § 199A survived. Moreover, passthrough owners would continue to have an incentive to recharacterize labor income as business profits, exacerbating the problem of reasonable compensation already rampant in S corporations.

Given the 2017 rationale for § 199A as providing parity for passthrough owners, Congress may face pressure to significantly revise or eliminate the deduction if corporate tax rates are increased. As currently structured, the tax savings from the § 199A deduction overwhelmingly benefit high-income taxpayers. In addition, Congress could address the ability of active S corporation owners to avoid employment taxes and the 3.8% tax under § 1411. Business tax reform cannot be divorced from broader reform of the individual income tax, especially since such a large portion of business net income is currently taxed as passthrough income at individual tax rates. Ideally, business tax reform could give new impetus to efforts to improve the passthrough system for nonpublicly traded businesses.

---

[23] Rather than raise the corporate tax rate, Congress recently imposed a 15% minimum tax on the adjusted financial statement income of certain large C corporations. *See* ¶ 5.07.

[24] If a C corporation earned income of $100 and distributed all of its earnings currently, the corporation would pay tax of $25 and the shareholders would pay tax of $18.75 (25% × $75 after-tax corporate distribution).

Appendices

USEFUL S CORPORATION REFERENCES

A. Professional, updated source books (available in print or on line):

Blau et al., S Corporations Federal Taxation (Clark Boardman Callaghan)

Christian & Grant, Subchapter S Taxation (WG&L)

Eustice, Kuntz & Bogdanski, Federal Income Taxation of S Corporations (WG&L)

Fass & Gerrard, The S Corporation Handbook (Clark Boardman Callaghan)

Jamison, S Corporation Taxation (CCH)

Maule, State Taxation of S Corporations (BNA Portfolio 1510—2nd)

Robinson, et al., Tax Planning for S Corporations (Matthew Bender)

Sobel & Starr, S Corporations: Corporate Tax Issues (BNA Portfolio 731—3rd)

Sobel & Starr, S Corporations: Formation and Termination (BNA Portfolio 730—4th)

Sobel & Starr, S Corporations: Shareholder Tax Issues (BNA Portfolio 732—1st)

Traum & Kosnitzky, The S Corporation: Planning & Operation (Wolters Kluwer)

B. Forms 2553 and 1120S

Form **2553**	**Election by a Small Business Corporation**	
(Rev. December 2017)	(Under section 1362 of the Internal Revenue Code) (Including a late election filed pursuant to Rev. Proc. 2013-30)	OMB No. 1545-0123
Department of the Treasury Internal Revenue Service	▶ You can fax this form to the IRS. See separate instructions. ▶ Go to *www.irs.gov/Form2553* for instructions and the latest information.	

Note: This election to be an S corporation can be accepted only if all the tests are met under *Who May Elect* in the instructions, all shareholders have signed the consent statement, an officer has signed below, and the exact name and address of the corporation (entity) and other required form information have been provided.

Part I Election Information

Type or Print	Name (see instructions)	A Employer identification number
	Number, street, and room or suite no. If a P.O. box, see instructions.	B Date incorporated
	City or town, state or province, country, and ZIP or foreign postal code	C State of incorporation

D Check the applicable box(es) if the corporation (entity), after applying for the EIN shown in A above, changed its ☐ name or ☐ address

E Election is to be effective for tax year beginning (month, day, year) (see instructions) . . . . . . ▶ _____

   Caution: A corporation (entity) making the election for its first tax year in existence will usually enter the beginning date of a short tax year that begins on a date other than January 1.

F Selected tax year:
   (1) ☐ Calendar year
   (2) ☐ Fiscal year ending (month and day) ▶ _____
   (3) ☐ 52-53-week year ending with reference to the month of December
   (4) ☐ 52-53-week year ending with reference to the month of ▶ _____
   If box (2) or (4) is checked, complete Part II.

G If more than 100 shareholders are listed for item J (see page 2), check this box if treating members of a family as one shareholder results in no more than 100 shareholders (see test 2 under *Who May Elect* in the instructions) ▶ ☐

H Name and title of officer or legal representative whom the IRS may call for more information | Telephone number of officer or legal representative

I If this S corporation election is being filed late, I declare I had reasonable cause for not filing Form 2553 timely. If this late election is being made by an entity eligible to elect to be treated as a corporation, I declare I also had reasonable cause for not filing an entity classification election timely and the representations listed in Part IV are true. See below for my explanation of the reasons the election or elections were not made on time and a description of my diligent actions to correct the mistake upon its discovery. See instructions.

Sign Here	Under penalties of perjury, I declare that I have examined this election, including accompanying documents, and, to the best of my knowledge and belief, the election contains all the relevant facts relating to the election, and such facts are true, correct, and complete.	
▶	Signature of officer	Title	Date

For Paperwork Reduction Act Notice, see separate instructions.   Cat. No. 18629R   Form **2553** (Rev. 12-2017)

Form 2553 (Rev. 12-2017) Page **2**

Name					Employer identification number

Part I   **Election Information** *(continued)* **Note:** If you need more rows, use additional copies of page 2.

J Name and address of each shareholder or former shareholder required to consent to the election. (see instructions)	K Shareholder's Consent Statement Under penalties of perjury, I declare that I consent to the election of the above-named corporation (entity) to be an S corporation under section 1362(a) and that I have examined this consent statement, including accompanying documents, and, to the best of my knowledge and belief, the election contains all the relevant facts relating to the election, and such facts are true, correct, and complete. I understand my consent is binding and may not be withdrawn after the corporation (entity) has made a valid election. If seeking relief for a late filed election, I also declare under penalties of perjury that I have reported my income on all affected returns consistent with the S corporation election for the year for which the election should have been filed (see beginning date entered on line E) and for all subsequent years. Signature	Date	L Stock owned or percentage of ownership (see instructions) Number of shares or percentage of ownership	Date(s) acquired	M Social security number or employer identification number (see instructions)	N Shareholder's tax year ends (month and day)

Form **2553** (Rev. 12-2017)

Form 2553 (Rev. 12-2017)   Page **3**

Name	Employer identification number

Part II   **Selection of Fiscal Tax Year** (see instructions)

Note: All corporations using this part must complete item O and item P, Q, or R.

O   Check the applicable box to indicate whether the corporation is:

    1. ☐ A new corporation **adopting** the tax year entered in item F, Part I.

    2. ☐ An existing corporation **retaining** the tax year entered in item F, Part I.

    3. ☐ An existing corporation **changing** to the tax year entered in item F, Part I.

P   Complete item P if the corporation is using the automatic approval provisions of Rev. Proc. 2006-46, 2006-45 I.R.B. 859, to request (1) a natural business year (as defined in section 5.07 of Rev. Proc. 2006-46) or (2) a year that satisfies the ownership tax year test (as defined in section 5.08 of Rev. Proc. 2006-46). Check the applicable box below to indicate the representation statement the corporation is making.

1. Natural Business Year ▶ ☐ I represent that the corporation is adopting, retaining, or changing to a tax year that qualifies as its natural business year (as defined in section 5.07 of Rev. Proc. 2006-46) and has attached a statement showing separately for each month the gross receipts for the most recent 47 months. See instructions. I also represent that the corporation is not precluded by section 4.02 of Rev. Proc. 2006-46 from obtaining automatic approval of such adoption, retention, or change in tax year.

2. Ownership Tax Year ▶ ☐ I represent that shareholders (as described in section 5.08 of Rev. Proc. 2006-46) holding more than half of the shares of the stock (as of the first day of the tax year to which the request relates) of the corporation have the same tax year or are concurrently changing to the tax year that the corporation adopts, retains, or changes to per item F, Part I, and that such tax year satisfies the requirement of section 4.01(3) of Rev. Proc. 2006-46. I also represent that the corporation is not precluded by section 4.02 of Rev. Proc. 2006-46 from obtaining automatic approval of such adoption, retention, or change in tax year.

Note: If you do not use item P and the corporation wants a fiscal tax year, complete either item Q or R below. Item Q is used to request a fiscal tax year based on a business purpose and to make a back-up section 444 election. Item R is used to make a regular section 444 election.

Q   Business Purpose—To request a fiscal tax year based on a business purpose, check box Q1. See instructions for details including payment of a user fee. You may also check box Q2 and/or box Q3.

1. Check here ▶ ☐ if the fiscal year entered in item F, Part I, is requested under the prior approval provisions of Rev. Proc. 2002-39, 2002-22 I.R.B. 1046. Attach to Form 2553 a statement describing the relevant facts and circumstances and, if applicable, the gross receipts from sales and services necessary to establish a business purpose. See the instructions for details regarding the gross receipts from sales and services. If the IRS proposes to disapprove the requested fiscal year, do you want a conference with the IRS National Office?

☐ Yes   ☐ No

2. Check here ▶ ☐ to show that the corporation intends to make a back-up section 444 election in the event the corporation's business purpose request is not approved by the IRS. See instructions for more information.

3. Check here ▶ ☐ to show that the corporation agrees to adopt or change to a tax year ending December 31 if necessary for the IRS to accept this election for S corporation status in the event (1) the corporation's business purpose request is not approved and the corporation makes a back-up section 444 election, but is ultimately not qualified to make a section 444 election, or (2) the corporation's business purpose request is not approved and the corporation did not make a back-up section 444 election.

R   Section 444 Election—To make a section 444 election, check box R1. You may also check box R2.

1. Check here ▶ ☐ to show that the corporation will make, if qualified, a section 444 election to have the fiscal tax year shown in item F, Part I. To make the election, you must complete **Form 8716,** Election To Have a Tax Year Other Than a Required Tax Year, and either attach it to Form 2553 or file it separately.

2. Check here ▶ ☐ to show that the corporation agrees to adopt or change to a tax year ending December 31 if necessary for the IRS to accept this election for S corporation status in the event the corporation is ultimately not qualified to make a section 444 election.

Form **2553** (Rev. 12-2017)

Form 2553 (Rev. 12-2017)   Page **4**

Name	Employer identification number

Part III Qualified Subchapter S Trust (QSST) Election Under Section 1361(d)(2)* **Note:** If you are making more than one QSST election, use additional copies of page 4.

Income beneficiary's name and address	Social security number

Trust's name and address	Employer identification number

Date on which stock of the corporation was transferred to the trust (month, day, year) . . . . ▶

In order for the trust named above to be a QSST and thus a qualifying shareholder of the S corporation for which this Form 2553 is filed, I hereby make the election under section 1361(d)(2). Under penalties of perjury, I certify that the trust meets the definitional requirements of section 1361(d)(3) and that all other information provided in Part III is true, correct, and complete.

Signature of income beneficiary or signature and title of legal representative or other qualified person making the election   Date

*Use Part III to make the QSST election only if stock of the corporation has been transferred to the trust on or before the date on which the corporation makes its election to be an S corporation. The QSST election must be made and filed separately if stock of the corporation is transferred to the trust **after** the date on which the corporation makes the S election.

Part IV Late Corporate Classification Election Representations (see instructions)

If a late entity classification election was intended to be effective on the same date that the S corporation election was intended to be effective, relief for a late S corporation election must also include the following representations.

1   The requesting entity is an eligible entity as defined in Regulations section 301.7701-3(a);

2   The requesting entity intended to be classified as a corporation as of the effective date of the S corporation status;

3   The requesting entity fails to qualify as a corporation solely because Form 8832, Entity Classification Election, was not timely filed under Regulations section 301.7701-3(c)(1)(i), or Form 8832 was not deemed to have been filed under Regulations section 301.7701-3(c)(1)(v)(C);

4   The requesting entity fails to qualify as an S corporation on the effective date of the S corporation status solely because the S corporation election was not timely filed pursuant to section 1362(b); **and**

5a The requesting entity timely filed all required federal tax returns and information returns consistent with its requested classification as an S corporation for all of the years the entity intended to be an S corporation and no inconsistent tax or information returns have been filed by or with respect to the entity during any of the tax years, **or**

b   The requesting entity has not filed a federal tax or information return for the first year in which the election was intended to be effective because the due date has not passed for that year's federal tax or information return.

Form **2553** (Rev. 12-2017)

Form **1120-S**	**U.S. Income Tax Return for an S Corporation**		OMB No. 1545-0123
Department of the Treasury Internal Revenue Service	▶ Do not file this form unless the corporation has filed or is attaching Form 2553 to elect to be an S corporation. ▶ Go to *www.irs.gov/Form1120S* for instructions and the latest information.		**2021**

For calendar year 2021 or tax year beginning			, 2021, ending		, 20

A S election effective date		**Name**		**D** Employer identification number
	TYPE OR PRINT			
B Business activity code number (see instructions)		Number, street, and room or suite no. If a P.O. box, see instructions.		**E** Date incorporated
		City or town, state or province, country, and ZIP or foreign postal code		**F** Total assets (see instructions)
C Check if Sch. M-3 attached ☐				$

G Is the corporation electing to be an S corporation beginning with this tax year? See instructions. ☐ Yes ☐ No

H Check if: **(1)** ☐ Final return **(2)** ☐ Name change **(3)** ☐ Address change **(4)** ☐ Amended return **(5)** ☐ S election termination

I Enter the number of shareholders who were shareholders during any part of the tax year . . . . ▶

J Check if corporation: **(1)** ☐ Aggregated activities for section 465 at-risk purposes **(2)** ☐ Grouped activities for section 469 passive activity purposes

Caution: Include **only** trade or business income and expenses on lines 1a through 21. See the instructions for more information.

Income	1a	Gross receipts or sales	1a		
	b	Returns and allowances	1b		
	c	Balance. Subtract line 1b from line 1a		1c	
	2	Cost of goods sold (attach Form 1125-A)		2	
	3	Gross profit. Subtract line 2 from line 1c		3	
	4	Net gain (loss) from Form 4797, line 17 (attach Form 4797)		4	
	5	Other income (loss) (see instructions—attach statement)		5	
	6	**Total income (loss).** Add lines 3 through 5 . . . . ▶		6	
Deductions (see instructions for limitations)	7	Compensation of officers (see instructions—attach Form 1125-E)		7	
	8	Salaries and wages (less employment credits)		8	
	9	Repairs and maintenance		9	
	10	Bad debts		10	
	11	Rents		11	
	12	Taxes and licenses		12	
	13	Interest (see instructions)		13	
	14	Depreciation not claimed on Form 1125-A or elsewhere on return (attach Form 4562) . .		14	
	15	Depletion **(Do not deduct oil and gas depletion.)**		15	
	16	Advertising		16	
	17	Pension, profit-sharing, etc., plans		17	
	18	Employee benefit programs		18	
	19	Other deductions (attach statement)		19	
	20	**Total deductions.** Add lines 7 through 19 . . . . ▶		20	
	21	**Ordinary business income (loss).** Subtract line 20 from line 6		21	
Tax and Payments	22a	Excess net passive income or LIFO recapture tax (see instructions) . .	22a		
	b	Tax from Schedule D (Form 1120-S)	22b		
	c	Add lines 22a and 22b (see instructions for additional taxes)		22c	
	23a	2021 estimated tax payments and 2020 overpayment credited to 2021 .	23a		
	b	Tax deposited with Form 7004	23b		
	c	Credit for federal tax paid on fuels (attach Form 4136)	23c		
	d	Add lines 23a through 23c		23d	
	24	Estimated tax penalty (see instructions). Check if Form 2220 is attached . . . . ▶ ☐		24	
	25	**Amount owed.** If line 23d is smaller than the total of lines 22c and 24, enter amount owed . . .		25	
	26	**Overpayment.** If line 23d is larger than the total of lines 22c and 24, enter amount overpaid . . .		26	
	27	Enter amount from line 26: **Credited to 2022 estimated tax** ▶ Refunded ▶		27	

Sign Here	Under penalties of perjury, I declare that I have examined this return, including accompanying schedules and statements, and to the best of my knowledge and belief, it is true, correct, and complete. Declaration of preparer (other than taxpayer) is based on all information of which preparer has any knowledge.		
	▶ _____ _____ ▶ _____ Signature of officer Date Title		May the IRS discuss this return with the preparer shown below? See instructions. ☐ Yes ☐ No

Paid Preparer Use Only	Print/Type preparer's name	Preparer's signature	Date	Check ☐ if self-employed	PTIN
	Firm's name ▶			Firm's EIN ▶	
	Firm's address ▶			Phone no.	

For Paperwork Reduction Act Notice, see separate instructions.   Cat. No. 11510H   Form **1120-S** (2021)

Form 1120-S (2021) Page **2**

Schedule B	Other Information (see instructions)			Yes	No

1 Check accounting method: **a** ☐ Cash **b** ☐ Accrual

c ☐ Other (specify) ▶ _____

2 See the instructions and enter the:

a Business activity ▶ _____ **b** Product or service ▶ _____

3 At any time during the tax year, was any shareholder of the corporation a disregarded entity, a trust, an estate, or a nominee or similar person? If "Yes," attach Schedule B-1, Information on Certain Shareholders of an S Corporation . .

4 At the end of the tax year, did the corporation:

a Own directly 20% or more, or own, directly or indirectly, 50% or more of the total stock issued and outstanding of any foreign or domestic corporation? For rules of constructive ownership, see instructions. If "Yes," complete (i) through (v) below . . . .

(i) Name of Corporation	(ii) Employer Identification Number (if any)	(iii) Country of Incorporation	(iv) Percentage of Stock Owned	(v) If Percentage in (iv) Is 100%, Enter the Date (if applicable) a Qualified Subchapter S Subsidiary Election Was Made

b Own directly an interest of 20% or more, or own, directly or indirectly, an interest of 50% or more in the profit, loss, or capital in any foreign or domestic partnership (including an entity treated as a partnership) or in the beneficial interest of a trust? For rules of constructive ownership, see instructions. If "Yes," complete (i) through (v) below . . . .

(i) Name of Entity	(ii) Employer Identification Number (if any)	(iii) Type of Entity	(iv) Country of Organization	(v) Maximum Percentage Owned in Profit, Loss, or Capital

5a At the end of the tax year, did the corporation have any outstanding shares of restricted stock? . . . .

If "Yes," complete lines (i) and (ii) below.

(i) Total shares of restricted stock . . . . ▶ _____

(ii) Total shares of non-restricted stock . . . . ▶ _____

b At the end of the tax year, did the corporation have any outstanding stock options, warrants, or similar instruments? .

If "Yes," complete lines (i) and (ii) below.

(i) Total shares of stock outstanding at the end of the tax year . ▶ _____

(ii) Total shares of stock outstanding if all instruments were executed ▶ _____

6 Has this corporation filed, or is it required to file, **Form 8918**, Material Advisor Disclosure Statement, to provide information on any reportable transaction? . . . .

7 Check this box if the corporation issued publicly offered debt instruments with original issue discount . . . . ▶ ☐

If checked, the corporation may have to file **Form 8281**, Information Return for Publicly Offered Original Issue Discount Instruments.

8 If the corporation **(a)** was a C corporation before it elected to be an S corporation **or** the corporation acquired an asset with a basis determined by reference to the basis of the asset (or the basis of any other property) in the hands of a C corporation, **and (b)** has net unrealized built-in gain in excess of the net recognized built-in gain from prior years, enter the net unrealized built-in gain reduced by net recognized built-in gain from prior years. See instructions . . . . . . ▶ $ _____

9 Did the corporation have an election under section 163(j) for any real property trade or business or any farming business in effect during the tax year? See instructions . . . .

10 Does the corporation satisfy one or more of the following? See instructions . . . .

a The corporation owns a pass-through entity with current, or prior year carryover, excess business interest expense.

b The corporation's aggregate average annual gross receipts (determined under section 448(c)) for the 3 tax years preceding the current tax year are more than $26 million and the corporation has business interest expense.

c The corporation is a tax shelter and the corporation has business interest expense.

If "Yes," complete and attach Form 8990.

11 Does the corporation satisfy **both** of the following conditions? . . . .

a The corporation's total receipts (see instructions) for the tax year were less than $250,000.

b The corporation's total assets at the end of the tax year were less than $250,000.

If "Yes," the corporation is not required to complete Schedules L and M-1.

Form **1120-S** (2021)

Form 1120-S (2021)   Page **3**

Schedule B   Other Information (see instructions) (continued)

		Yes	No
12	During the tax year, did the corporation have any non-shareholder debt that was canceled, was forgiven, or had the terms modified so as to reduce the principal amount of the debt?		
	If "Yes," enter the amount of principal reduction ▶ $		
13	During the tax year, was a qualified subchapter S subsidiary election terminated or revoked? If "Yes," see instructions		
14a	Did the corporation make any payments in 2021 that would require it to file Form(s) 1099?		
b	If "Yes," did the corporation file or will it file required Form(s) 1099?		
15	Is the corporation attaching Form 8996 to certify as a Qualified Opportunity Fund?		
	If "Yes," enter the amount from Form 8996, line 15 ▶ $		

Schedule K   Shareholders' Pro Rata Share Items

				Total amount
Income (Loss)	1	Ordinary business income (loss) (page 1, line 21)	1	
	2	Net rental real estate income (loss) (attach Form 8825)	2	
	3a	Other gross rental income (loss)	3a	
	b	Expenses from other rental activities (attach statement)	3b	
	c	Other net rental income (loss). Subtract line 3b from line 3a	3c	
	4	Interest income	4	
	5	Dividends: a Ordinary dividends	5a	
		b Qualified dividends	5b	
	6	Royalties	6	
	7	Net short-term capital gain (loss) (attach Schedule D (Form 1120-S))	7	
	8a	Net long-term capital gain (loss) (attach Schedule D (Form 1120-S))	8a	
	b	Collectibles (28%) gain (loss)	8b	
	c	Unrecaptured section 1250 gain (attach statement)	8c	
	9	Net section 1231 gain (loss) (attach Form 4797)	9	
	10	Other income (loss) (see instructions) Type ▶	10	
Deductions	11	Section 179 deduction (attach Form 4562)	11	
	12a	Charitable contributions	12a	
	b	Investment interest expense	12b	
	c	Section 59(e)(2) expenditures Type ▶	12c	
	d	Other deductions (see instructions) Type ▶	12d	
Credits	13a	Low-income housing credit (section 42(j)(5))	13a	
	b	Low-income housing credit (other)	13b	
	c	Qualified rehabilitation expenditures (rental real estate) (attach Form 3468, if applicable)	13c	
	d	Other rental real estate credits (see instructions) Type ▶	13d	
	e	Other rental credits (see instructions) Type ▶	13e	
	f	Biofuel producer credit (attach Form 6478)	13f	
	g	Other credits (see instructions) Type ▶	13g	
International Transactions	14	Attach Schedule K-2 (Form 1120-S), Shareholders' Pro Rata Share Items—International, and check this box to indicate you are reporting items of international tax relevance ▶ ☐		
Alternative Minimum Tax (AMT) Items	15a	Post-1986 depreciation adjustment	15a	
	b	Adjusted gain or loss	15b	
	c	Depletion (other than oil and gas)	15c	
	d	Oil, gas, and geothermal properties—gross income	15d	
	e	Oil, gas, and geothermal properties—deductions	15e	
	f	Other AMT items (attach statement)	15f	
Items Affecting Shareholder Basis	16a	Tax-exempt interest income	16a	
	b	Other tax-exempt income	16b	
	c	Nondeductible expenses	16c	
	d	Distributions (attach statement if required) (see instructions)	16d	
	e	Repayment of loans from shareholders	16e	
	f	Foreign taxes paid or accrued	16f	

Form **1120-S** (2021)

Form 1120-S (2021)   Page **4**

Schedule K	Shareholders' Pro Rata Share Items *(continued)*				Total amount
Other Information	**17a** Investment income			**17a**	
	b Investment expenses			**17b**	
	c Dividend distributions paid from accumulated earnings and profits			**17c**	
	d Other items and amounts (attach statement)				
Reconciliation	**18** **Income (loss) reconciliation.** Combine the amounts on lines 1 through 10 in the far right column. From the result, subtract the sum of the amounts on lines 11 through 12d and 16f . .			**18**	

Schedule L	Balance Sheets per Books	Beginning of tax year		End of tax year	
	Assets	**(a)**	**(b)**	**(c)**	**(d)**
1	Cash				
2a	Trade notes and accounts receivable . . .				
b	Less allowance for bad debts	( )		( )	
3	Inventories				
4	U.S. government obligations				
5	Tax-exempt securities (see instructions) . .				
6	Other current assets (attach statement) . . .				
7	Loans to shareholders				
8	Mortgage and real estate loans				
9	Other investments (attach statement) . . .				
10a	Buildings and other depreciable assets . . .				
b	Less accumulated depreciation	( )		( )	
11a	Depletable assets				
b	Less accumulated depletion	( )		( )	
12	Land (net of any amortization)				
13a	Intangible assets (amortizable only)				
b	Less accumulated amortization	( )		( )	
14	Other assets (attach statement)				
15	Total assets				
	Liabilities and Shareholders' Equity				
16	Accounts payable				
17	Mortgages, notes, bonds payable in less than 1 year				
18	Other current liabilities (attach statement) . .				
19	Loans from shareholders				
20	Mortgages, notes, bonds payable in 1 year or more				
21	Other liabilities (attach statement)				
22	Capital stock				
23	Additional paid-in capital				
24	Retained earnings				
25	Adjustments to shareholders' equity (attach statement)				
26	Less cost of treasury stock		( )		( )
27	Total liabilities and shareholders' equity . .				

Form **1120-S** (2021)

Form 1120-S (2021) Page **5**

Schedule M-1 — Reconciliation of Income (Loss) per Books With Income (Loss) per Return

Note: The corporation may be required to file Schedule M-3. See instructions.

1	Net income (loss) per books		5	Income recorded on books this year not included on Schedule K, lines 1 through 10 (itemize):	
2	Income included on Schedule K, lines 1, 2, 3c, 4, 5a, 6, 7, 8a, 9, and 10, not recorded on books this year (itemize)		a	Tax-exempt interest $	
3	Expenses recorded on books this year not included on Schedule K, lines 1 through 12 and 16f (itemize):		6	Deductions included on Schedule K, lines 1 through 12 and 16f, not charged against book income this year (itemize):	
a	Depreciation $		a	Depreciation $	
b	Travel and entertainment $		7	Add lines 5 and 6	
4	Add lines 1 through 3		8	Income (loss) (Schedule K, line 18). Subtract line 7 from line 4	

Schedule M-2 — Analysis of Accumulated Adjustments Account, Shareholders' Undistributed Taxable Income Previously Taxed, Accumulated Earnings and Profits, and Other Adjustments Account (see instructions)

		(a) Accumulated adjustments account	(b) Shareholders' undistributed taxable income previously taxed	(c) Accumulated earnings and profits	(d) Other adjustments account
1	Balance at beginning of tax year				
2	Ordinary income from page 1, line 21				
3	Other additions				
4	Loss from page 1, line 21	( )			
5	Other reductions	( )			( )
6	Combine lines 1 through 5				
7	Distributions				
8	Balance at end of tax year. Subtract line 7 from line 6				

Form **1120-S** (2021)

Table of Cases

Table of Cases

Table of I.R.C. Statutes

Table of Regulations

Table of Rulings and Procedures

Index

References are to Paragraph Number